Advance Praise for *Keyword Intellige*

Keyword Intelligence by internet marketing legend Ron Jones represe [...] *step guide on how to effectively use keyword research to improve all* [...] *online marketing efforts, including search-engine optimization, pay pe*[...], *local, and social media. Get your sticky notes and highlighter ready because this book is a must-share resource that you can leverage to take your business to the next level.*
　　—KRISTOPHER JONES, Founder and CEO, ReferLocal.com, Best-Selling Author
　　of *Search Engine Optimization: Your Visual Blueprint to Internet Marketing*

If you're looking to find new customers through online marketing, this book is for you. It's a great read for anyone in online marketing with specific and actionable tips for your paid search, organic, and social efforts. With a large collection of recommended tools and hands-on examples of how to use these to mine for your perfect keywords, this book will be your guide to getting started on a path to growing your business through successful online marketing.
　　—FREDERICK VALLAEYS, AdWords Evangelist, Google

If you have ever struggled with how to achieve a happy marriage between keywords and your social media strategy then Chapter 8 of Ron Jones' book provides the insight you need.
　　—ERIK QUALLMAN, Author of *Socialomics*

We use words in all forms of communication; and they are the lifeblood of search marketing. Choosing the correct words is essential in all forms of online marketing. Ron does an excellent job of walking the reader through not just researching keywords; but also in showing the user how to use those keywords in your marketing efforts from SEO, PPC, social, and even content development. If you are involved in online marketing, this book will help you strengthen your keyword research and execution skills.
　　—BRAD GEDDES FOUNDER, Certified Knowledge & Author of *Advanced
　　Google AdWords*

Search engine marketing continues to become more complicated and knowing how to find and use the best keywords is a critical component for search marketers and business owners alike. Ron Jones has used his vast experience and expertise in writing a book that covers this topic concisely and is a must have for anyone wanting the best placement in the major search engines.
　　—JAY BEAN, CEO, OrangeSoda

Developing a successful keyword strategy is an oft-overlooked, yet critical component of any serious Internet marketing strategy. Strategic decisions are always based on good keyword research. This book is a useful read for junior, middle weight, and senior marketers alike, providing a solid foundation for thought processes and tools required for actionable, insightful keyword research projects.
    —RICHARD BAXTER, CEO SEOgadget.co.uk

Understanding how humans search on the Internet is to understand who we are, what we want, and where we are going. But current techniques for interpreting this data are often overly complicated and elusive. Ron is an expert at distilling the complexities of search and keyword intelligence, offering practical recommendations for how to best tackle these problems and come out on top in the competitive world of SEM, SEO and Social. His impressive experience in the search arena, coupled with his exhaustive research methodology, make this book an excellent addition to any search marketer's library!
    —ELI GOODMAN, Search Evangelist, comScore

In Keyword Intelligence, Internet marketing expert Ron Jones touches on important topics like SEO and PPC but takes the reader further beyond by providing valuable insights on how keyword research impacts social media, information architecture, branding, and mobile marketing. This is a must read book for any Internet marketing professional whether they be novice or professional.
    —JEFF PRUITT, CEO Tallwave

What others shroud in secrecy, Ron Jones shares openly. From the history of Search, to choosing keywords to tracking and rating success and the connectedness of these to our other marketing efforts, Ron give us a playbook for success online and ultimately in our businesses.
    —DOUG BRISOTTI, CEO, Eleven

Most marketers know that keyword research is important for SEO and PPC campaigns, but many don't recognize that it can be highly effective for social media marketing as well. That's why I strongly recommend reading Keyword Intelligence. Unlike other keyword research books, Ron outlines the use of keywords in social media, specifically how to put user intent into context. Additionally, he provides tips on using keywords within social media sites.
    —GREG JARBOE, Author of *YouTube and Video Marketing: An Hour a Day*

Keyword Intelligence

Keyword Research
for Search, Social,
and Beyond

Keyword Intelligence

Keyword Research for Search, Social, and Beyond

Ron Jones

WILEY

John Wiley & Sons, Inc.

Senior Acquisitions Editor: Willem Knibbe
Development Editor: David Clark
Technical Editor: Matt Van Wagner
Production Editor: Christine O'Connor
Copy Editor: Judy Flynn
Editorial Manager: Pete Gaughan
Production Manager: Tim Tate
Vice President and Executive Group Publisher: Richard Swadley
Vice President and Publisher: Neil Edde
Book Designer: Franz Baumhackl
Compositor: JoAnn Kolonick, Happenstance Type-O-Rama
Proofreader: Adept Content Solutions
Indexer: Nancy Guenther
Project Coordinator, Cover: Katherine Crocker
Cover Designer: Ryan Sneed

ISBN: 978-1-118-06183-1
ISBN: 978-1-118-21685-9 (ebk.)
ISBN: 978-1-118-21691-0 (ebk.)
ISBN: 978-1-118-21689-7 (ebk.)

Library of Congress Control Number: 2011938577

Dear Reader,

Thank you for choosing *Keyword Intelligence: Keyword Research for Search, Social, and Beyond*. This book is part of a family of premium-quality Sybex books, all of which are written by outstanding authors who combine practical experience with a gift for teaching.

Sybex was founded in 1976. More than 30 years later, we're still committed to producing consistently exceptional books. With each of our titles, we're working hard to set a new standard for the industry. From the paper we print on, to the authors we work with, our goal is to bring you the best books available.

I hope you see all that reflected in these pages. I'd be very interested to hear your comments and get your feedback on how we're doing. Feel free to let me know what you think about this or any other Sybex book by sending me an email at nedde@wiley.com. If you think you've found a technical error in this book, please visit http://sybex.custhelp.com. Customer feedback is critical to our efforts at Sybex.

Best regards,

Neil Edde
Vice President and Publisher
Sybex, an imprint of Wiley

To my wife, Stacey, for all of your love and for being by me these many years.

To my children, Amanda, Grayson, Leah, and Ethan, for showing me that joy is endless.

And to the entire search engine marketing community because I feel I need to give back to the industry that has been so kind to me. As I spent time serving on the board of SEMPO, I realized the value of having great knowledge resources available with which to stay fresh. So this book is my contribution to the industry and a way of saying thank you to the many people who have imparted their knowledge to me.

Acknowledgments

Like most projects, writing this book is a culmination of the time and effort of many people who have helped me so much. First, I need to thank my wife, Stacey, for putting up with me these past several months—keeping the family going while I was tucked away writing. I could have not done this without your love, support, and encouragement. Thanks also to my kids, Amanda, Grayson, Leah, and Ethan, who are the loves of my life and have supported me with "quiet time" when I needed it the most. A special thanks goes to my father, who provided me encouragement and support not only with this book but throughout my entire career.

I need to thank my colleagues at Symetri Internet Marketing for their inspiration, dedication, and insights while I was somewhat preoccupied with this project. Thanks for all your hard work.

A huge thanks to Tim Ash, Kris Jones, and David Szetela, whose friendship I have valued for the past few years. Thanks for twisting my arm to write a book, for introducing me to the great people at Wiley, and for all of your advice and wisdom.

Thank you to the great people at Wiley and Sybex for all of your help in this process. There is much more that goes into writing a book than I ever imagined. I especially want to thank Willem Knibbe for his coaching and encouragement. His "Gooooo Ron" emails had the effect of picking me back up when I felt overwhelmed. David Clark deserves thanks for keeping me in line and on task. And thank you to Christine O'Connor for keeping the project moving steadily forward and Judy Flynn for making sure the i's were dotted and the t's crossed—thanks for your patience. Also, a thank you goes to Pete Gaughan, Connor O'Brien, and Jenni Housh for their fine editorial management skills—I would've never figured out the Word template without you!

My technical editor, Matt Van Wagner, from FineMeFaster, was indispensable as the voice of reason and in verifying all of my facts and figures. I very much appreciate his no-nonsense approach and honesty and how he forced me to take things one step further.

The content on international keyword research (Chapter 13) was developed with the help of Bill Hunt with Back Azimuth. He was a great friend and mentor as I wrote this book. I felt it appropriate to have him write the Foreword. Thank you Bill for all of your help and direction!

To the many others that I always look forward to seeing at SES and other conferences, you have been great friends and have taught me many aspects of this industry through your brilliant ideas at sessions and in person. Many thanks to friends like Matt Bailey, Kris Jones, Tim Ash, Christine Churchill, David Szetela, Jessica Bowman, Li Evans, Mark Jackson, Eli Goodman, Jay Bean, Scott Sorokin, Greg Jarboe, Lee Odden, and Eric Quallman.

Additionally, I would like to thank all of the industry leaders I worked with at SEMPO while I served on the board of directors for two years. They have taught me many things about this industry. I am passionate about search because of leaders like Dana Todd, Kevin Lee, Jeff Pruit, Bill Hunt, Massimo Burgio, Sara Holubek, Chris Boggs, Gord Hotchkiss, Dave Fall, Duane Forrester, Bruce Clay, and others I served with on committees and working groups. A special thanks to Terry Plank and the team that I worked with at the SEMPO Institute for their time and effort in developing the beginners and advanced courses on keyword research.

Finally, I would be remiss if I did not thank the great people at Incisive Media and the folks who work tirelessly to put on all of the events for SES: Mike Grehan, Marilyn Crafts, and Jackie Ortez, who have continued to have me speak and conduct training sessions on keyword research. A special thanks to Matt McGowan, who got me started. Remember that time we spent running the SEMPO booth at SES? Thanks for your introductions and help.

About the Author

Ron is an Internet marketing consultant, trainer, columnist, and owner of Symetri Internet Marketing, which provides strategic consulting and Internet marketing solutions for medium to large organizations. Ron has served as president and key Internet strategist since its inception in 1998. He has provided consulting services for companies like Sealy, Inc. as well as Broyhill Furniture, Kimberly Clark Healthcare, Wachovia, Shaw Industries, Kayser Roth, and many other notable organizations.

Ron has been an avid proponent of the Internet marketing industry by hosting and speaking at industry seminars and conferences. Ron's 20 years' of experience working with clients and traditional advertising agencies around the world make him one of the industry's leading authorities on Internet marketing strategy.

Prior to Symetri, Ron served as director for MCI, where he led market strategy and execution of web-based initiatives for many of MCI's clients, including Macy's, Brook Brothers, Crutchfield, and Nieman Marcus. Ron was also a consultant on MCI's branding campaign, Gramercy Press, and launched subbrands internetMCI and emailMCI.

Ron has served on the board of directors for SEMPO (Search Engine Marketing Professional Organization) and as one of its officers from 2008 through 2010. He is also one of the authors for the SEMPO Institute *Insider's Guide* and advanced courses on the topic of keyword research.

Ron is currently a columnist for *ClickZ* and *Search Engine Watch*.

Contents

Foreword

Most people think of keywords and "Keyword Intelligence" as being unique to Search Marketing. Keywords are what we try to rank for, try to create social media mentions for, and are the exact point of intersection between a consumer looking for content or products like yours. The better you can understand your keyword universe, searcher intent, and now, social media conversations, the more opportunities you will have to connect with consumers, identify new products, and expand into new markets.

In late 1994, my business school thesis was "Using the Internet to Reach Overseas Markets," which was based on my own experience of finding customers using message boards. As I got better at matching the board topics to product categories and the probability of interest, I saw significant increases in leads and sales from around the world. I demonstrated that a small company based in Los Angeles, using various Internet properties, relevant content, and an understanding of participant interest could inexpensively use the Internet to generate sales around the world.

Fast-forward to today's hyper-competitive online world where billions of dollars are spent with Google on Paid-Per-Click advertising. Hours are spent mining and optimizing keywords and copy to minimize click costs and maximize conversion opportunities.

Recently, when trying to explain the importance of keyword research and searcher intent modeling to a group of traditional marketers, I used the following analogy to help them understand the valuable asset they have been missing out on.

> "Let's pretend keywords are nails. Now picture the average construction site or your last remodeling project. There are boxes of them in different sizes and uses. We grab them by the handful to connect the wooden frame, the flooring, the sheet rock on the walls, fasten the shingles to the roof, and, finally, hang the picture frames on the wall. Nails are used in nearly every building component of our house yet we often use the wrong size or type, scatter them on the ground or simply discard them to rust without giving them the slightest respect for the significance they play in the foundation of our structure."

Like the nails of a house, keywords are the binding element of any digital marketing program. They are your ad copy, they support your branding message, and now, more than ever, it is how consumers ask for, praise, and complain about your products and services.

It is this lack of respect for keywords that explains why it has taken so long for someone to write a book on Keyword Intelligence. Ron pays homage to the lowly keyword phrase and offers a wealth of ideas, techniques, and process that will guide you through the process of not only finding the gold mine but knowing exactly where and how to dig to find the biggest nuggets of keyword gold.

Beyond finding keywords, it is what you do with them that matters the most. Companies that understand their consumers' voice use this data to influence every potential connection opportunity with their target market.

Companies like IBM and National Instruments have used keyword research and keyword intelligence techniques to identify new products or product modifications that have resurrected old products and created new opportunities with new or existing products that may have passed them by.

Small and large companies are now using keyword intelligence to understand market opportunities in emerging markets. It is far cheaper to run search ads to test interest and awareness than TV or other sales channels in new markets.

Brands like Tide detergent can use information on "how to" queries to understand consumer needs and problems and use them to create new products or shift brand messages to integrate new or changing needs quicker.

Mining social media conversations can help companies understand what consumers like or dislike about their products as well as new applications of the product that may not have been considered or mentioned in the feature function messaging.

There is no limit to what you can do with this data, and Ron offers a number of great strategies and tactics for businesses to leverage Keyword Intelligence to increase customer satisfaction, product awareness, and insight that will have a distinct impact on improving your bottom line.

I wish you the best of luck and success with your keyword adventure.

BILL HUNT
President
Back Azimuth Consulting

Introduction

This book represents an evolution in thinking about keyword research. Many consider the task of researching keywords to be tactical and a necessary evil because it is so time consuming and tedious. This book was written with the idea that the knowledge, or "intelligence," gleaned from keyword research will help you not only with your SEO and PPC campaigns but also with many other marketing channels.

More importantly, it will provide you with insights into your target audience and their expectations, wants, and needs. You can therefore become more knowledgeable about those you wish to attract and provide marketing materials and content that fulfills their expectations. In our world of social media and with the ubiquitous nature of information and collaboration, it is more important than ever to be able to tap into this stream of thought and act to provide products and services in a manner that is inviting and compelling to the new online consumer.

This book will start by teaching you principles of keyword research that can be applied whether you are a small company or a large enterprise. It will map out a process you can use to identity, refine, organize, and test your keywords for optimal performance. You can take what you have learned and apply it toward not only your SEO and PPC campaigns, but also your social, mobile, and local campaigns. You can even use it for traditional marketing campaigns, including branding and messaging.

Finally, you can apply your keyword research to your site's informational structure. As you understand new topics on keyword segmentation and categorization, you can apply them as new models for designing your websites around the very needs and intent of your target audience. Doing so will set the stage for the development of dynamic, rich, and engaging content that will resonate with your visitors and lead to higher conversions.

The vision for this book is to open your eyes to new ways of looking at keyword research. It is also meant to guide you in plotting a course for exploring new opportunities that will provide you with a competitive advantage and a strategic edge to help you achieve your business goals and objectives.

Who Should Buy This Book

This book is intended for the business owner, marketing manager, or any team member who in any way touches the marketing process. In fact, it is for anyone who works in or manages search marketing, social media, and content development within an organization or agency.

This book is designed for the beginner and advanced alike, because few follow this approach to researching, managing, and implementing keywords.

What's Inside

Here is a glance at what's in each chapter:

Chapter 1, "Keyword Research History and Its Evolving Role in Marketing," lays the foundation for understanding keywords and how they have evolved into the formidable resource they are to marketers today.

Chapter 2, "How to Develop a Successful Keyword Strategy," provides you with the latest tips and insights for establishing, measuring, and implementing a successful keyword strategy.

Chapter 3, "Keyword Research Tools," outlines the types of tools you should have in your toolbox and reviews some of them to show you how they can work to help you with your keyword research activities.

Chapter 4, "Finding Keywords," outlines processes and methodologies to help you brainstorm and find all possible keywords that are candidates you can use within your campaigns.

Chapter 5, "Refine Your Initial List of Keywords in Seven Steps," provides a set of processes and filters you can use to help you refine the list of keywords and identify which ones are most likely to succeed and perform.

Chapter 6, "Using Keywords for SEO," gives you tips for taking the keywords that you have identified as your top performers, integrating them within strategic places to enhance your search engine marketing campaigns.

Chapter 7, "Using Keywords for PPC," provides tips on using your keywords to assist you in developing your campaign structure and examples on integrating keywords for ad copy and landing pages for optimal relevancy.

Chapter 8, "Using Keywords for Social Media," helps outline the use of keywords in social media to put context into user intent. Additionally, there are tips on using keywords within your blogs or other social media sites, like Facebook, Twitter, and YouTube.

Chapter 9, "Using Keywords for Mobile and Local," brings into focus the use of keywords in the new and emerging world of local and mobile marketing, especially with many of the new portable devices and smartphones.

Chapter 10, "Keywords and Site Architecture," explains the unique insight that comes from keyword research and what keywords tell us about user intent. This knowledge can be used to assist in building a site structure that contains relevant content and compelling user experience.

Chapter 11, "Creating Great Content with Keywords," shows you how to take the next step in applying keyword intelligence and using it to build content that will engage your visitors and keep them on your site longer while meeting their search expectations in the process.

Chapter 12, "Using Keywords for Branding and Messaging," covers a unique opportunity to use keywords in branding and messaging with traditional channels.

Chapter 13, "International Keyword Research," explores the world of keyword research within other cultures, regions, and languages. It will caution you on the pitfalls and provide direction on the best ways to conduct keyword research outside of the United States.

Chapter 14, "Keyword Measurement," walks you through some procedures to test your keywords and their overall performance.

How to Contact the Author

I welcome feedback from you about this book or about books you'd like to see from me in the future. You can reach me by writing to rjones@symetri.com. Additionally, you can go the companion book site at www.sybex.com/go/keywordintelligence.com and interact with me there.

Sybex strives to keep you supplied with the latest tools and information you need for your work. Please check the website at www.sybex.com, where we'll post additional content and updates that supplement this book should the need arise. Enter Skin in the search box (or type the book's ISBN—9781118061831), and click Go to get to the book's update page.

Keyword Intelligence

Keyword Research
for Search, Social,
and Beyond

Keyword Research History and Its Evolving Role in Marketing

How have we used keywords in the past? What role do they play in our lives today? Can keyword research be a strategic tool for all of your marketing initiatives? Can keyword research increase your conversions and make you more money? This chapter will examine these questions and outline the principles you need to know to be successful at mining the powerful knowledge you can gain through keyword research.

1

Chapter Contents

How Keyword Research Has Evolved

Finding and refinding information and documents after they have been created and stored has been a challenge since the establishment of the printed word. "Findability" is unequivocally more important to us as we deal with the plethora of information that is available to us today.

Time is conceivably one of the most valuable assets we have. Information seekers value tools that help them quickly find the information they are looking for and manage the quantity of information they come into contact with. One of the tools used early on is called *indexing*, and it's fundamental to information organization and retrieval.

So let's look at what an index is. Fundamentally, it is a list that includes names, places, and topics and the page numbers for the pages where they are mentioned.

Most of us are familiar with the indexes in the backs of books, especially reference books, where there is a list of words and phrases that are accompanied by page numbers leading us to more detailed content. These words and phrases are also referred to as *keywords*. We have grown accustomed to finding information in dictionaries, encyclopedias, and libraries by searching on keywords.

Thus we have been trained to find what we want based on keywords. By definition, a keyword is a word or phrase that represents a larger concept or idea. It can be a word that is memorable and used to form the basis for a complex thought. So when we are searching for something, our brain attempts to break down what we are searching for into a small set of words known as a keyword phrase or a search query. Then we use an index of a book or a search engine on the Internet and find what we are looking for. Sometimes we are successful and sometimes we aren't. The reason we fail to find what we are looking for usually stems from the search query we came up with and the keyword phrase the content developer uses. With search engines today, there is usually an attempt to fix this by asking the searcher, "Did you mean to search for...?" This wasn't always the case.

Since the beginning of the information age, the first search engines were designed with the same premises. Enter a search query and results would be generated and presented to you in the form of a list of web pages that contain keywords matching your search query.

According to Search Engine History (http://searchenginehistory.com), one of the first search engines that surfaced before 1993, which was when websites began to show up on the Internet, was called Archie (Figure 1.1). It was created in 1990 by Alan Emtage, a student at McGill University in Montreal. The name was originally meant to be archives, but it was shortened to Archie. Many new search engines came on the scene after Archie to provide even better search results from related keyword queries.

Figure 1.1 Archie Query Form (1990)

Today we have full-blown search engines that provide us all with the information we want through the use of keywords. Essentially, keywords are the gatekeepers of information. You just need to know the right password to get in. It all began in 1993 with the appearance of websites on the Internet. Very soon afterward, the following search engines started to emerge:

- 1994 – Excite, InfoSeek, WebCrawler, and the Yahoo! Directory
- 1995 – Lycos, AltaVista
- 1996 – Ask Jeeves
- 1997 – LookSmart
- 1998 – Google

With many of these search engines pulling content from the websites that were up at the time, search engine optimization started getting under way.

The idea of having visible sites in the search engines brought site owners valuable business results. Additionally, the idea of gaining higher rank, which brought with it higher visibility, would drive increased traffic. This insight, together with search engine technology, marked the beginning of search engine optimization (SEO) as an industry. One of the key fundamentals of SEO is keyword research. Website owners started finding ways to conduct research on which keywords were right for them to use for SEO purposes.

Later, as search engines offered pay-per-click (PPC) services, keywords and keyword research really ramped up. The basis of the PPC program is that you bid on the keywords for which you want your ads to show upon the keywords that will trigger your ad. This required a better understanding of the right keywords to buy or to bid for.

Soon after, keyword tool vendors started popping up, providing a way to research the best keywords to be used for search engine marketing (SEM), which has been loosely defined as all online marketing channels that involve search engines, like SEO and PPC. Some of the first were Wordtracker and Keyword Discovery.

Now keywords and keyword research are understood by many marketers as the foundation to all you do with SEO and PPC. With this book you'll learn tips, tools, and principles for just that...and more.

Why Keywords and Keyword Research Are Vital for Success

As keywords and keyword research have evolved over the years, more and more marketers are seeing the importance of adding this most important function to their processes. They may see keyword research more as a tactical rather than a strategic aspect of their campaigns, but they are realizing that it plays an important part in their Internet marketing initiatives.

In the following sections, we will look at the obvious reasons keyword research is important, especially since the first thing people do when they begin a search is to type the words that describe what they are looking for into a search bar. Then I will outline the more subtle reasons and examine the power of making this keyword research function the foundation of success with all of your marketing channels.

Online Searching Begins with a Search Query or Keyword Link

Think about how you have found information on the Internet. You typically either started with a search query in a search engine or found a keyword link on a website or blog that interested you enough to click, right? You may even have typed in a URL, or searched for words you read or heard about from an offline marketing campaign or promotion. Either way it was a keyword that represented what you were looking for.

If keywords are almost always at the beginning of all that we search for, then wouldn't you think that identifying the right keywords for your campaign is highly important? It is. Keyword research is more than just finding keywords for your PPC campaign. It is also important when managing search expectations.

Keyword Research Is a Strategic Function

I have asked students and clients alike about their thoughts on the process of doing keyword research. Most indicate that they feel keyword research is tactical and mundane. They fail to see it as more of a strategic step in the overall process of developing and deploying Internet marketing campaigns.

Not only is it strategic, but if understood correctly, it can be central to many things you do within your company. I have applied the knowledge of targeted keywords to many facets within a company with great success.

The foundation of your strategy is a list of tested, verified keywords that is organized to complement your marketing channels like SEO and PPC. They should be organized into themes that correspond and are relevant to your target audience. When this is done correctly, it will form the basis for much of your content development and messaging to your visitors.

Without a strategy, you will become lost in the depths of random pages of web content without a core meaning or focus.

Form the Foundation for *All* Marketing Campaigns

After conducting keyword research on my clients for the past several years, I began to realize that much of the information gathered could be used for more than just search engine optimization or pay-per-click advertising. If a company wanted to be known for a particular keyword, then shouldn't that keyword be used ubiquitously throughout the company? Usually when research like this is done, it typically stays within the confines of the marketing department. This kind of information needs to be shared because it affects all parts of the organization.

Once a keyword research study is complete and foundational keywords are selected, the keywords should be distributed to all divisions of the company. Consider the implications of having a keyword used in a company's positioning, mission, or vision statement. Or how about using the keyword in press releases, or even TV, radio and print advertising? The more the keyword is used, the more you are attaching it to the company's brand. Let's look at all of the places keywords and keyword research can be used in both online and offline marketing campaigns:

Online Campaigns

- Search engine optimization (SEO)
- Paid search advertising (PPC)
- Social media marketing
- Local search
- Mobile search
- Video and image search
- Display and banner ads
- Email marketing
- Real-time search

Offline Campaigns

- Print advertising
- TV advertising
- Radio advertising
- Public relations
- Positioning and branding
- Direct marketing
- Billboard advertising

If all of these functions were privy to the core set of keywords that came from a solid keyword research study, a consistent message would surface about what the organization really stands for. In reality, keyword research is and should be part of a good branding campaign. Copywriters can use keywords as they craft the important positioning statements or product and service descriptions.

What if we take this a bit further and explore the use of keywords in mission and vision statements for an organization? These declarations are designed to affect leaders, managers, and workers who attempt to internalize the messages and use them to make important decisions in their various roles.

So keywords can affect public perception, employee mentality, and of course, search engine rankings. If organizations can catch the vision of the power of consistent use of the right keywords, it can be the silver lining that can help to propel organizations to success.

Let's take a closer look at online marketing and how keyword research plays a role in its success. It has already been established that Internet searches begin with keywords. We typically have an idea of what we seek on the Internet and so type the keyword that best represents that expectation into a search engine. Throughout this book, I'll refer to the words people type into a search engine as *search queries*, *searches*, or simply, *queries*. We then are confronted with search results, that is, a list of choices in the form of links to different sites that may have what we are looking for.

Most of these links contain the keyword we used in our search query. So it becomes an exercise in following the links that we think will lead us to our desired content. There are two primary types of links on the search engine results pages (SERPs), organic listings and text ads. Organic listings are the "free" listings that the search engines present as the most relevant sites it believes match the users' search query. Ads, which the search engines place in and around the search results, are the other type of links.

Marketers wishing to have their listings appear in the SERPs use SEO and PPC. Both of these types of listings require the use of best practices to help marketers connect with their target audience. Because most searches begin with a keyword, researching keywords that your target audience will use to find you is essential.

The same principles apply to video and image search listings that appear in local and mobile search. Videos and images need to be tagged with the right keywords in their descriptions. If that's done properly, a searcher may connect with them as they search for image or video content. Local and mobile search companies need to have their listings filled out properly using keywords that are at the core of what they do. This helps searchers who are looking for local content or stores to make the right connection.

Additionally, you will want to use the right keywords in your conversations with blogs, Facebook, Twitter, and other social media sites. Doing so will help to establish keyword relevance and recognition with your web content.

As we move on to display and banner advertising, we transition to online billboards on our journey to our desired content. Sometimes these are distractions, but aside from pretty pictures and flashy animations, there still lies the message of the ads that mostly contain text, or keywords. Those ads need to keep company with sites that are relevant and contain similar keywords. If done properly, an ad would steer a searcher to the advertiser's website. Having a solid knowledge of relevant keywords will help marketers construct and place display advertising correctly to maximize success.

Most marketers would agree that keyword research is a core function for all of their online marketing initiatives, but they really don't think about how it can be instrumental for their offline or traditional advertising. Next let's look at how keyword research can play a role in offline marketing.

Keyword Research's Role in Offline Marketing

If you work earnestly at identifying the right keywords for your SEO and PPC campaigns and you then include your core keywords in your online content, why not continue to use the same content offline? In fact, much of what happens offline eventually gets posted online. For example, TV commercials are now appearing online through YouTube or other social media sites.

Press releases often go out to the newswire but eventually get picked up through online news sites. Likewise, public relations content finds its way to news and social media sites. Many marketers are turning to social media to help them with reputation management.

Even promotional couponing is finding its way online in the form of Groupon and other online couponing sites.

Radio can also be found online through streaming audio sites, and the media content may get archived on other websites. Speech-to-text systems are now mainstream. Google can take an audio file and convert the speech to text and then index the text to help searchers find that content.

Print will of course always be around, but with iPads and other tablet devices, many print publications are being digitized and pushed online for us to read. Some of the content is actually linked to online content or websites.

There are of course still other marketing tools, but I would suggest to you it is all about messaging and branding. Whether consumers see an ad online or offline, there is usually a central message that the advertiser is trying to get across. For instance, let's say you are developing a TV commercial and you arm your copywriter with the list of targeted keywords you are using for SEO and PPC. When your core keywords are used visually and orally within the commercial, those keywords are planted in the minds of the viewers. When those viewers are in the market for your product or service and they think of the words they are going to use as their search query to find you, what words do you think they will use?

No matter what your promotional vehicle (online and offline), many sales are made through the Internet and, in particular, through search engines. Having a unified keyword strategy improves your likelihood of ranking well with search engines by focusing all of your online content intently on your most important keywords.

Essentially, you are not only influencing the way people think about your brand but also the search queries they will use to find you on the Internet. Personally, I think this is big. It opens up a whole new way of thinking about the use of keywords and keyword research for both offline and online marketing.

Picking the Wrong Keywords Can Waste Time and Money

I have run into many companies who approached their keyword research rather haphazardly and really didn't take the assignment seriously. The most common excuse is that keyword research is a tedious job and it is difficult to automate. In our time-deprived lives, we typically put off those things that are time consuming and mundane.

Ask anyone how long it takes to get the search engine ranking you desire and you will get many answers. Some lucky souls will report that they have achieved good results in two to three months, while some will tell you it took them a year or two to get their targeted results. Think now if you embarked on this assignment using a haphazard set of keywords and finally achieved your desired rankings, let's say in six months, and realized that you were driving the wrong traffic to your site! You checked your site analytics and found that the traffic you were bringing to your site with those keywords just didn't convert.

You would have visitors, but they would not fill out any forms or purchase anything. Or maybe you had keywords for which there was very little search traffic regardless of how well you ranked. Now think about how much time and money was spent getting you to this point. Many people waste significant resources because they do not take the time to carefully identify the right keywords from the beginning.

A good example of this is choosing keywords like "cheap fares" versus "inexpensive fares". Both mean roughly the same thing, but a quick peek at keyword research numbers from Google tells us that "cheap fares" is searched on 165 thousand (K) times per year while "inexpensive fares" is searched on only 260 times. If you chose the latter, then you will not get nearly as much traffic and therefore are missing out on a big opportunity.

You also need to look at the type of traffic you will get with your keywords. This can be done only by testing your core keywords with analytics to observe the type of visitors that come to your site and what they do.

The sad part is that many don't even have site analytics set up and are not monitoring their overall site performance, much less their keyword performance. So they report to their boss that they are ranked on the first page of results but don't realize they are gaining little benefit. I am a very big proponent of setting up, analyzing, and interpreting site analytics. If you are not doing this, you should stop everything you *are* doing and insert this very important function into your daily processes. This is vital to running any successful marketing campaign. More on this topic later.

Suffice it to say that embarking on any online marketing campaign without having a solid keyword research study will come back to haunt you. Make sure you take the time to get this done correctly, and test and validate your list to ensure that you have identified the right keywords for your campaigns.

The Six Principles of Keyword Research

Before I reveal this first principle, I should say that it is the most important. In fact, I will be referring to it many times throughout this book.

1. The Secret Formula of Success

Let's start with an observation. Think back to when you searched for something online. You went to a search engine and typed in a search query. Let's stop there. While you typed in those words, didn't you have an expectation of what you would find? You may have struggled to find the right words to represent what you were looking for. Say you were searching for a digital camera as a birthday present. You had pretty good idea of what you ultimately wanted to find but you were not exactly sure how to phrase your words correctly so the search results would deliver what you seek. You can almost see the camera you want but are cautious to pick your words carefully.

I recently had this assignment and was searching for a digital camera for my daughter. Her only criterion was that it had to be orange. That was good for me since I haven't seen too many orange digital cameras. I thought this would make it easy to find. I had an image of a medium-sized pocket digital camera in my head. So I started with words "digital camera orange".

Now let me stop here and switch roles from searcher to marketer. When I as a marketer decide to employ keywords in my marketing campaign, I have a responsibility to deliver on a searcher's expectations. This is a very important statement. Many do not think of keywords this way. If I use SEO or PPC, for instance, and set up a campaign around "digital camera orange", I should design the campaign in such a way as to deliver what the searcher is likely expecting. You almost need to get into their head, walk in their shoes, if you will. See what they are seeing. Then when they are confronted with an ad or link description and click on to your website or blog, they will get what they were looking for.

That needs to be your mental attitude as you approach keyword research. Anticipate what searchers are looking for when you employ your targeted keywords. When you use keywords, you are essentially setting or reinforcing searchers' expectations about what they will find. Picking the right keywords becomes even more important. It has already been established that picking the wrong keywords wastes time and money. Make every effort to choose the keywords that will work for you and your searchers.

So the first variable in our formula is choosing the right keywords.

Now let's look at what the searcher finds as they click a link or an ad from a SERP. They will end up on a landing page where they will make a split-second decision on whether or not that page meets their expectation. They may invest a few more seconds looking the page over for more clues that they have landed on the right place. If the content on that page is relevant to the keyword they typed in, then they will likely take more time on the site.

The key word (no pun intended) here is *relevance*. If I am looking for an orange digital camera and I land on a page that has cameras of a different color, then I am likely to return to the SERP and click another link. If on the other hand I land on a page that has an orange digital camera, I will feel that I have landed on a qualified page and will invest the time to look at the specs and make a decision about whether or not I want to purchase that specific camera. The point here is that you need to match your landing page content with your keyword. By doing so, you have a significantly better chance that a conversion will take place, which is, of course, what most are in business for. By conversion, I mean they will purchase, download, fill out a form, or do whatever it is you want them to do when visiting your site.

So now let's put these variables together into a formula.

The Right Keywords + Relevant Destination Content = Conversions

By identifying the right keywords and then connecting them to relevant destination content, you will achieve a higher conversion rate. Again, think about your own experience as you surf the Internet looking for something. Think about how you feel when you type in a keyword and end up on a page with just what you are looking for. And if the web page is user friendly enough, you are likely to be led to a conversion.

Although I will be discussing landing page content and conversions, the main objective of this book is how to find the right keywords.

2. Keyword Relevance

I will take this idea of relevance a bit further by stating that each keyword you choose to use in your campaign needs to be relevant to all searcher touch points and ultimately lead to a conversion. So let's first take a look at these various touch points, as shown in Figure 1.2.

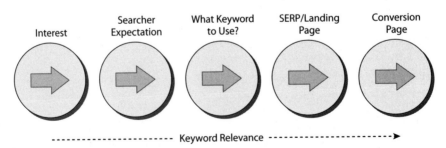

Figure 1.2 Keyword relevance

The first touch point may be some kind of message from an advertiser or even word of mouth. These messages can have the effect of triggering a response to act which leads one to seek more information before they make a purchase. Before they do they form an expectation in their mind about the item and how it might appear online. The struggle comes when they have to condense this expectation into what I call "the language of search" or keywords that represent the expectation they have in their mind. This can be a challenge as they try to come up with the keyword phrase that will lead them to the content they are looking for. Once the listings appear in the SERPs they pick one and click a link, where they are taken to a page on a website where they make a quick judgment as to whether or not they landed in the right place. If the content is relevant to the search query and the listing, it is more likely they will end up making a purchase or otherwise convert. Let's say the user's search query matches a keyword that appears in a PPC ad. If it does, the ad has a better chance of being clicked because users expect to see some clue that they are on the right path. So they click the ad, which takes them to a landing page. Now if the keyword they originally typed in appears not only in text format on the page but is also manifest with graphics or video content, then the searcher is going to feel right at home. They will feel content that their journey has taken them to the right place.

Of course, the journey typically doesn't end on this first landing page. It should provide them with enough information to lead them to other pages of relevant content that again supports their original search query and ultimately leads them to where a conversion takes place, be it contact form, final shopping cart, or download page. Each stop along the way is a touch point with the searcher. If with each touch point they are confronted with keywords and content that is relevant to their original search query, they will be much more receptive to interacting with the site.

It is important, then, to think about your marketing campaigns holistically from beginning to the end with keywords and content that are relevant to each other.

I would like to make a point here, which I will cover more in Chapter 12, "Using Keywords in Traditional Marketing Channels," that if the keywords that have been researched can then be shared with those who are driving the messaging, there can be another great benefit. If the core keywords can be embedded into the messages from the beginning, then they can actually influence the keywords that are chosen to be used in a search query. This is powerful. For those that are trying to condense their expectation into keywords, it is possible to help them with messaging that includes your targeted keywords. So don't underestimate the power of other channels to influence your target audience.

3. Keywords and the Buying Cycle

The third principle to understand is the relationship between keywords and the buying cycle of your visitors. Most companies have done some kind of research on the typical buying cycle of their customers. The buying cycle runs from the time they are "in the market" for your product or service to the time they actually make a purchase, and it can be measured and recorded. Some companies have a buying cycle of about two to three days; others two to three months or even two to three years, such as one client I know who sells timberframe home kits. You should find this information or begin the process of conducting this research within your company. Understanding the buying cycle will help you determine where your audience is as they use various keywords to find you.

Let's walk through a typical scenario. Say I am in the market for a new road bike. I have decided that it is time for me to get some more exercise and find a bike I can use to ride with my friends. I go to a search engine and type in the word "bike". What does typing in such a broad term tell you about me? It could suggest that I am in the beginning of my buying cycle and I am just beginning the process to collect information. Am I ready to purchase road bike yet? Of course not; I am merely starting my search.

When I type in the word "bike", I see results for mountain bikes, motorcycles, bike clothing, bike parts, and so on. All of this, of course, is dependent on where I am located and my searching history. Since the search engine is smart enough to know basically where I am and they have information about other related searches I may have made, it will attempt to prescribe to me the type of results I might be looking for. Still, the word "bike" is a general term, and the results I get are not specific. What am I likely to do next? Yes, I will refine my search to something more specific. So I type in "road bike". Now I start seeing better results. At this point I may click a few links and look at a few road bikes. I may even look at a review or two. After I have done a little research, I realize I would like to see one up close. So I go back to the search engine and type in "road bike greensboro, nc", because I want to find local retailers who sell road bikes so I can see them.

After I take the time to visit these retail stores and start narrowing down my search to the two or three brands I am most interested in, I may come back to a search engine and get even more specific. This time I type in "trek bikes", "specialized bikes", and "cervelo bikes". I will take the time to study each of these brands in more detail, looking for the features that impress me the most. Finally I narrow down my choice. I think I want to purchase a Madone 6.7 SSL. So now am approaching the end of my buying cycle and looking for the best price. I type in "trek madone 6.7 ssl" and begin searching for online or local retailers who can offer me the best price.

Now that I have typed in a very specific query like "trek madone 6.7 ssl", what does that tell you about me? It tells you that I may be at the end of the buying cycle and very close to a conversion. So if you have what I am looking for at the right price, I would likely purchase from you.

What does all of this mean? If I choose keywords that are general or broad, I am likely to attract visitors who are not ready to convert, who are just looking for information. If I chose more specific keywords, then I am likely to attract an audience who is ready to convert. Which audience would you rather have? I am not saying that attracting a broad audience is bad, but you need to have a different expectation from that group. You need to treat them differently. Teach them what to look for in a bike, for instance, and be a good resource for them as they collect their needed information. Then, if they have a good experience, they might return and buy from you.

Have you ever gone into a store and found a salesperson who was very knowledgeable and really helped you understand the product related to your situation? They took the time to help you out. Even if they didn't have the best price, didn't you purchase from them because of their expertise and how they took care of you? I know I have.

Let's take a closer look. In Figure 1.3, you can see that searchers who type in broad search terms are just beginning the buying cycle. As they become more informed and educated, they start typing in more specific terms. Then they find the content they are looking for and finally narrow their decision down to one or two items and start looking for those that have the best features, benefits, or price. They may even look for who can provide them with the product or service the quickest. Either way, they are ready to buy or convert. This is where they will be using search terms that are very specific.

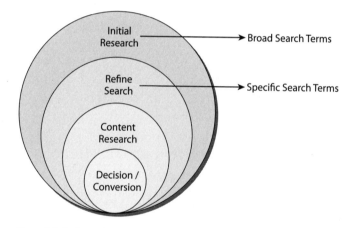

Figure 1.3 Buying cycle

Understanding this cycle can help you understand how you should approach your campaign and which keywords you should use.

4. Broad Keywords vs. Specific Keywords

For this next principle I will expand on the terms *broad* and *specific*. You have already learned that broad search queries are typically used at the beginning of the buying cycle and represent a searcher who is just getting started. These search terms are searched on more often and are pretty popular.

On the other hand, a searcher using specific words in their search query typically knows exactly what they want and is in a later phase of their buying cycle. These keywords are not searched on that often and aren't as popular.

Let's take a closer look at the differences in popularity. I will use the Google AdWords Keyword Tool to gather some quick stats about the keywords related to my bike search I used earlier. (I will cover keyword tools and how to use and understand them in more detail in Chapter 3.)

Look at Table 1.1. If I look up the word "bicycle" and "bicycle shop" I get a larger number of global monthly searches. If we then look at keywords that are much more specific we get a lower number of searches.

▶ **Table 1.1** Broad keywords versus specific keywords

Keyword	Global Monthly Searches
bicycle	5,000,000
bicycle shop	90,500
trek madone 6.7	170
bicycle shop san diego	1,900

As you consider your use of broad keywords versus specific keywords, you should understand the dynamics between the two. Generally, you will get more impressions with broad keywords, but your conversion rate, and in many cases the conversions themselves, will be low. This again is because people are in the beginning of their buying cycle and are starting their search. In my example earlier, I started by using the term "bike". Once I saw the results, I really didn't click anything because I realized the term was too broad. I immediately refined my search to "road bike," which is a little more specific. It was then that I started clicking links.

Broader, generic keywords will give you more impressions. If you are running a PPC campaign and use general, nonspecific keywords, you are likely to get many impressions and your click-through rates (CTRs) will be lower. However, you are also likely to get many more unproductive clicks that can run up your costs and lower your conversion rates.

On the other hand, if you were to use very specific keywords, you will not get as many impressions, but the number of clicks and your CTR will be a lot higher. This is mainly because people who use those keywords know exactly what they are looking for, and if you ad shows up, they are likely to click on to your landing page.

The strategic decision you need to make is whether to make your campaign more branding oriented or more conversion oriented. If you are out to gain impressions and that is the success metric you are focusing on, then broad keywords will work best for you. On the other hand, if you are looking for searchers to become customers, specific keywords should be in your strategy.

In Chapter 5, I will discuss some methods of refining your keyword search, and you will be able to decide whether broad or specific keywords will serve you best. You at least need to be able to see the dynamics between the two and plan accordingly. There is a hybrid strategy that includes both branding and acquisition. That means you will be using a set of keywords just for branding and another to draw traffic to your site for a conversion. Table 1.2 outlines the different strategies:

▶ **Table 1.2** Keyword strategies

Strategy	Tactic
Branding strategy	Broad keywords
Conversion strategy	Specific keywords
Hybrid strategy	Broad and specific keywords

5. The Long Tail

Another thing that is related to broad and specific keywords is the long tail. The term *long tail* was popularized by Chris Anderson of *WIRED* magazine who later wrote a book on the topic. The example he used was how Amazon generates most of its revenue from a large number of specialized titles, not necessarily the big, high-selling blockbusters you come across in bookstores. The idea is that each specialized title may only sell small quantities per year, but there are enormous amounts of them.

This same principle applies to keywords you may use for Internet marketing, as illustrated in Figure 1.4. The more generic, or broad, keywords are more popular, but they are more costly and competitive. On the other hand, more descriptive, or specific, keyword phrases are less popular but are often also less costly and less competitive.

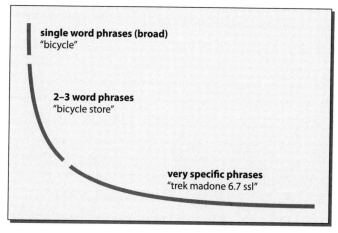

Figure 1.4 The long tail

Long-tail keywords tend to be easier to rank well for than the more generic or single- or double-keyword phrases, mainly because there is less competition. This coincides with my earlier discussion on broad versus specific. It really is the same principle, but it's important for you to understand as you make goals for how you want your keywords to perform.

The shorter, more generic keywords, often referred to as *head terms*, are those that are more popular and more competitive. These are the "best sellers" if you will. Unless you have a large budget and staff, you may not get the results you are looking for by going after those terms.

Here are some benefits of using long-tail keywords:

- In bulk, they can generate a large amount of search volume to your site.
- They are usually less competitive and therefore result in a lower cost per click (CPC) and higher click-through rates (CTRs).
- Since they are more specific, ads and landing pages can be better tailored and more relevant to match searchers' needs.
- Searchers using long-tail keywords are often further along the buying cycle and are closer to making purchase decision.
- With lower CPC, higher CTR, and higher conversion rates (CVRs), long-tail keywords can be very profitable.

So let's take a closer look at how search volume, CTR, CPCs, CVR, and cost per acquisition (CPA) differ for searches containing varying numbers of keywords. You will also see how long-tail keywords can be beneficial.

For this example, I will use the combined average results of three PPC campaigns over a four-month period of time. I will go into more detail about using keywords in your PPC campaign in Chapter 7, but here I just want to help you better understand the power of these long-tail keywords. Also, even though this example is based on a PPC campaign, the principle will work for other types of Internet marketing campaigns.

Search Volume or Impressions

Let's start with search volume and number of long-tail searches. In Figure 1.5, the first column represents the number of words per keyword phrase. Note that there seems to be more searches for three- to five-word phrases. As the search queries go beyond six-word phrases, you see a drop in the number of searches.

One important observation, however, is the accumulated volume of all of the long-tail keywords. On average, they made of 24 percent of all the impressions. So a keyword campaign made up of many of these long-tail keywords can be a significant source of traffic.

Click-Through Rate (CTR)

Let's now look at CTR and see if it, as suspected, is higher for long-tail keywords. As mentioned, long-tail keywords are less competitive, so you have more of a chance that someone will click to find you. Additionally, you can create more relevant and specific ads or descriptions that help encourage searchers to click.

So let's add the click-through rate layer onto our previous illustration to visualize the behavior against searches and the number of keywords, as shown in Figure 1.6. Notice how the keyword one to three words in length have lower CTRs than keywords made up of four+ words. This illustrates how long-tail keywords that are more specific and relevant are also more likely to be clicked by searchers.

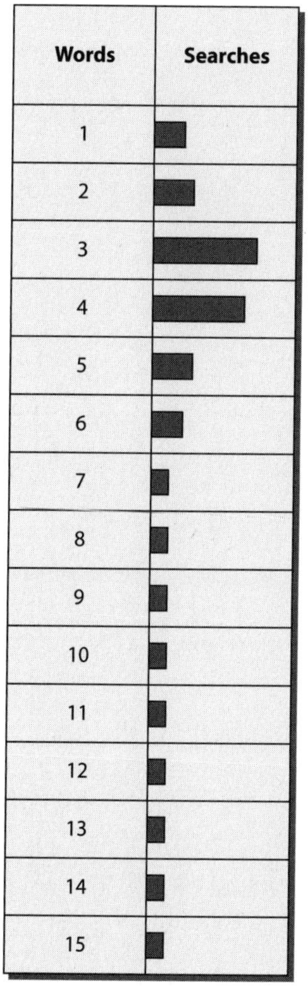

Words	Searches
1	
2	
3	
4	
5	
6	
7	
8	
9	
10	
11	
12	
13	
14	
15	

Figure 1.5 Search volume profile for head and long-tail keywords

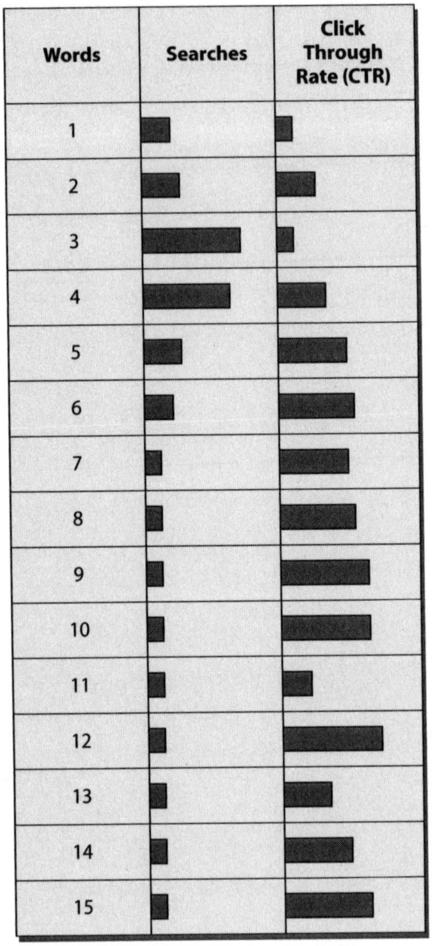

Words	Searches	Click Through Rate (CTR)
1		
2		
3		
4		
5		
6		
7		
8		
9		
10		
11		
12		
13		
14		
15		

Figure 1.6 Click-through rate performance of long-tail keywords

Cost Per Click (CPC)

Now, let's look at the effect of the cost per click on long-tail keywords. Are they as cheap as you would expect? Since fewer people are bidding on them and there is less competition, you would think so, right?

In Figure 1.7 you can see that for searches of 13 words or more, CPCs are a bit cheaper (longer bar represent higher cost). On the other hand, searches for 13 words or less result in CPCs that are relatively similar. It also appears that a 9-word keyword phrase seems to cost as much as a 3- to 4-word search query.

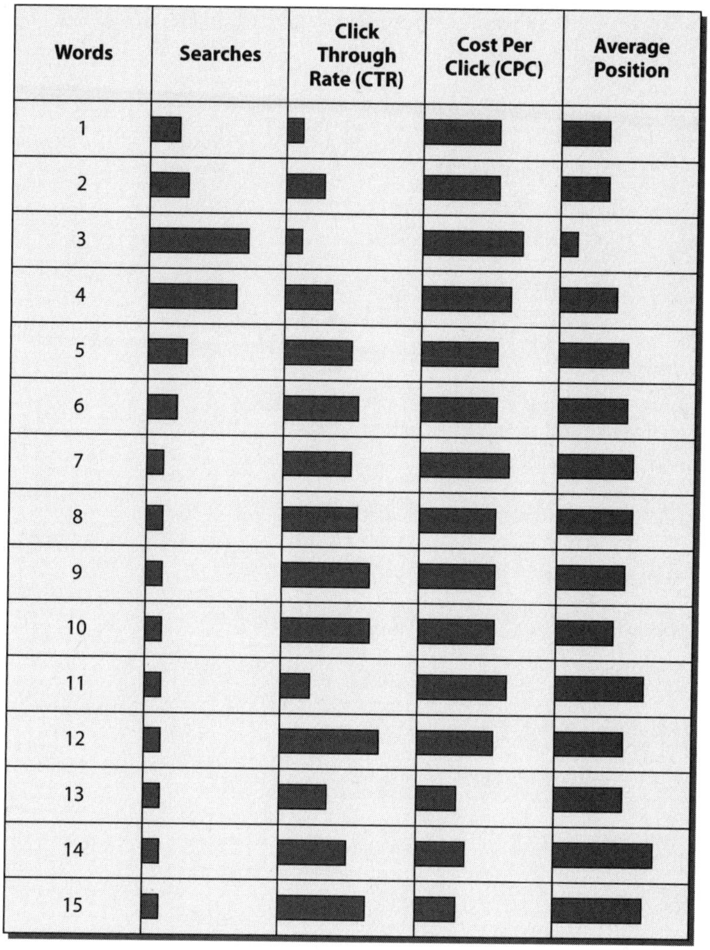

Figure 1.7 Impact of long-tail keywords on cost per click

Now if you factor in average position (a longer bar on the chart represents a higher ad ranking) to the equation, you will see that one- to three-keyword phrases net a lower ad ranking and ads will appear at the lower end of the search engine results page. As words get beyond the three-word phrase, their ad rank starts rising significantly.

So even though CPCs are similar for searches on all word counts, the long-tail keywords typically enjoy a higher position.

Conversion Rate

I think that most people would agree with the assumption that the conversion rate for long-tail keywords will be higher. Based on the logic of the consumer buying cycle, we would guess that searchers who are using long-tail keywords know what they are looking for. They are making their final decisions and are ready to buy.

As you can see from Figure 1.8, as the number of words used in the keyword phrase increases, so does the conversion rate.

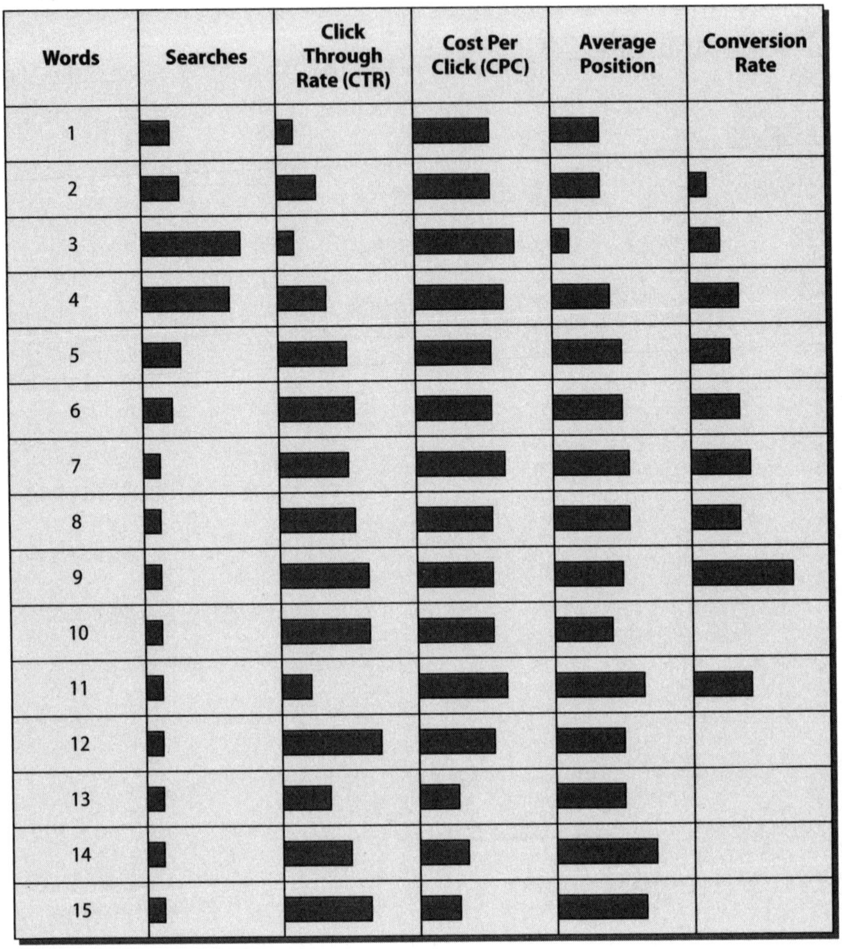

Words	Searches	Click Through Rate (CTR)	Cost Per Click (CPC)	Average Position	Conversion Rate
1					
2					
3					
4					
5					
6					
7					
8					
9					
10					
11					
12					
13					
14					
15					

Figure 1.8 Conversion rate

Cost Per Acquisition (CPA)

CPA, or cost per acquisition, is the amount of money you are willing to spend to acquire a new customer or lead. Let's say your usual new customer represents $100 in gross profit to you. If it takes $50 of your PPC campaign to produce a new customer, then your CPA is $50. Your net profit is $50.

Let's look at what effect the long tail has on CPA. In Figure 1.9, you see that as the word count increases, the CPA decreases. This essentially means that long-tail keywords convert at higher rates and lower costs than head keywords. The cost to get a new customer will decrease as you employ long-tail keywords.

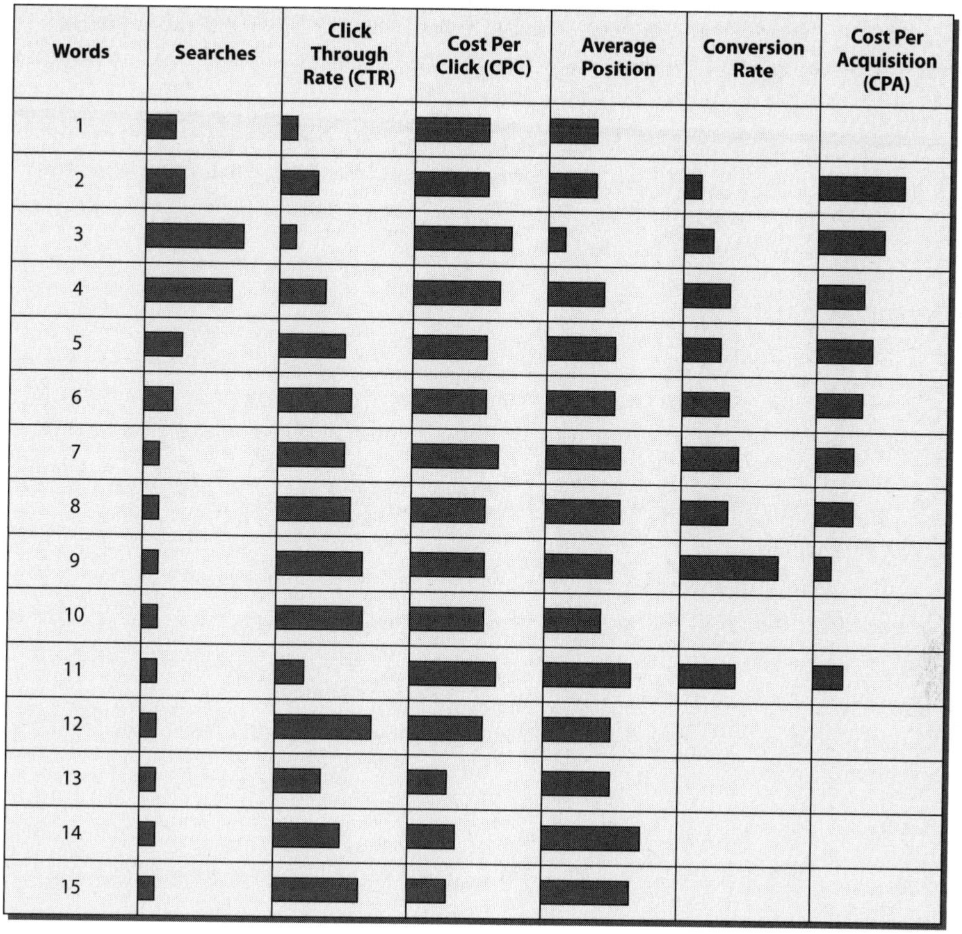

Words	Searches	Click Through Rate (CTR)	Cost Per Click (CPC)	Average Position	Conversion Rate	Cost Per Acquisition (CPA)
1						
2						
3						
4						
5						
6						
7						
8						
9						
10						
11						
12						
13						
14						
15						

Figure 1.9 Cost per acquisition

Let's summarize our findings with an observation of the benefits of using long-tail keywords:

- Significant search volume
- Higher CTR
- Cheaper CPCs (or better ad positions at same CPCs)
- Higher conversion rates
- Lower CPA

I hope that this has illustrated the power of going after the long-tail keywords and opened your mind to the possibilities. It will take more work to find these keywords and organize them into relevant groups, but, as you can see, it will be worth it.

Now, head keywords do have a place. Remember, if you are not interested in conversion and are aiming more at impressions, then keywords should be your choice. They are also good for branding and awareness.

From a strategic point of view, you should consider both a long-tail keyword strategy and a head-term strategy if needed. Make sure you take time to measure your own performance. What works for one company many not work for you and your industry, so see what works best for you.

6. Keyword Interpretation

This last principle delves into using keywords to better understand your target audience and those that actually visit your website. It goes without saying that you should have an analytics tool installed on your website. If you don't have one, please install one as soon as possible! The same goes for those who have an analytics tool installed but do not take the time to dig into the keyword portion of the reports to learn a wealth of information.

Once you mine this information, I recommend getting your team together and have a healthy discussion about what you see and how you interpret it. If you see that a particular keyword is bringing traffic to your website but those visitors aren't converting, you need to ask yourself why. What can you do to get them to convert? Or do you need to eliminate that keyword from your campaign and target a different set of visitors who will convert?

Peek Inside the Minds of Searchers

As marketers, we thrive on research and the idea of learning more about our target audience. How about learning more about how they search? By analyzing the keywords that are driving traffic to your website, you can find out how your customers search to find your site. Learn which phrases they commonly use. Many times we *think* we know which keywords they are using, but if we look closely, we can *really* know.

These and other gems are waiting for you as you study the analytics reports. Again, there is a lot of value in pulling together your team to study the results. I have sat in many meetings with my own staff or with a client to scrutinize the keyword analytics reports. Sometimes most of us will miss an important observation, but there is usually one team member who will see something important and interpret it correctly. This can make all of the difference.

Observe Which Keywords Are Performing for SEO and PPC

If you observe that your site is showing up on the first page for specific keywords, congratulations. But don't stop there. Look closely at how much traffic you get from those keywords. I have talked to many people whose only goal is to get ranked on the first page for their keywords. Many don't measure the traffic or, more important, the conversions from those keywords. Many times they learn that the highly ranked keywords are driving hardly any traffic to their site.

So it is important to pay close attention to actual traffic and the sales you gain from your keywords and not just your ranking in search engines. You will often be surprised at which keywords are really performing and which are not.

With PPC you have a lot more flexibility on your use of keywords. You can decide quickly which ones to use and which ones not to use. You also can use many keywords at a time and test to see which work and which do not. If you find some keywords that are performing well for you, you might decide to add them to your SEO campaign. Generally speaking, searchers click more often on the natural listings than on PPC ads.

So using PPC to test your keywords and learn about how they perform is a great way to study your target audience and learn their behavior.

Get Ideas for New Content, Services, or Products

As you observe the types of search keywords visitors use to get to your site, you might find that many of them prefer a certain phrase that you haven't thought of. If those keywords are popular enough, you might want to consider using them for new content. Or you may even decide to use a popular keyword for naming a product or service. What a great market research idea.

Summary

You have learned about keywords and how people are accustomed to condensing large concepts into a keyword phrase to help them find what they are looking for, whether it is in a book, at the library, or online. More importantly, you have learned the importance of conducting keyword research correctly from the beginning. The failure to do so can be costly—in time and money.

The six principles of keyword research will help form a solid foundation as you build your knowledge of keyword research in the following chapters.

How to Develop a Successful Keyword Strategy

Does your organization have a short-term or long-term strategy? Do you know what it is? How will you measure success? What is the right process for implementing a solid keyword strategy plan? What can you learn from your competitors?

In this chapter, I will answer these questions and arm you with the latest tips for establishing, measuring and implementing a successful keyword strategy.

Chapter Contents

Develop Your Marketing Strategy, Plan, and Goals

In Chapter 1, we established that keyword research is a strategic component of any marketing campaign. As such, it is important to integrate it into the overall goals and objectives of your organization.

Does your organization have a marketing strategy? Do you know what it is? Your marketing strategy is really a tool to help you focus your energy on the greatest opportunities to increase sales. A written marketing strategy is shaped by your overall business goals and can include the following items:

- A definition of your business
- A description of your products or services
- A profile of your target audience
- Your company's role in relation to your competition
- The unique positioning of your company
- Why you are unique and compelling to your customers
- Your pricing strategy
- Your distribution channels
- Your competitive market segments

This strategy document should be used to judge the appropriateness of business actions. If business actions take a course that isn't outlined, then you should reassess your actions to get back on course. Strategies should be written to be measurable and actionable. This is key. Your strategy sets the criteria in which you will be able to measure success.

Your marketing plan is the practical application of your marketing strategy. While your marketing strategy outlines your goals, your marketing plan outlines the specific actions or tactics you will use to reach those goals. You really need both documents working together to be successful. Furthermore, you will achieve better performance with your plan if it is understood and realized by all parts of the organization.

So what does this have to do with keyword research? The basis of a keyword research project is to develop a list of core and foundational keywords for which your organization wishes to be known. These keywords should not only be integrated into the marketing plan, they should also be ingrained into the minds of all constituents. The more these keywords are known by all, the more they will be used and the more consistent they are to the overall plan, just like a well-worded, heartfelt mission statement.

Let's say that your marketing strategy dictates that your goal is to obtain 14 percent market share within your industry in the next five years. Your marketing plan should outline the tactics or marketing campaigns you will use to achieve this. Some of these campaigns could focus on the following goals:

- Generating awareness and branding
- Increasing consumer confidence
- Increasing customer satisfaction

There can be more, but let's start with generating awareness and branding. Online tactical campaigns can include Search Engine Optimization (SEO), Pay-Per-Click Advertising (PPC), social media marketing, and mobile and local search. Offline campaigns can include print, TV, radio, and public relations (PR).

One of the steps in using any of these channels is to write the copy and content for each one. This is where keyword research should be added to your arsenal, to better understand the mindset of your target audience and which keywords will resonate with them the most. The keywords can be incorporated into any of the previously mentioned channels. When used consistently, they will help to form the basis for your goal of generating awareness and branding.

This also creates relevancy between your campaign and landing page messaging. Relevancy is the glue that will keep your visitors on your site longer and lead them to a conversion.

Decide Which Marketing Channels You Will Use

A strong marketing strategy will form the basis of your marketing plan. This plan outlines all of the specific action items needed to successfully implement the organization's strategy. So your marketing plan is essentially made up of a list of tactics you will use. In Figure 2.1 you can see the interrelationship of these different channels and how they can work together.

I like to think of these tactics as *drive-to-site* campaigns. Essentially that is what they accomplish. They catch the attention of your target audience and invite them to your website or blog. This is their purpose. The purpose of your website is to convert them into customers. This is a very important point to understand. If you find you have a poor conversion rate, that is a symptom of your website's inability to "close the sale," if you will.

It is not the job of your drive-to-site tactics to convert. However, it is their job to set an expectation. When visitors arrive on your site, its function is to deliver on that expectation, providing visitors with the information they need and leading them down the path to a conversion.

When you develop your site, there are three aspects to the development process:

- Visual design
- Technical design
- Behavioral design

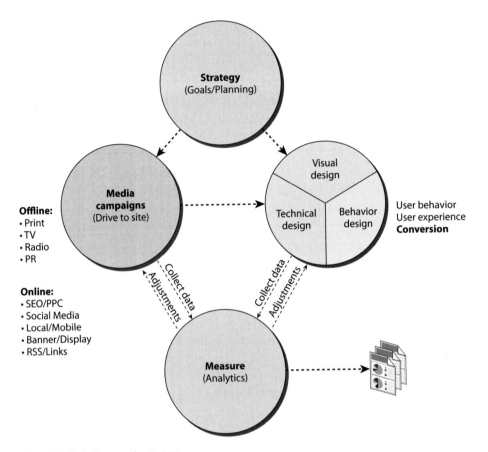

Figure 2.1 Marketing campaign strategy

Visual design is the creative and visual aspect to your site. It is typically in harmony with elements of the brand's style guide. It is important when visitors see your brick-and-mortar store, your advertising, and your website that there is a common visual thread that is woven through each. This helps with brand consistency.

Technical design is planning and orchestrating all of the technical components that make up the website. It includes server architecture, web applications, and databases that work together to make your site function as it is intended to function. When implemented correctly, the technology seems invisible. It is not until errors start popping up that the technology is noticed.

Behavioral design is, in my opinion, the most important because it speaks to learning the behavior of your audience and then designing accordingly. I have personally conducted many one-on-one interviews with people to learn about their likes and dislikes and their preferred processes and features. When this information is collected at the beginning of a campaign, you have a basis for developing the visual and technical. Too often a look-and-feel treatment is designed first without any consideration for the audience and its participation on the site. Then when a visual skin is applied to the technical infrastructure, behavioral factors are considered as an afterthought. This is a recipe for failure.

All three are integral to the process, but behavioral design provides the psychological insight that helps you structure the information flow, the navigational elements that get visitors what they need and in the order that leads to a conversion.

For example, suppose you operate week-long kayaking trips. As you conduct your research and learn about your customers and how they make purchase decisions, you learn that many of them first look on your website for available dates and pricing. Once the dates and prices match up to their family's availability and budget, they spend more time on your site. This may cause you to make date and price information more accessible on the home page and strip out other content that distracts. You learn essentially what questions your customers need to answer first, second, third, and so on. This helps you build the visual and technical elements to support your customers' needs. When this happens, you have happy visitors that are more likely to convert.

Keyword research play a role in the behavioral design process by giving you insights into search queries that are commonly used or that resonate well with your audience. You may identify keyword trends or demographic data that is associated with certain keywords. Finally, as you categorize your keywords into relevant themes, it will help you as you construct your information architecture and content design, which helps to anticipate users' needs and fulfill expectations.

Finally, you want to set up your analytics infrastructure or your mechanisms for measuring success. This should be done for both your drive-to-site channels and your website. Your marketing plan should outline the budget and percentage of use for each online and offline channel you use to drive traffic to your website. Then outline what you hope to achieve with each one. You will need to measure the effectiveness of both drive-to-site tactics and website performance. Analytics is the process that allows you to measure which channels are succeeding and which are not. It also shows you how well your website performs by itself and against each channel. Once you identify things that aren't working, make the necessary adjustments to increase effectiveness.

How Will You Measure Success?

What does it mean to measure success? Is it just a matter of tagging your site and viewing the analytics? Or is it just looking at keyword ranking? Success can be measured in several different ways. Mainly it means you have thought ahead of the process and have visualized what success looks like. If you apply what we previously discussed, then you should visualize success in the form of overall business goals.

For example, I frequently have the opportunity to provide consulting to organizations as I travel, speak, and train. Many ask me to evaluate their websites and their SEO efforts. One of the first questions I ask them is, "Do you have any metrics in place?" Many will tell me that they are monitoring their keyword ranking and seem to be doing well with some keywords and are falling behind with the others.

In this case, the metric for success is keyword ranking. This is not a bad metric. It basically means that the higher their rank, the more visibility they will achieve. The more visibility, the more brand awareness and possibly more traffic. What's missing is tying this into the overall goals of the organization. Let's say that one of the overall goals is to increase the amount of sales and leads by 7 percent within the next six months. How would you link keyword ranking to this goal?

First you need to connect keyword performance to the website analytics to identify which keywords are driving traffic to the website and generating conversions such as leads or orders. Next you should look at the keywords that are not driving the traffic or conversions and try to understand why they are not. Then make necessary changes to get them to perform better.

The problem with just focusing on keyword ranking is that you may have keywords that rank on the first page of Google, but if they are not driving any traffic, they are doing you no good. Furthermore, if they are not bringing you more traffic, they are probably not converting. So having a solid understanding of business goals will help you better define your success metrics for each campaign.

I remember in the late 1990s when the primary metric for website traffic was the number of hits. Then it quickly evolved into a more meaningful metric, which was the number of unique visitors. We now have more channels than just our website to focus on. We have SEO, RSS feeds, email marketing, social media, PPC, and other channels that need to be factored in.

With all of these variables, it becomes more and more complicated to determine how success is measured from one campaign to another. I suggest defining success metrics within your marketing plan and then defining them for each campaign. Take a look at Table 2.1 to see an example of how you can measure multiple campaigns against ROI.

▶ **Table 2.1** Campaign dashboard

	Traffic/				Cost/		Conversion			
	Impressions	Clicks	CTR	Conversion	Investment	CPA	Value	Revenue	Profit	ROI
SEO	10,000	400	4.00%	20	$300	$15	$100	$2,000	$1,700	467%
PPC 1	500	10	2.00%	2	$500	$250	$100	$200	-$300	-160%
PPC 2	2,000	50	2.50%	8	$700	$88	$100	$800	$100	-86%
Email 1	500	30	6.00%	5	$200	$40	$100	$500	$300	50%
Email 2	1,000	50	5.00%	10	$300	$30	$100	$1,000	$700	133%
Print 1	20,000	150	0.75%	25	$2,000	$80	$100	$2,500	$500	-75%

You can see that we have a mix of online and offline campaigns here. Some columns might not match up directly, but do your best to include as much detail as possible. For example, for SEO it is difficult to know the number of impressions. It is important to identify the value of a conversion. If you are selling products online, this would be the value for products sold through each channel. Or maybe you sell an annual subscription for $100. This number is important to calculate ROI.

With the information outlined in Table 2.1, you would conclude that SEO and Email 1 provided the largest profits and the best ROI. The point here is to help you understand how you can tie all of your marketing campaigns to a single goal, in this case, profit and ROI. With a dashboard like this, it is much easier to keep your eye on the ball and on track with goals.

Another way to look at success metrics is to divide your analytics data into two camps: qualitative and quantitative. *Qualitative* data provides insights into categories based on subjective or intangible ideas. A qualitative analysis would seek to answer these questions:

- Are you reaching the right audience?
- Are you providing valuable content?
- Does your brand have a positive sentiment?

Quantitative analysis, on the other hand, looks at more verifiable data that is statistical in nature. Quantitative data would answer these questions:

- How much traffic came from a specific campaign?
- How many followers did we gain?
- What was our click-through rate (CTR)?

You may have specific goals to reach that were reported in Table 2.1; however, you may also want to consider adding to your processes the qualitative results of your campaigns. This is where you will learn more about human characteristics. It will also provide insight into ways to improve your campaign, which will improve the quantitative results.

Setting Up SMART Goals

We have all learned the importance of setting goals. It is a critical factor in setting up the right success metrics for your digital marketing campaign. Armed with your organization's strategic vision and overall business objectives, you can start the process of setting up individual goals for each channel you use. A great approach is to use *SMART goals*. It takes more time and energy to set them up, but using SMART goals helps to ensure quality. *SMART* is an acronym that stand for the following attributes:

S = Specific

M = Measurable

A = Attainable

R = Realistic

T = Timely

I will cover each attribute because they are important. First, define a goal that is clearly stated and *specific.*—for example, "Increase our average monthly unique visitors to our website from 10,000 to 15,000 within six months with top five targeted keywords." Not only is this specific, it is also *measurable*. Any good web analytics program can track that performance. Contrast that goal with "Increase our website traffic this year." Can you see the difference? Even though this may seem like a simple concept, how many of us take the time to set up a clearly defined goal.

The next thing to consider is making the goal *attainable*. We would all like to be ranked No. 1 for our target keywords in our SEO campaign. Is this really attainable? Is it *realistic*? Probably not. How about "Increase our ranking for [target keyword] from page 6 to page 2 within the next six months"? This might be more attainable and realistic. Any past analytics you have should help you identify the right trends to help you set a realistic and attainable goal.

The final attribute is *timely*. It is okay to have long-term goals and five-year strategic plans to help provide a vision for where your organization is going. For the purpose of measuring success, you need to have short-term milestones that help you feel you are hitting targets in a timely manner. In the last two examples, I used a time span of six months. You might consider monthly, quarterly, or another short-time segment for your success metrics. Either way, by setting up short-term goals, you'll be in a better position to measure your long-term successes.

Benchmarking

Another consideration when establishing success metrics is benchmarking. *Benchmarking* is evaluating or checking data or a statistic by comparing it to a standard. For example, when you first launch your site and gather statistical data like number of visits, that becomes the standard or benchmark to measure future successes or failures. You may have ever heard someone rattle off a statistic like "We have 560 followers on Twitter," or "Our site had four thousand visits this month." These common statistics don't say much unless they are placed in the context of your competition, your industry, or even within your own company.

Have you benchmarked your competition or other similar sites within your industry? How many followers do they have on Twitter? How about internally? What was your traffic like a month ago or at the beginning of your search campaign. Benchmarking is a simple concept, but it will help to put your statistics in a clearer context that has more meaning. To gain a little more insight into benchmarking, you might find SEOmoz's blog post on SEO and social media benchmarking useful: www.seomoz.org/blog/seo-and-social-media-benchmarking.

Team Members and Their Roles and Goals

There is usually a fair amount of attention on the development of Internet marketing programs, but what sometimes gets overlooked is the ongoing work after development. Marketing programs can be difficult to operate and maintain. It can also be a challenge to integrate them with other marketing efforts. More importantly, the ability to set up the ROI model can be a headache.

These issues are not necessarily centered on the *what*, but the *who*. Is your marketing team organized to handle these issues? Are there clear role descriptions and performance goals in place for all team members?

Before I dive into organizational scenarios, I would like to outline some of the general challenges that face Internet marketing teams:

- Content
- Clear strategies and goals
- Success metrics and methodology
- Competitive response

Content

Let's begin with a look at website content issues like product images, text, and video, for example. Especially if you are a larger organization, gathering and managing the site content in a timely manner can be a real challenge. Usually the problem lies not in finding knowledgeable people to write the content but rather no one takes ownership. The content stakeholders are not part of the marketing team, and getting them to produce and keep up with online content is a struggle. The goal here would be to pull them into the process of keeping content up-to-date and to do it in a way that makes them feel they have ownership and are a critical part of the team.

Clear Strategies and Goals

This, of course, has been mentioned previously, but all team members having a clear sense of direction of the overall strategy is important for success. You might have all of the skills you need to implement your marketing plan, but if your direction is not clear, you will find that performance will be less than desirable. Make sure the message and direction are clear and you have the right leadership in place. This will help to ensure that your plan is implemented toward a common brand goal.

Success Metrics and Methodology

It is important that all marketing efforts have a common analytics framework to evaluate performance across all channels. There will always be plenty of data to sift through, but aligning goals for each channel and making sure performance can be measured "apples to apples" can be tricky. Clear success metrics need to be established so all team members have a clear understanding of what real performance is, not to mention having the right ROI data or dashboard metrics (as was demonstrated in Table 2.1) to bring to the leadership hierarchy and be understood by all.

Competition

It can sometimes be difficult to focus on only your own business goals without being distracted by what your competition is doing. While you are working on internal issues, your competition has already launched a social media campaign and is ahead of the game. You may be so focused internally that you neglect to see what is happening in the marketplace and fail to take advantage of new approaches or leveraging new marketing channels.

Organization Design

There are several ways to structure a team for maximum performance. This is somewhat dependent on whether you are a small or large organization. I will outline six types of structures you might consider to help your team become more successful and help meet your business goals.

Matrix Organizational Structure

This first structure is one of my favorites because I have personally used it to build a highly efficient and innovative team. As you can see in Figure 2.2, this structure is organized with members reporting primarily to some kind of director or supervisor on a day-to-day basis. Additionally, each discipline is grouped together and meets regularly to share ideas and innovations. So each column represents accounts, while each row focuses on the discipline. However, the team sits together daily as an account team, which is made up of creative, technical, and behavioral roles, for example. This will also work for other disciplines you might have.

In many organizations, members of a department (say the creative department or the technical department) sit together, mainly because they have the same interests. The problem with this structure is isolation from other groups. The goal is to get more of an interdisciplinary collaboration to take place.

	Account Team 1	Account Team 2	Account Team 3	Account Team 4
Discipline Leader Creative	**Creative** Team Member	**Creative** Team Member	**Creative** Team Member	**Creative** Team Member
Discipline Leader Technical	**Technical** Team Member	**Technical** Team Member	**Technical** Team Member	**Technical** Team Member
Discipline Leader Behavioral	**Behavioral** Team Member	**Behavioral** Team Member	**Behavioral** Team Member	**Behavioral** Team Member

Figure 2.2 Matrix organization structure

It is an interesting thing to have people from multiple disciplines sit together as a team and work on a project. At first it can be a challenge as the team members struggle to relate to one another. But soon they learn to see things from another point of view. They start to relate more to other team members and their roles. Once the creative person understands the point of view of the technical person and vice versa, learning takes place. I have seen teams modify their processes and approach to become more efficient as a result. The collaboration and innovation that comes from this kind of structure is incredible.

A multimillion-dollar client once came to us for a spot visit to basically "look under the hood" before they made a decision to work with us. They asked to interview one of our teams to gain some insights into our processes and methodologies. So I pulled one of our teams at random into a conference room to be interviewed. A very interesting thing happened. When a technical question was asked, it was the creative person who answered first. Then when a creative question was asked, the technical person was excited to answer. They worked so closely with each other that they knew each other's discipline and processes very well, more so than if they were sitting by themselves with people from the same discipline. The prospective client was completely blown away. They had never seen anything like this. As a result of this, and some other factors, they gave us the business on the spot.

The nice thing about a matrix structure is that you can still satisfy the need for each team member to work and collaborate with their own discipline. We identified a discipline leader to organize a regular meeting with the group to discuss and collaborate on issues related to them. For instance, the technical folks would talk about and discuss any advances in tools, protocols, and processes. I highly recommend this kind of structure.

Embedded Structure

You can take the idea of a matrix structure to a new level and embed certain team members into other divisions or departments. They can have a dotted line report to the management within that division as well. What this accomplishes is that this individual becomes a team member in that department and is the subject matter expert for the group. They build a closer relationship with members of the department and help to educate them on best practices for SEO, let's say. This way, key information from a keyword research study for SEO can organically (no pun intended) grow within that department.

Direct Report Structure

Another variation of the matrix structure is to literally place a team member within another department and have them report directly to that department. This allows the SEM team member, for example, to be accountable to the department and not to the SEM team. They can then meet with a leader of the SEM group to stay grounded and be trained in the latest best practices and share knowledge and ideas.

Training Structure

If you do not have enough SEM personnel to go around, you can set up a training team to conduct training for each division or department so they can become more knowledgeable about important processes, best practices, and methodologies.

To take this one step further, you can identify champions or advocates within each division and provide extra training for them so they can represent your interests with their own department. Make sure you keep the lines of communication and training open to these people. Share insights and learning with them, especially keyword research data.

Outside Vendor Structure

If you cannot afford to have your own team of SEM professionals on board, you can reach out to other Internet marketing vendors. I highly suggest that if you consider this model, you treat them as team members within your own organization and not as vendors who do a project and then walk away. Treat the relationship more like a partnership than a vendor relationship. Have them train you on their processes and find opportunities for collaborative meetings.

As you review regular analytics for your website or SEO performance, make sure it is not a report that gets emailed around. Set up a face-to-face (or voice-to-voice) meeting to discuss the key takeaways and recommendations for improvements. This way your vendors learn more about your company and its needs, which will make them more of a value to you and your team. You then learn more about Internet marketing and are generally more educated and enabled to make wiser marketing decisions.

There are probably more structures you can use, but I hope you at least see the principle of cross-pollination and collaboration. You will help to ensure that important information like keyword research data can be shared with more members of the organization than just the marketing team. If you need help with organizing your internal marketing teams, you should contact Jessica Bowman with SEOinhouse.com. She has helped many organizations to develop successful team structures as they bring internet marketing disciplines in house.

Keyword Research Brief

This next idea is not so much a structure as it is an idea to help get information gathered from keyword research data into the hands of important stakeholders within and without the organization. This idea comes from Sarah Fay, an executive advisor who used to be CEO of Aegis Media in the United States. She and I were discussing ideas around this topic and the idea of a keyword research brief came up.

Just as a creative or technical brief outlines general strategy, the *keyword research brief* would be a one-pager that outlines the targeted keywords that are to be used for marketing purposes and any related, insightful data around these keywords. It would also include the proper use of the keywords in editorial, print, and other content that is developed for the company.

The brief is then to be shared and/or presented to all stakeholders, including C-level execs, product development teams, outside agencies, copywriters, and so on. The idea here is that if these stakeholders are aware of this information, it can influence their approach to their use of these keywords in their own roles within the company.

If, for example, the copywriters have this brief, they can use the keywords in scripts for TV and radio spots or in print. These media help create impressions for us as consumers. Then when we are in the market for a product or service and we head to a search engine to point us in the right direction, the keywords are likely to pop into our head. It all then comes full circle. Is that not SEO? Think of how much more can be accomplished if a simple thing like keyword research data was shared with more people within your company. You can go to the website www.keywordintelligencebook.com and download a sample keyword research brief that you can use as a template. Modify it as you will to your own liking.

Keyword Competitive Intelligence

Do you know who your competition is? Do you know if they are engaged in any Internet marketing campaigns? If so, do you know what keywords they seem to be using in those campaigns? In this section, I will show you how to identify methods your direct and indirect competition uses so you can identify what keywords they are using and where.

This knowledge will give you insight into what your competition is, or is not, doing. Armed with this information, you can keep your competitors in your sights and identify new opportunities that may not have been exploited.

For our purpose, a *competitor* is any known organization you are competing against or an organization who is similar to you in some respect.

Let's start by identifying your online competition. If you are unsure, you can use some online tools to help you do the research. For example, look up www.nationwide.com using a competitive keyword research tool called SpyFu (www.spyfu.com). As you can see in Figure 2.3, I have discovered a list of organic and paid, or Ad, competitors. This can be handy tool to help you build out a list of your competition. You might know the main players, but you could be missing some of the lesser-known ones. If you wish to dig a little deeper, you can click any of links representing the competitors to get a list of their competitors.

There are many tools like SpyFu to help you learn who your competition is. Tools like iSpionage and Keyword Spy will also provide similar information. I will touch on each of these in more detail later. Additionally, you can go to www.keywordintelligencebook.com for an updated list of keyword competition tools.

Now that you have a good list of your competitors, let's look at some methods for learning more about which keywords they strive to be known for or are using in their online marketing campaigns.

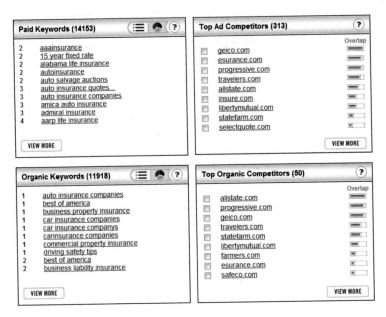

Figure 2.3 Top competitors found with SpyFu

Look at Your Competitors' Metadata

One simple way to learn more about what keywords your competition is using is to go to any page of their website and view the page source to look at their HTML tags. As you can see in Figure 2.4, there is an option on the View menu in most browsers. In this example, I am using Firefox.

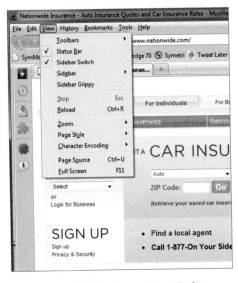

Figure 2.4 The View Page Source option in Firefox

This lets you see the HTML code that makes up the web page. You are just looking for the keywords used in the title, meta keyword, and meta description tags. These are placed where organizations will place their keywords to optimize for search engine rankings or SEO.

Several years ago, SEO was simply done by placing your keywords in the meta keyword tag. Today that practice has very little, if any, value for SEO. But since many people still feel that this is how SEO is done, they will insert their keywords here. It may not help with SEO, but it serves us as we look under the hood and see what our competition intends to be ranked for. So let's take a look at Nationwide and see what keywords they wish to be known for. You can see there are three HTML tags: `title`, `meta name="description"`, and `meta name="keywords"`.

```
<title>Nationwide Insurance - Auto Insurance Quotes and Car Insurance
Rates</title>
<meta name="description" content="Auto insurance from Nationwide - Save up
to $43 every month on car insurance! Get your insurance quote online and
start saving today! Learn more about our competitive auto insurance rates -
Get a quote online or contact us to speak to an insurance agent."/>
<meta name="keywords" content="car insurance, auto insurance, online auto
insurance, auto insurance rates, car insurance quote" />
```

Those who know how to do SEO today will find good keywords in the title tag. This is one of the best places to put your keywords to help you for natural search engine rankings. The keywords I would derive from this are "nationwide insurance", "auto insurance quotes", "car insurance", and even "insurance". You now have the brand name and two very specific keywords that describe what this web page is all about.

Next is the meta description tag, which should contain a description about the page content. If this is the home page, it might be a description of the whole site. You can see the text:

```
Auto insurance from Nationwide - Save up to $43 every month on car
insurance! Get your insurance quote online and start saving today! Learn
more about our competitive auto insurance rates - Get a quote online or
contact us to speak to an insurance agent.
```

The keywords that have any meaning for our purpose would be as follows:

- auto insurance
- nationwide
- insurance
- insurance quote online
- competitive auto insurance rates
- insurance agent

- auto insurance

- insurance quote

- car insurance

As with most competitive keyword research, you will need to interpret intent—that is, are they looking to make a purchase or just gathering information? In this case, we do not know if these keywords are being used in their SEO or PPC campaign or not. With a little more research, we can find out. In any case, it is good to include your core keywords in the description as well as the title tag and in other key places. Your core keywords are those that are strategic to your company's goals like "auto insurance" is for Nationwide. These are likely to be found on most home pages because those pages include core message that that are representative of your entire website. Furthermore, the title and description tags act like ads. The search engines will often grab this text and use it as the description for the search engine results page (SERP). Figure 2.5 shows the search results for Nationwide when I did a search for "auto insurance" on Google.

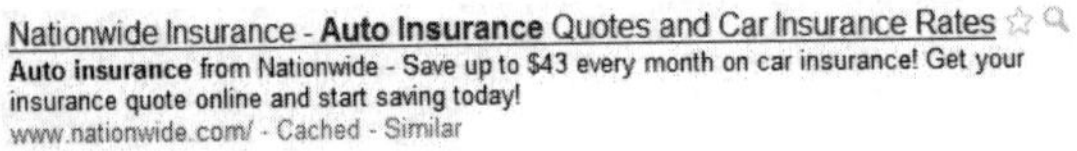

Nationwide Insurance - **Auto Insurance** Quotes and Car Insurance Rates ☆ ⚲
Auto insurance from Nationwide - Save up to $43 every month on car insurance! Get your
insurance quote online and start saving today!
www.nationwide.com/ - Cached - Similar

Figure 2.5 Nationwide natural listing

Now, let's look at the meta keyword tag. Here we find the following keywords:

- car insurance

- auto insurance

- online auto insurance

- auto insurance rates

- car insurance quote

These are five good keywords that describe what this site does and what it represents. It is a good guess that these are used in their PPC and other marketing campaigns.

It is important to note here that when you use this method to look at the page source for other websites, you should consider looking at more than just the home page, especially if the organization is doing SEO the right way. When you are optimizing your site for search engines, you are not just optimizing the home page; you should optimize each and every page on your site. So if you wish to get more keywords from your competitors, you should try this method on other pages on the site.

To do this might require a lot of time; however, there tools that can help you analyze websites and gather keywords from their metadata as well as pull keywords from body copy on each page. This helps to automate the process a bit more. We will cover keyword tools in Chapter 3.

Keyword Gap Analysis

A keyword gap analysis is analyzing the keywords being used and noting those that should be there but are missing. In some cases it may not be the keywords you see, but the keywords you don't see that matter. This might present itself as a great opportunity. As you do your research on your competitors, you should conduct a kind of gap analysis. Find out what keywords are not being used and add them to your keyword list. You can also use tools like the Google AdWords Keyword Tool (https://adwords .google.com/select/KeywordToolExternal), Keyword Discovery (www.keyworddiscovery .com), Word tracker (www.wordtracker.com), or Wordstream (www.wordstream.com) to help you find words that are less competitive. Keywords that fall in the gap are usually easier to rank for organically and cost less with paid search.

We have already taken a look at SpyFu (www.spyfu.com) for identifying who your competition is; however, it provides us with more competitive data to look at. If you look back at Figure 2.3, you will see two boxes I didn't mention previously. One is labeled "Paid Keywords" and one is "Organic Keywords". They show keywords that the company may be bidding on for PPC and which words their sites are ranking well for through SEO.

As you can see, there are more keywords to look at but you need the premium version of SpyFu to access them. Most of these tools will provide you with a free version or a 30-day trial. But to get the real good stuff, you need to upgrade to the paid versions.

If you wish to go beyond just keyword gap analysis, there is more competitive detail to view. In Figure 2.6 you will see information about the domain's adwords ad budget, average ad position, and organic SEO traffic, just to name a few. Additionally, you can identify the top paid keywords as well at the top organic keywords. This is obviously very helpful as you consider building your own paid search campaign.

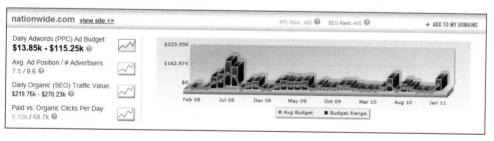

Figure 2.6 SpyFu dashboard

iSpionage (www.ispionage.com) is another great tool that will provide information on an organization's PPC and SEO efforts. It helps you gain insight into your competitors' ads and their ad budgets and top performing keywords. You can even do a keyword search instead of a domain search. Figure 2.7 shows a snapshot of a search on the keyword "web hosting". You can view the top advertisers as well as the top keywords.

Rank	Advertiser	Monthly Budget	Keyword Count
1	godaddy.com	$119,373 - $221,597	32,743
2	top5hosts.ipage.com	$43,374 - $83,374	3,993
3	fatcow.com	$42,417 - $81,330	4,434
4	google.com	$849,559 - $1,466,138	695,182
5	hostgator.com	$67,706 - $128,688	12,098
6	consumer-rankings.com	$79,804 - $144,779	22,634
7	1and1.com	$91,162 - $170,166	32,072
8	top10hostinglist.com	$16,323 - $30,193	2
9	webhosting.yahoo.com	$59,485 - $110,480	16,629
10	top-10-web-hosting.com	$34,246 - $66,175	4,961

Number of Advertisers

Figure 2.7 iSpionage

KeywordSpy (www.keywordspy.com) is similar to the others and helps you keep track of the most highly searched keywords. It can also provide insight into which ads are the most profitable as well as cost-per-click (CPC) information. You can look at the actual ads, PPC competitors, and organic competitors.

Other notable keyword competitive tools you should look at are Compete (www.compete.com) and Quantcast (www.quantcast.com). Both of these tools go beyond finding your competition's keywords. They provide insight into your competitors' site traffic and demographic data. There are more great tools out there, but these will get you started. Again, I will review these tools in more detail in Chapter 3. Additionally, you can check out for the latest tools as new ones emerge frequently.

What Is Your Competition Seeing about You?

You may think that these tools are pretty cool. But note that your competitors can use these same tools to look at your site. So use these tips and tools on your own site to see what you are revealing about yourself.

Keyword Research Process

The process for conducting a keyword research project can be a daunting task. It is not easy or fun, but having the right process in place can make it more meaningful and efficient. Whether you use online tools or work the steps manually, you will find that this process can be a real benefit to you. Figure 2.8 shows each step in this process.

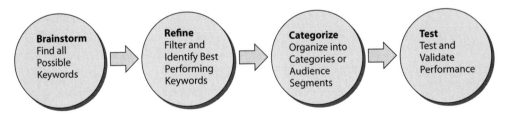

Figure 2.8 Keyword research process steps

The purpose is to develop an efficient workflow, from identifying your initial set of keyword all the way to utilization. You might make some slight variations depending on your own approach, but the principles in this four-step process will help you get the results you want quickly.

Brainstorming: Find All Possible Keywords

The first step is to brainstorm all of the possibilities of keywords that might be candidates. This can be done using some tools I will outline in Chapter 3 or with methods I will outline in Chapter 4. The tools will help to automate the process a bit more and allow you to export your work into a spreadsheet, which will make it a lot easier.

If you are using a keyword tool, you need an initial set of phrases called *seed* keywords. These are the keywords that you feed the tool to get an output that includes a larger set of keywords that are related in some way. You may start with 10 seed keywords, and your keyword tool of choice returns a hundred or even a thousand terms. This is another method for brainstorming. You can go through this extended list of terms and see if any stand out as candidates for your overall list.

The methods in Chapter 4 will provide some creative places to look to uncover a gold mine of keyword choices that may turn out to be your best performers. You can still use some tools to automate this process, but uncovering all of the keywords you need in this first phase will take some time. You should recruit as many team members as you can to help you with this. The more heads the better.

One of the key points in this phase is that you rule nothing out. You are interested in the whole gamut, keywords that are even remote possibilities, and the more the better. Sometimes we have a tendency to discard keywords after we find them, thinking that they will not work. Try to avoid doing so during this phase. You will have time in the next phase to filter out any unwanted keywords. Let you mind flow with all the possibilities and collect as many as you can. All keyword ideas that you identify in this phase should make it on the list.

Some keywords you find might give you or another team member a creative idea for another, better keyword phrase. I have seen many situations where others have reviewed my master list and have come up with keywords I would have missed. So whether you are a large or small organization, you should get as many people involved in this process as practical. The old adage is true: two heads are better than one.

One more point in this phase is that you need some sort of tool to keep all of your keywords organized, I suggest a spreadsheet. As you will see in the next phase, it will help you in the refining process with some methods I will teach you in Chapter 5.

In Chapter 4, I will outline many methods and tactics for identifying your initial keyword list.

Refine: Identify High-Potential Keywords

In this next refining stage you take all of the keywords you brainstormed and attempt to filter the list so you can identify high-performance keywords. This is where you can start making a judgment on which you will keep and which you will discard.

Again, there are tools you can use (which I will cover in Chapter 3) that will help you with the refinement process. Many of these tools will provide you with data that can give you more insight into how the keywords might perform. Or it might show you historical data on a keyword to illustrate how it has performed in the past.

This may include the following types of data:

- How many annual searches there were for the keyword
- How those annual searches trended from month to month
- The percentage of search share from each search engine
- The keyword's current maximum bid for a given search engine
- The keyword competition index or the relationship of demand to competition

As you can see, with information like this you can now make educated decisions on which keywords you use for your campaigns. Learning how to interpret this data and make sense of it will serve you well as you sift your way through your large keyword list and start narrowing it down.

I will teach you scoring methods in Chapter 5 that will help you evaluate your keywords based on some of the important data you get from your keyword tools. Then you can systematically sort your keywords into meaningful groups and prioritize them so that the keywords with the greatest potential come out on top and keywords with lower potential end up toward the bottom of the list. Scoring will help you filter a large set of keywords by using important evaluation criteria such as these:

- How popular is the keyword?
- How competitive is the keyword?
- How broad or how specific is the keyword?
- How relevant is the keyword to your business?
- How relevant is the keyword to your website?

This scoring method will help you evaluate each keyword phrase holistically and evaluate its real potential rather than just its popularity as many people do. You will learn that while popularity is an important factor, you should also consider the other variables and weight them accordingly to give you a better perspective on overall keyword potential for your business.

Ultimately you want to create a smaller set of keywords that you can start working with and determining how they play out in various campaigns. You may have a small set of core keywords that you will decide to use for SEO purposes or for social media. You then might have a larger list made up of very specific keywords that can be grouped nicely for your PPC campaign.

The refining process will give you peace of mind knowing you have a solid list of keywords that have been filtered and scored and are now ready for the next phase, categorization.

Categorize: Organize into Categories or Audience Segments

You should now have a refined list of keywords that have been filtered and are ready to be grouped into categories or audience segments. One of the main reasons for this step is all about relevancy. Remember the second factor in our success formula?

The Right Keywords + **Relevant Destination Content** = Conversions

Categorizing your refined keywords by common themes enables you to more easily pair them up to their corresponding and relevant destination content. In fact, I have used this as a method to build out wireframes or sitemaps for a new website. If you start outlining the content for your site and you start matching your refined and grouped keywords to the correct pages, you are essentially building out your website's information architecture which will be discussed in more detail in Chapter 10.

If you are updating an existing site, you might simply match your keywords to the correct pages. However, in some cases you might have a category of keywords that do not match with any relevant landing pages on your site. This is not a bad thing. It basically means you now need to add pages that correspond to these keywords. You can't dictate what pages a search engine will rank for any particular keyword, so you can't know which page a user will land on. It is very important for your visitors and especially for search engines that you have solid, keyword-focused pages that search engines can find, index, and rank you for. The more relevant the page content to your keywords, the higher your conversion rate. A higher conversion rate equals more money and more success for your organization.

Again, there are methods to help with the categorization process, and I will review them in more detail in Chapter 5. If you are using a spreadsheet, you can create more tabs for each of your categories to keep them organized.

Some people like to categorize keywords during the brainstorming process, before refining their lists. That is okay to do. You might want to group your keywords while you are in the brainstorming phase to keep them in logical groups. Then when you refine, you can refine them by group instead of the whole list at once. On the other hand, grouping keywords into themes may be easier with a smaller, refined list. Either way is fine. Just identify what seems to work best for you and be consistent.

Deeper insights on how to map segmented keywords into relevant buckets that will help with the design of your site will be covered in Chapter 10. Additionally I will discuss persona design and how this can help you understand your audience, their needs and their intent. With this kind of information in hand, you provide more keyword rich, relevant content that will be more engaging. The refinement step is often overlooked by people because they are in such a rush to get their keywords and start working on their campaigns. Adding this step to will greatly help your campaigns to succeed.

Test: Test and Validate Keyword Performance

The final step in the keyword research process is to test your keywords and validate their performance. Just because you used a keyword tool or two and have found some cool data that makes you feel better about using a set of keywords doesn't mean they will perform as you wish. There may be something about your industry or other factors that will cause your keywords to perform poorly.

Do you want to find out late in your campaign that your keywords didn't bring you the conversions you thought they would? It is best then to add this important step to your process and test them to see how they will perform.

This is especially important if you are using your keywords for SEO or other campaigns that take time to get off the ground. I have seen many organizations that jump right in and spend a great deal of time on their campaigns without testing the keywords first. Then later, sometimes much later, they realize they are driving traffic to their site but the traffic is not converting. So they have to go back to the drawing board and identify new keywords to use. This time they usually take the time to test and validate their keywords before they get used. This can be a sore lesson to learn and one you can avoid if you add this final step to your process.

One way to test is to organize a mini PPC campaign for the keywords you plan to use. This is a good way to test your keywords. I typically like to plan on 5 to 10 percent of my Internet marketing budget for testing my keywords in a PPC campaign before using them in any sort of meaningful marketing channel. This provides a comfort level, knowing that your keywords have been tested to perform the way you want them to.

Summary

At this point you should have a better idea what your organization's strategies and goals are. With these goals in mind, you should be able to build a solid marketing plan with each of the channels you plan to use. Additionally, you can design the specific success metrics for each channel and develop a dashboard to connect these metrics to your overall business objectives.

Furthermore, you should explore organizational structures that will help you share keyword research data with more stakeholders within your company. This will ensure that anyone who is developing any content to be published or used in messaging will also use these same keywords.

You should now be able to peek in on your competition and learn from them based on keywords they are using. By doing so, you may uncover opportunities that have not been exploited yet.

Finally, you should have a clearer idea of how to go about finding the right keywords to use in each of your campaigns. The details of each of these keyword research steps will be outlined in the next few chapters.

Keyword Research Tools

Keyword research tools are an important part of Internet marketing because they provide information on keyword intelligence throughout the search funnel spectrum. You can use them to manage your keyword research projects automatically, which will help you save time. This chapter covers the various types of keyword research tools and how they work.

3

Chapter Contents

Keywords and the Search Funnel

There are many keyword tools out on the market, and they all perform in different ways. It can be a challenge to sort out what each one does and which ones you might need. One way to make sense of these tools is to align them to the four stages of the search funnel. Each stage represents an action or a search event, as you can see in Figure 3.1.

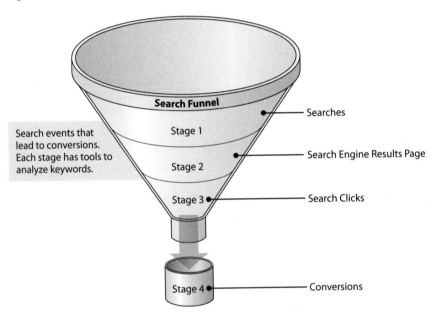

Figure 3.1 The search funnel

Searches

This first stage represents the actual search phrases that people type into a search engine's search box. It is that "language" of search that represents the expectations of the searcher. The keyword tools that include information about the type of search terms used and the volume of searches can help provide behavioral insights and predictive models for your keyword campaigns.

The tools that provide insight into this pre-click data are the search engine tools themselves as well as a handful of other keyword suggestion tools:

- Google AdWords Keyword Tool
- Microsoft adCenter Advertising Intelligence
- Trellian Keyword Discovery
- WordTracker
- WordStream
- SEOmoz

These tools are great to help get you started as you look for search phrase candidates, not to mention they are free! They also provide keyword suggestions based on searcher behavior. They can help you size up the marketplace in the keyword space.

However, there are limits to what these tools can offer:

- They may be limited to a specific search engine.

- They are limited in competitive information. In other words, they cannot provide data on their clients.

- They are focused on only pre-click funnel metrics.

Search Engine Results Page

After a search query is entered, a search engine results page (SERP) lists the organic and paid search listing in a ranked order. The ranking provides insight into how you and your competition are performing in relation to the search query. Keyword analysis tools within this stage can include rich analytics regarding your website and your competition, such as page and position rank, copy analysis, cost per click, and recommendations for performance improvements. Tools that analyze the SERPs can help you understand all things related to paid search impressions and organic search impressions.

These tools are not free however. Most offer tiered pricing based on your company and campaign size. Also, there is no click-through data. That is the next stage. These tools can help you understand how you should best position yourself and what you should value as it relates to page, position rank, copy analysis for your campaign, and competitive insights.

Here are some of the paid search keyword tools that are available:

- AdGooroo

- SpyFu

- The Search Monitor

These are organic search keyword "software" tools:

- Conductor

- Covario

- Rank Above

- BrightEdge

- SEOmoz

These keyword tools provide the kind of intelligence that helps you study the SERPs and understand what you can do with that real estate.

Search Clicks

The next stage in the funnel represents the analysis of clicks from the SERPs. Where the second stage focuses on impressions, this stage focuses on conversions, or "search clicks." So in this stage you look at how many clicks are available in the marketplace around your keyword terms and where searchers go after they click. Are they going to your site, to your competition's site, or to other informational sites?

These tools show what is working for your competition—not just what they are bidding/optimizing for, but what is driving traffic. Like the tools in the previous stage, they provide paid and organic click analysis, including varying metrics like:

- Click-through rates
- Full funnel analysis (all four stages)
- Market sizing metrics and recommendations

These tools are generally very expensive, and there are few vendors to choose from. Some offer some free analytics like Alexa, and others are expensive from the start. The following keyword tools are among those in this stage:

- comScore Search Planner
- Hitwise Search Intelligence
- Compete Pro Search Analytics
- Trellian Search Term Intelligence Tool
- Alexa
- AdGooroo

Conversions

Only after searchers have clicked through can you competitively analyze how well you are leading them to a conversion with your search terms. The keyword tools in this stage provide conversion analytics. When visitors reach your site via search, these tools will help you understand the competitive landscape.

Furthermore, they allow you to follow search terms through all stages of the search funnel. What you learn using these tools can help you figure out whether your visitors are shopping or buying and whether you are maximizing your dollars and labor investments appropriately.

The following tools are among the few players in this segment:

- comScore Search Planner
- Hitwise Search Intelligence
- Compete Pro Search Analytics

These tools are very expensive and have a limited vendor set as you can see, and because they pull their data from panels and poll groups, sample size can be an issue. Typically, these tools are used for extremely large sites and market segments.

In Figure 3.2, I have aligned these tools to each stage in the search funnel as they relate to paid or organic search. This should help you to better understand the various keywords tools on the market and how they function.

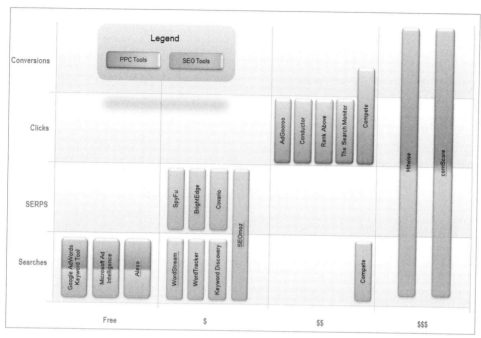

Figure 3.2 Keyword tools comparison chart

You can see that there are specific keyword tools that provide insight and analytics for specific search events within each stage.

Building Your Toolset

As you have seen, there are many tools that will help you in your keyword research process of collecting data (from pre-click to post-click data). What type and how many tools you will need will depend on whether you are a small business with a small number of keywords in your campaign or a very large organization. It is always good to start with the basics and move up the search funnel and the tools within each segment as you learn how to use them and can afford them.

Where Does Keyword Data Come From?

Before you start putting together your shopping list, there is another aspect to search tools that is important to understand: the sources from which each tool collects its data and the type of algorithm it uses to render keyword statistics.

Many of these tools come in pretty wrappers, but you need to take a look inside to get the real picture. After all, it's the data you are after first and foremost. The more accurate it is, the better the results. Here are the various sources these tools use to get their data:

- Search engines (For example, Google collects its own data.)
- Search engine APIs
- Browser toolbars
- Purchases from ISPs
- Panels of selected participants

Obviously, Google and Bing provide tools that analyze their own data and then provide you with the results. Many other keyword tools have an application programming interface (API) for Google or other search engines. This means they have a conduit directly into Google's keyword data. The difference between these tools and Google is the algorithms and how the data is interpreted. Some try to filter out bot searches and nonessential searches to provide true searcher behavior. However, the core data all comes from the same source.

Some get data from a browser toolbar. Toolbars are given away for free with the understanding that search behavior is collected and analyzed. ISPs also collect data on search behavior and sell it to keyword tool vendors. These two methods usually result in lower search volumes but the data is cleaner because it represents human search behavior rather than machine. It is the humans you are interested in at the end of the day.

Finally, the big players like comScore and Hitwise use panels of human participants. The resulting data is even truer, but the costs are higher because of the expense of data collection.

Why Do Different Tools Report Different Numbers?

If you have used two or more keyword tools, you have probably asked yourself why different tools report different numbers. When you use one keyword tool and then compare the results to another, they will likely be different—in some cases, very different. Understanding where the data comes from plays an important part in answering this question. As I just explained, the keyword tools not only get their data from different sources, they also use unique algorithms to interpret the data and provide you with the results. Even the tools that tap into Google's database through an API start with the same data, but they may adjust their algorithm differently and provide you with what they consider the best results.

With that said, how do you need to look at the data from different keyword tools? The key is to look at the results in relative terms. For instance, if you look at Table 3.1, you will see wildly different search volumes for the keywords "bike", "mountain bike", and "road bike".

Keyword	Google Keyword Tool	Keyword Discovery Global Premium	Word Tracker US Database	WordStream
bike	24,900,000	35,220	1,905	412,942
mountain bike	2,240,000	10,712	536	36,334
road bike	673,000	3,576	97	13,008

You will notice that the relative difference between keyword results roughly corresponds from one tool to another. The Google Keyword Tool tends to have the higher numbers. This is mainly because it represents all searches by anyone and anything. The other three tools account for match types, bots, rank checkers, geography, and so on, thus resulting in smaller numbers.

So when you look at your results, you need to look at them in relative terms. Because none of the keyword tools provide perfect numbers, it is important to not take them too literally. Another way to deal with this is to pick the keyword tool of your choice and stick with it as a base. Then as you observe and even challenge the base numbers, you can make any adjustments you feel are necessary. For purposes of keyword research, you want to get a general idea of search volume. In this case, we can observe that the word "bike" is searched on many more times than "mountain bike" is and "mountain bike" is searched on more than "road bike".

In Chapter 5, I will show you a way to score your keywords and how to convert these numbers into relative terms on a scale of 1 through 10. This helps to put these varying numbers in the proper perspective. As you use multiple keyword tools, you can weight this scale accordingly based on your results.

Keyword Tools That Streamline Processes and Save Time

The next thing to consider in a tool is the degree to which you can save time in conducting your research. Does the tool help you organize your work projects to save time? What are the various files types you can use to export the data? Will they handle a large amount of keywords or just a few?

You will invariably end up with a handful of tools that you enjoy working with and that you will use within your organization. Be on the lookout for new tools or even tool upgrades. There are too many tools to include in this book, so I will cover only the more popular ones. However, I will be posting all of the keyword tools I can find on the book site at www.keywordresearchbook.com, so check frequently for updates on new and discontinued keyword tools.

Stage 1 and 2 Keyword Tools

As mentioned, I obviously do not have the space to go into all of the keyword tools that are out there, but I have decided to pick a select few to discuss for a couple of reasons.

After you have seen the general capabilities and functionality of the tools in this chapter, you will have a good idea how the others will likely function. They are all unique in features and user interface, but they all provide similar keyword intelligence insights.

I will begin with a review of three keyword tools that have a good installed base and are found in many companies' toolboxes. Each tool has been around for a while, has matured, and is well respected among search marketers.

All three tools outlined in the following sections are good and solid keyword tools. They have similar features and benefits, and each has unique selling points. They all pull data that represents searches from multiple search engines. I will present them in alphabetical order.

Keyword Discovery

Trellian's Keyword Discovery tool (http://keyworddiscovery.com) is first in our lineup of general-use, all-around keyword tools. It is one of the tools that has been around for several years and have grown and matured over time. Keyword Discovery draws its data from over 200 search engines worldwide. This, of course, includes statistics from those with the largest market share: Google, Yahoo!, Bing, Ask, and AOL.

Additionally, Keyword Discovery includes behavioral data such as search volume per month and other insightful trends from its Premium database, which is derived exclusively from user panel information through toolbars used by over 5 million users. This means the data represents real searches made by real people and not skewed searches made by bots and automated rank checkers, which artificially inflate search volumes.

Keyword Discovery follows a model that's similar to the model other tools follow and allows marketers to access some tools for free. As you would expect, the free tools are limited in features and functionality, but they do give you a flavor for how the tools work. As this book is being written, Keyword Discovery is $69.00 per month or $599.40 for a 12-month standard subscription. If you need enterprise level tools or API access, the vendor offers those as well.

As you look at Figure 3.3, you will see Keyword Discovery's main interface with all of its different features and modifiers.

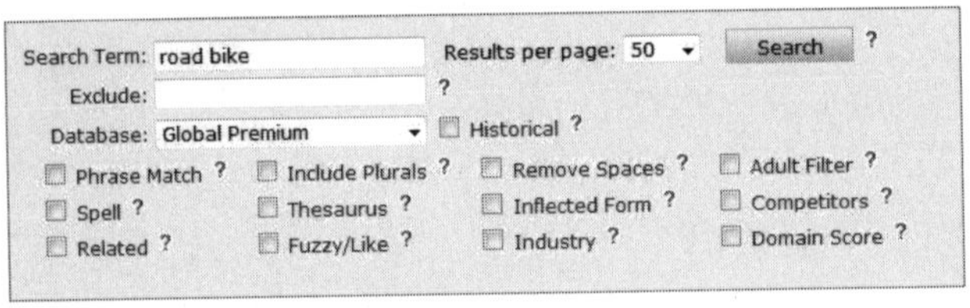

Figure 3.3 Keyword Discovery interface

As with all keyword research tools, you enter your search term and simply click the Search button to get your results. However, to do so without taking advantage of choosing the right database or any of the fully featured modifiers is like taking only two licks from a lollipop. You won't get the full experience.

I will briefly describe each of these features, but if you get stuck you can roll your mouse over any of the question marks to get a mini help window.

Working with Projects

One of the nice things about Keyword Discovery is the ability to research your keyword and place it into separate projects. These projects might represent clients, campaigns, or even ad groups. You will find the Project drop-down menu at the top of your browser in the application strip, as seen in Figure 3.4.

Figure 3.4 Working with Projects

Simply select the project for which you wish to do research and then start researching your keywords. When you find the search terms you wish to add, simply check the box next to the word and click the Add button. The terms will then be added to your selected project.

Keyword Discovery Databases

Before you start researching keywords, you need to decide which database you wish to use. Figure 3.5 shows several types of databases to choose from. The two primary databases are the Global Premium and Historical Global databases. The Global Premium database represents the purest database of true searches and by default presents the last 12 months' worth of search data. If you do a search on a keyword in October 2011, the results you will get will likely be those from September 2010 to September 2011. This is because it takes a couple of weeks to update the databases with the most current search results. You can also grab data from as far back as August 2006 by clicking the Historical check box to the right of the database selection.

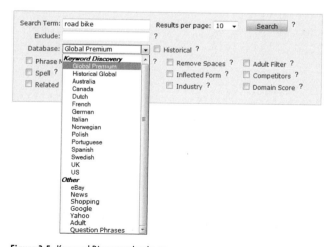

Figure 3.5 Keyword Discovery databases

For most cases, I recommend using the Global Premium database because it is based entirely on data collected from the toolbars of over 5 million users, which means it is based on real searches made by real users. The Historical Global database is fundamentally different than the Global Premium in that it collects data from over 200 search engines going back as far as June 2005 and includes searches made by automated rank checkers and bots, which artificially inflate search volumes. I do not recommend using the Historical Global database unless you wish to compare the relative difference from one term to another *and* from one database to another. Otherwise, it doesn't represent the best numbers to work with.

Don't get the Historical check box confused with the Historical Global database. Clicking the Historical check box will give you search results from August 2006 to the present for all databases *except* the Historical Global database. The Historical Global database always includes all data, going back to June 2005.

Now look at Figure 3.6 and see how these choices will affect the results for the term "road bike". The first number represents the result from the Global Premium database, with 3,576 searches. When you select the Historical check box, the result is 24,575 searches, which is the number of searches from August 2006 to present time.

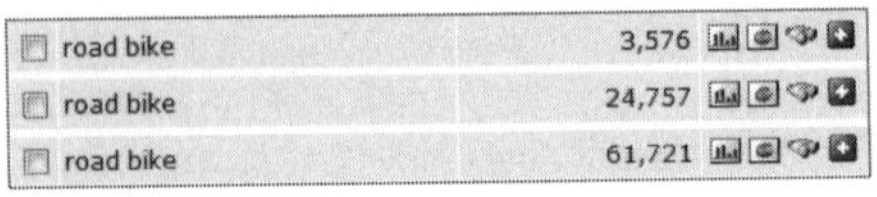

☐ road bike	3,576
☐ road bike	24,757
☐ road bike	61,721

Figure 3.6 Database search comparisons

The Historical Global database, which is skewed by bots and automated rank checkers and includes data back to June 2005, returns the result of 61,721 searches.

If you are using Keyword Discovery, it is very important that you understand these differences so you have a clearer picture of what your data truly represents. Using this tool without this knowledge could adversely affect your numbers and skew your results, which could lead to you having unreasonable expectations. So please make sure you and your team understand this concept.

Now return to Figure 3.5 and you will see that there is a listing of regional databases:

- Australia
- Canada
- Dutch
- French
- German
- Italian
- Norwegian
- Polish

- Portuguese
- Spanish
- Swedish
- UK
- US

If you are conducting keyword research for any of these regions, you may want to check your results against the corresponding databases. Of course, you will get lower numbers, but they will be filtered by the region you select. Also notice that you have the option to check the Historical box to get the past several years of data as opposed to the last 12 months.

If you scroll down the list of database, you will find a third set of choices in the Other category. These are select databases that represent unique cases in which to search, such as Shopping, eBay, News, Google, Yahoo, and Adult.

Most of these choices are self-explanatory. For example, if you wish to search keyword phrases for only eBay searches, you would select eBay. I would, however, like to draw your attention to the last choice, which is Question Phrases. As searchers become more savvy about using search engines, they are finding that a straightforward question sometimes gets the best results. So as this trend continues to grow, Keyword Discovery has provided a tool to help visualize which keyword "question" phrases are most popular. I especially like this feature.

Search Term Filters

Let's now look at the other ways to filter your keyword search using Keyword Discovery. If you will refer again to Figure 3.3, you will find several filters that allow you to modify your results:

- Phrase Match
- Spell
- Related
- Include Plurals
- Thesaurus
- Fuzzy/Like
- Remove Spaces
- Inflected Form
- Industry
- Adult Filter
- Competitors
- Domain Score

By selecting any of these filters, you modify your search results. Many of these filters are self-explanatory, like Spell, Related, Include Plurals, and Thesaurus. Some are not so obvious. I recommend playing around with them until you have a solid grasp on what each modifier does. Some of these are very powerful tools, but you need to understand the results you get with each one to really appreciate them. You can always roll your mouse pointer over the question mark to get a clarifying description on what the modifier does.

Keyword Results and Graphs

Now that you have a foundational understanding of the interface and the various modifiers and features, let's look at the kinds of results you can get from the tool. We will start with a search on the keyword "jewelry". For this example, I will use the Global Premium database. Figure 3.7 shows keywords and their search volume from the last 12 months and three icons that give you more options for analyzing your keywords.

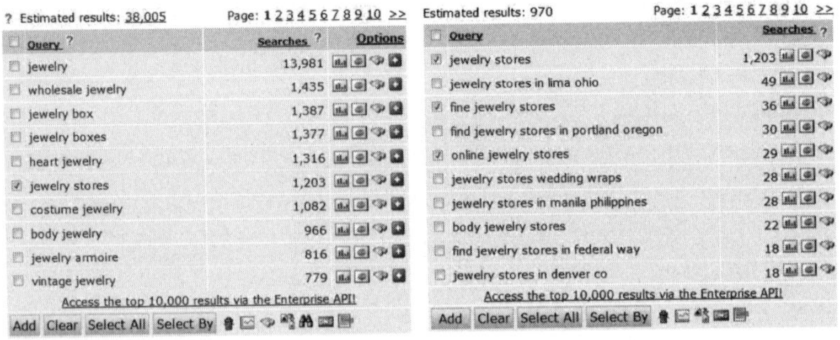

Figure 3.7 Keyword discovery search results

The list on the left shows the top 10 results for the search query "jewelry". If I want to drill down on the keyword "jewelry stores", I click the keyword itself and a new, similar window appears at right with a deeper level of data for that keyword.

As you find keywords you are interested in saving for your project, you can check the box next to them or click the Select All button on the bottom to select all of them. Then click the Add button to add them to your project. This saves your keywords into your currently open project folder, so make sure you have the right project selected before doing this. When you are done searching, you can view all keywords in your project and conduct further research or you can export them to a spreadsheet for further manipulation and analysis.

Let's take a closer look at those icons next to each keyword and what they mean. Keyword Discovery provides some amazing tools that provide better insight into keyword performance:

- Trends
- Search Market Share
- Industry Categories
- Add to Bid Manager

The Trends icon will provide you with three graphs that show search volume for the past 12 months (Figure 3.8, Figure 3.9, and Figure 3.10). Keep in mind that this data represents results from only the Global Premium database. Each graph shows the same data in a slightly different format. These trend graphs are great to identify seasonal trends in searcher behavior and help you forecast future search traffic. Due to the dynamic nature of the data and your choice of modifiers you may get different results as you follow these examples.

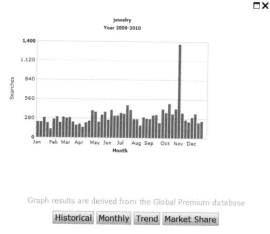

Figure 3.8 Historical graph

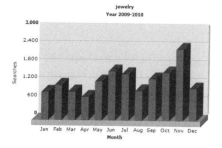

Figure 3.9 Monthly graph

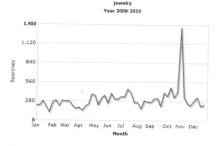

Figure 3.10 Trend graph

The next icon provides market share information. Since Keyword Discovery looks at many search engines, it provides information on where the searches are coming from. In Figure 3.11, you can see that for the search term "mountain bikes," the majority of searches come from Google.

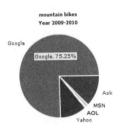

Figure 3.11 Search market share results

This graph also provides the exact percentage of market share in the legend; you can also roll your mouse pointer over each slice of pie. You can see that Google has 75.25 percent of the market share. This information is helpful as you plan your campaigns around specific search engines. In this case, you might consider doing some paid search on Yahoo! or Ask in addition to Google for the keyword "mountain bikes".

The next icon on the list is Industry Categories. The graph shows the top categories that receive the most traffic for the keyword researched. Notice in Figure 3.12 that there are four main categories that represent a fair amount of the searches:

- Business/Consumer Goods
- Sports/Cycling
- Shopping/Cycling
- Sports/Cycling

The last icon allows you to add the keyword right into the big manager for Trellian's Direct Search Network. This is a separate tool that allows you to bid on keywords to drive traffic to your website.

This information is helpful when you start segmenting the keywords into logical categories. This will be discussed in more detail in Chapter 5, and you will see how it will help your campaigns to achieve a high degree of relevance.

Keyword Trends

A new tool that has recently been added is Keyword Trends, shown in Figure 3.13. You can find it in the top navigation bar under Keyword Discovery. With this tool, you can enter up to five keywords and then compare trend information over the past 12 months to view comparative data across these dimensions:

- Search engine market share
- Search region demographics
- Keyword search trends

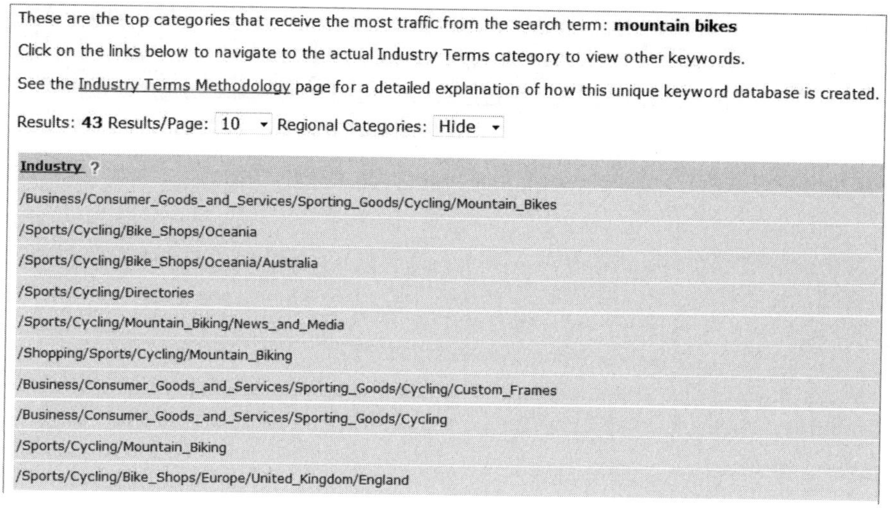

These are the top categories that receive the most traffic from the search term: **mountain bikes**

Click on the links below to navigate to the actual Industry Terms category to view other keywords.

See the Industry Terms Methodology page for a detailed explanation of how this unique keyword database is created.

Results: **43** Results/Page: 10 ▾ Regional Categories: Hide ▾

Industry ?

/Business/Consumer_Goods_and_Services/Sporting_Goods/Cycling/Mountain_Bikes

/Sports/Cycling/Bike_Shops/Oceania

/Sports/Cycling/Bike_Shops/Oceania/Australia

/Sports/Cycling/Directories

/Sports/Cycling/Mountain_Biking/News_and_Media

/Shopping/Sports/Cycling/Mountain_Biking

/Business/Consumer_Goods_and_Services/Sporting_Goods/Cycling/Custom_Frames

/Business/Consumer_Goods_and_Services/Sporting_Goods/Cycling

/Sports/Cycling/Mountain_Biking

/Sports/Cycling/Bike_Shops/Europe/United_Kingdom/England

Figure 3.12 Industry categories

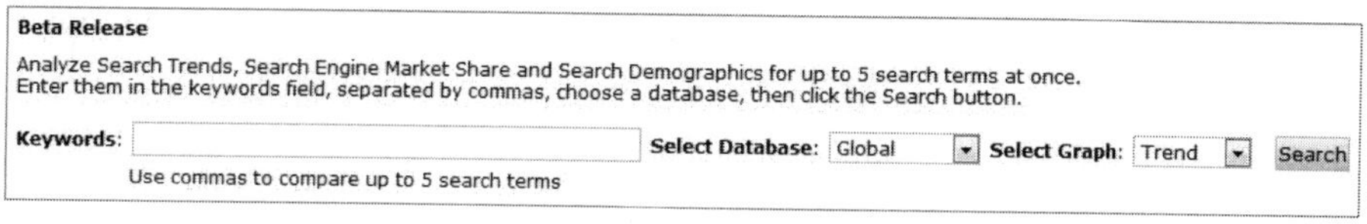

Beta Release

Analyze Search Trends, Search Engine Market Share and Search Demographics for up to 5 search terms at once. Enter them in the keywords field, separated by commas, choose a database, then click the Search button.

Keywords: [   ]   **Select Database:** Global ▾ **Select Graph:** Trend ▾ Search

Use commas to compare up to 5 search terms

Figure 3.13 Keyword trends

Keyword Discovery is one of the better all-around tools that will help you manage many aspects of your keyword research, and I recommend it as one of the tools you should have in your toolbox. When you sign up for a premium account, you have access to more tools and features, like these:

- Cross Reference Tool
- Domain Researcher Tool
- Google Formatting Tool
- Keyword Analyzer Tool
- Keyword Competitor Tool
- Keyword Density Tool
- Keyword Manager Tool
- Keyword Permutations
- Keyword Trends

Spend some time getting to know this tool and its features and I am sure you will find much of what you need to gather the right intelligence for your keyword research projects.

WordStream

Tools from WordStream are next in our lineup of research tools. Its main keyword research tool is called the Keyword Research Suite.

WordStream also offers a series of free tools that it makes available for a limited number of uses. The tools are fully functional but limited as to the number of times you can run them, currently set at 10 uses. Please note that three free tools are available at the home page, but they list five free tools here: www.wordstream.com/free-keyword-tools.

WordStream's data is derived from "blended" data that comes from multiple sources. According to the folks at WordStream, they purchase their keyword data from a number of search industry partnerships:

- Internet service providers (ISPs)
- Browser toolbars
- Search engines

Once this data has been acquired, they use their own statistical models to aggregate the different keyword data sets. Then they apply various weights and semantic algorithms to generate the terms that you and I see.

Free Keyword Tools

WordStream goes out of its way to offer several free keyword research tools. However, WordStream's tools lend themselves to better integration with Google AdWords and Google Analytics. Here are some of the free tools that Wordstream offers:

- Free Keyword tool
- Free Keyword Niche Finder
- Free Keyword Grouper
- Free Negative Keyword tool
- AdWords Performance Grader

Like most keyword suggestion tools, the WordStream Free Keyword tool serves up keyword data via its blended method. One nice thing about this free tool is that once you get your keyword results, you can download a whopping 10,000 keywords. Most free tools limit the number of results you can download. So this is truly a nice feature for those who are on a tight budget.

The Keyword Niche Finder helps you identify niches of any targeted keyword. It works best if you start with a broad keyword. When you enter a seed term, you are served up with a list of niches. You can eliminate niches you are not interested in and narrow your search to only the niche you are interested in. You can then have the results emailed to you as a CSV file that can easily be opened in Microsoft Excel.

The Keyword Grouper tool allows you to enter up to 10,000 keywords and have them grouped by category and word/modifier association. One way to use this tool is to pull data from your campaigns or web analytics program and dump them into this tool to get several new ideas back. Because the Grouper tool sorts by using modifier ("shop", "free", "new", etc.), it helps you to identify new keywords or keyword segments you may be missing.

Keyword Research Suite

For those who are willing to pay for a subscription, WordStream offers a set of four tools that make up its Keyword Research Suite:

- Keyword Suggestion tool
- Keyword Niche Finder
- Keyword Grouper
- Negative Keyword tool

The main difference between the paid and the free tools is an upgraded interface and unlimited searches per day.

WordStream for PPC offers a nice dashboard that groups your tools into logical sections.

Keyword Suggestion Tool

The keyword suggestion tool, as do all of the tools, provides a nice graphical user interface that has a couple of modifiers to make adjustments to your search. Figure 3.14 shows the basic layout of the tool. You simply enter your query and see the results. In this case, I used the keyword "personal injury". You can see that there is a column for monthly search volume and competition. This is very similar to the results you would get from the Google Keyword Tool.

You can select any or all of the keywords that have been served up and placed in or added to an ad group. You can export your list into tab-separated value (TSV) or comma-separated value (CSV) format for use in a spreadsheet. You can also order your spreadsheet by any of the visible columns.

The related keyword tool is exactly the same except you are served up keywords that relate to the seed word you entered.

Negative Keyword Tool

Negative keywords are mainly for PPC because they help to cancel out undesirable keywords that might drive the wrong traffic to your site. If, for instance, you sell premium leather furniture, you would not want broad match keywords like "discount" or "free" integrated into your keyword set. People using these keywords are likely not your target audience.

WordStream's negative keyword tool starts off as the others do but displays slightly different results. Once you enter a keyword, you are given a list of related keyword suggestions that include possible negative keywords. You then go through a kind of question-and-answer session by clicking Yes or No next to each negative keyword selection. As you do, your negative keyword list begins to populate.

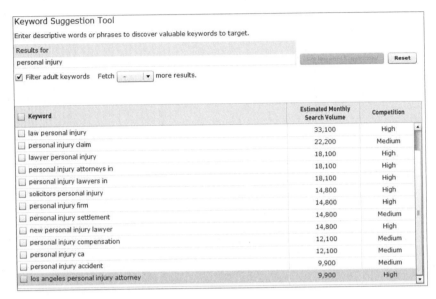

Figure 3.14 Keyword Suggestion tool

I really like this feature because it doesn't just crank out a list of negative keywords that are possible candidates but allows you to interact with the tool and builds your list based on your feedback.

Keyword Grouper

Being able to categorize keywords into groups or themes will help you in many ways. First, it is very helpful in organizing your ad groups, but it can also help you in organizing your website.

The WordStream Keyword Grouper first allows you to enter up to 1,000 keywords and then attempts to organize the keywords into logical and meaningful groups. As you can see in Figure 3.15, there is a list of finance keywords that have been organized using the keyword grouper tool. You simply select any of the terms either in the ad group section or the keyword selection to have them added to your ad group.

AdWords Performance Grader

This new tool to the line-up evaluates the performance of your AdWords account and ranks your performance against other advertisers with similar advertising budgets. Advertisers always want to know how they are doing relative to their competition and other related campaigns.

WordStream seems to offer very robust free keyword tools if you wish to do simple keyword research or spot checks. With the ability to import and export up to 1,000 keywords at a time, this tool rivals many others with this feature alone.

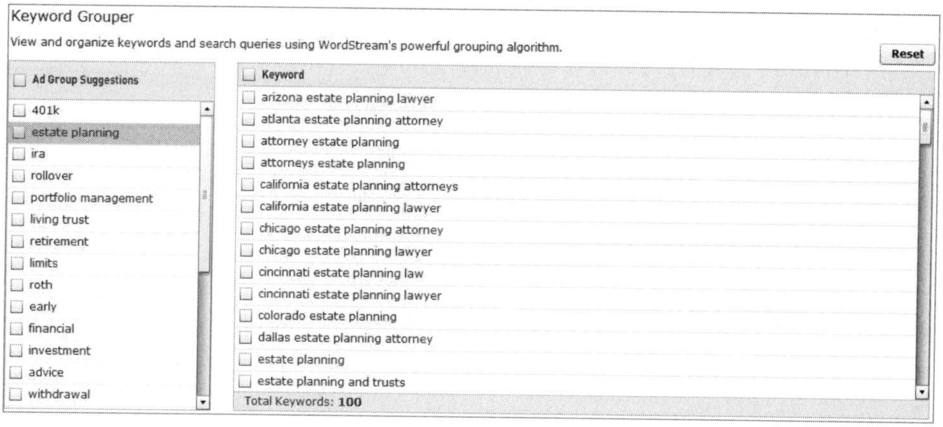

Figure 3.15 Keyword Grouper

Wordtracker

Wordtracker has become a trusted source for quality keyword research data and has evolved into the tool it is today based on past experience and user feedback.

Wordtracker also has a set of free tools that have limited functionality. A free trial is offered that gives you the ability to try out the tool before you purchase a subscription. As this book was being written, the monthly subscription prices were $69 and $379 for an annual subscription.

Wordtracker has developed its own proprietary databases for US and UK markets. The US data is derived from metacrawler data. A *metacrawler* is a search engine that doesn't actually perform the Web searches itself. It sends the user's search query to all the major search engines and then blends together those search results and presents the results to the user. Wordtracker collects search query data from actual searches made on the metacrawlers, Metacrawler.com and Dogpile.com. This approach to gathering keyword data means that Wordtracker's data does not include searches made by automated rank checkers and bots instead of humans. Wordtracker search volume data is based on true searches on the Internet. The UK database is compiled from two data sources, UK ISPs and UK search engines.

Wordtracker also allows you to access Google's keyword research in its interface and to break down regional results for the US, UK, Australia, Canada, India, South Africa, and New Zealand.

When you log in to the Wordtracker dashboard, you have the option to create new projects, as seen in Figure 3.16. You can have multiple projects, and each project can be broken down into lists, which is analogous to pay-per-click (PPC) account hierarchy, where projects correspond to campaigns and lists correspond to ad groups. So if you are organizing a PPC campaign, you can set up your Wordtracker projects similar to your PPC campaign. This will make for a smoother transition as you move your keywords into your PPC campaign.

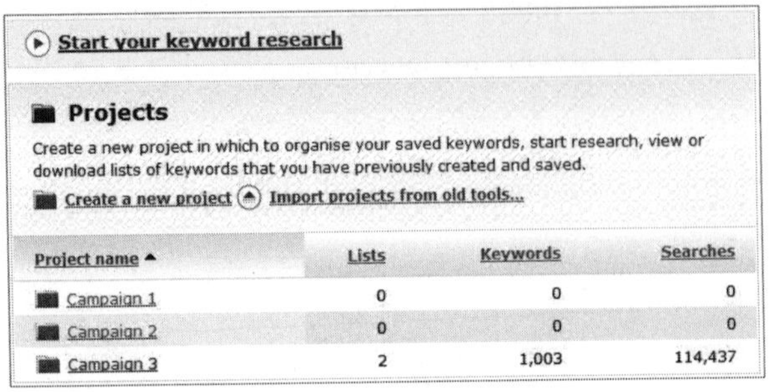

Figure 3.16 Wordtracker projects dashboard

Once you have created your projects and your list, you can begin your research on your keywords. As you can see in Figure 3.17, you have a rather large window to type or paste in your keywords. There is virtually no limit to how many keywords you can import.

Figure 3.17 Wordtracker keyword tool user interface

Once you have typed or pasted in your keywords, you have the option to choose a source for your keyword data. You can choose either a Google regional database or the US or UK Wordtracker database. If you choose one of the Wordtracker databases, you can also refine your search further by specifying a matching option and whether or not to include plurals and adult keywords:

- Keywords in any order = broad match
- Exact keyword inside a search term = phrase match
- Exact keyword only = exact match

Once you initiate a search, you will be served up a list of results that have the following statistics associated with each keyword, as seen in Figure 3.18:

- Number of searches
- Competition (IAAT)
- KEI
- KEI3

Search Count

The number of searches or search count is the number of times each keyword appears in the Wordtracker database of searches over the past 365 days. The data is gathered from metacrawler.com and dogpile.com. The database is updated every day and new data is between 15 and 30 hours old when it hits the live servers.

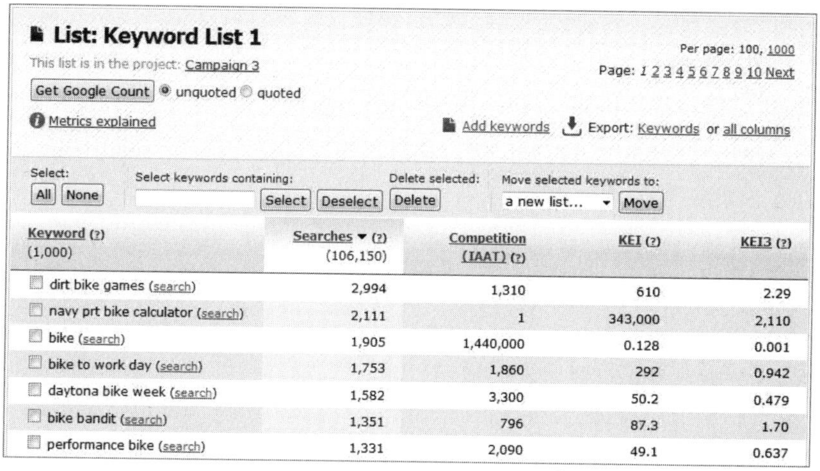

Keyword (?) (1,000)	Searches ▼ (?) (106,150)	Competition (IAAT) (?)	KEI (?)	KEI3 (?)
☐ dirt bike games (search)	2,994	1,310	610	2.29
☐ navy prt bike calculator (search)	2,111	1	343,000	2,110
☐ bike (search)	1,905	1,440,000	0.128	0.001
☐ bike to work day (search)	1,753	1,860	292	0.942
☐ daytona bike week (search)	1,582	3,300	50.2	0.479
☐ bike bandit (search)	1,351	796	87.3	1.70
☐ performance bike (search)	1,331	2,090	49.1	0.637

Figure 3.18 Wordtracker results panel

If you choose to search the Google data, the information comes directly from the AdWords API. It represents broad match data, which is the equivalent to Wordtracker's "keywords in any order" option. The search volumes are from the last calendar month.

Competition (IAAT)

IAAT stands for In Anchor and Title. The competition column more or less represents SEO competitiveness because it derives its data from web pages that are optimized for a particular keyword. It represents the number of pages for which the keyword appears in both the title tag of a page and the anchor text of an external link to the page. Based on current SEO best practices, these are two of the most important places to insert targeted keywords.

So the higher the number in this column, the more pages have been optimized for the keyword and thus the more competition there is.

KEI and KEI3

The keyword effectiveness index (KEI) is a metric that combines two important other metrics: the number of monthly keyword searches (popularity) and the number of websites (competition) that have that exact keyword in at least one of its incoming hyperlinks, which Wordtracker refers to as All in Anchor. There are two cases where this comes into play:

- The KEI figure will go up when the keyword's popularity increases.
- The KEI figure will go down when there is more competition for a keyword.

The KEI formula is as follows:

KEI =- (# of Searches ^2/ In Anchor)

KEI3 provides a slightly different calculation to assess the keyword popularity and the level of competition together in one metric:

KEI3 = (# of Searches / Competition "In Anchor and Title")

Wordtracker recommends that you should look at this number in relative terms instead of taking it too literally. I recommend this approach to any keyword tool. Many of these tools attempt to automate the tedious process of helping you find your best keywords, but you need to scrutinize your final list and test them to validate their potential.

Related Keywords

Another great tool built into Wordtracker is the ability to search for related keywords. As you can see in Figure 3.19, you simply type in a seed term and then you get a list of related keywords. This is very handy when you are building your keyword list and looking for all of the variations of your core terms. Using this tool will help you uncover terms you may never have thought of.

If you wish to drill down further on one of the keywords in your list, you simply click the "search" link next to the keyword. You then have an option to search and save to your list or just search.

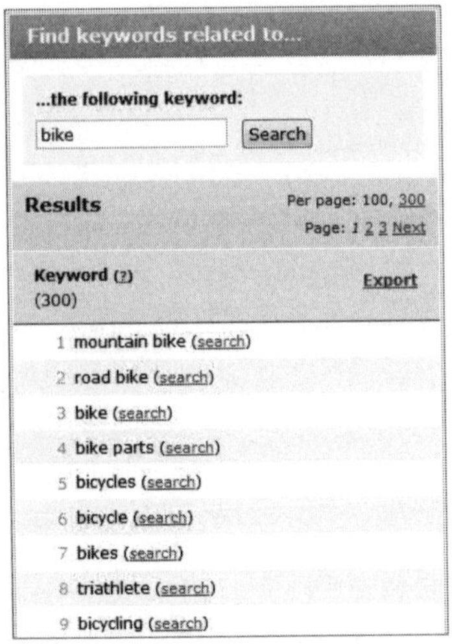

Figure 3.19 Wordtracker related keyword Tool

Wordtracker is a great keyword tool that has grown through the years and with its upgraded interface has become one of the primary tools for many marketers.

Search-Engine-Specific Tools

Now we shift gears to those keyword tools provided by the search engines. As you would expect, most of the keyword tools are provided by Google. If you are only optimizing for or doing PPC on Google's network, then these are certainly tools to use. So let's get started with the flagship keyword tool from Google.

Google AdWords Keyword Tool

The Google AdWords Keyword tool (`https://adwords.google.com/select/KeywordToolExternal`) is a tool that is used by many people because it is free and it provides results from Google's own network. Remember that this tool will not provide results from other search engines, only Google's. Be sure to set up your free Google account and sign in to the keyword tool before you use it. The benefits of this are full-featured results and you can avoid typing in the CAPCHA for each use. (This is that obscure string of letters you have type in to prove you are a human as opposed to an automated program.) This alone is a good enough reason.

The Google database is the source of many keyword tools, and Google provides an API to allow partners to tap into this data source for their own applications. Since everyone wants their campaigns to perform well on their search engine, having this tool in your toolbox is very wise. Keep in mind, however, that the results from this tool usually result in higher search volumes than others, as you saw demonstrated earlier in the chapter. This is mainly because they do not filter out rank checkers, bots, and so on.

As you can see on Figure 3.20, the main part of the interface allows you to input keywords into the box. You can also type a website URL to have the Google Keyword Tool find keywords from that website. This is a nice feature if you are trying to mine new keywords from scratch. Point this tool to pages on your site or your competitors' sites and see what keywords come up.

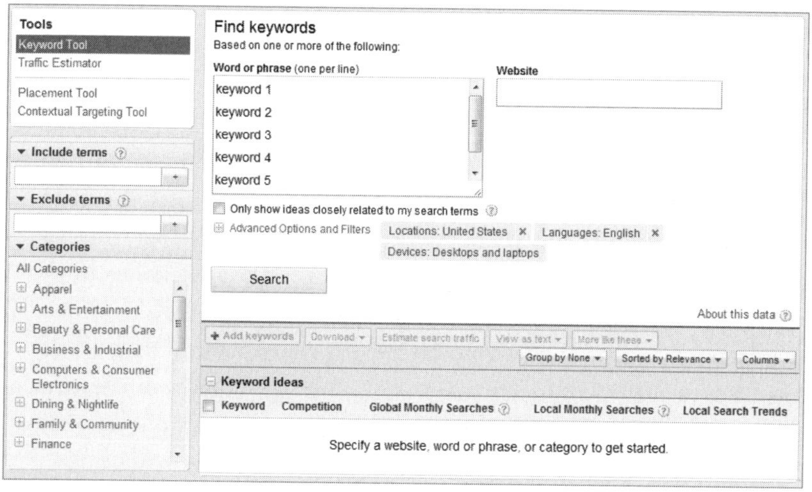

Figure 3.20 Google Keyword Tool

If you prefer to have Google provide you with exactly the keywords you typed in and not give you suggestions of related keywords, then check the box labeled "Only show ideas closely related to my search terms". If you select the Advanced Options And Filters box below that one (Figure 3.21), you will be able to filter your search by these variables:

- Locations
- Languages
- Adult content
- Various devices (laptop, desktop, mobile)
- Competition
- Monthly searches (Global and Local)
- Ad share
- Global monthly searches
- Search share
- Approximate CPC

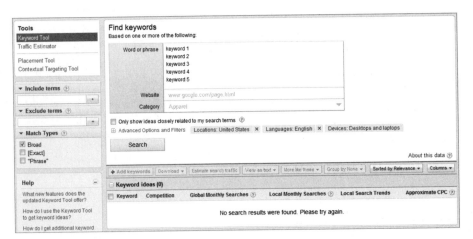

Figure 3.21 Google Keyword Tool advanced options

Google provides a list of categories, as shown in Figure 3.22, that you can drill down on to see which keywords go with each category. Simply pick a main category and drill down to your desired subcategory to find what you are looking for. Once a subcategory is selected, a list of related keywords will appear. If you are going after a niche, this approach will help you find keywords that are category related.

Another way to use this is to choose your targeted keyword list and then "look up" how Google groups their keywords. This might help you as you put your related keywords together to help you achieve the relevance you need. If you have an understanding how Google subdivides their categories of keywords, it is a safe bet you could do the same for optimal relevance.

Figure 3.22 Category search

Google Data

Once you have entered keywords, categories, or a website and selected your filtering preferences, you will get a nice selection of keywords with related statistics, as seen in Figure 3.23.

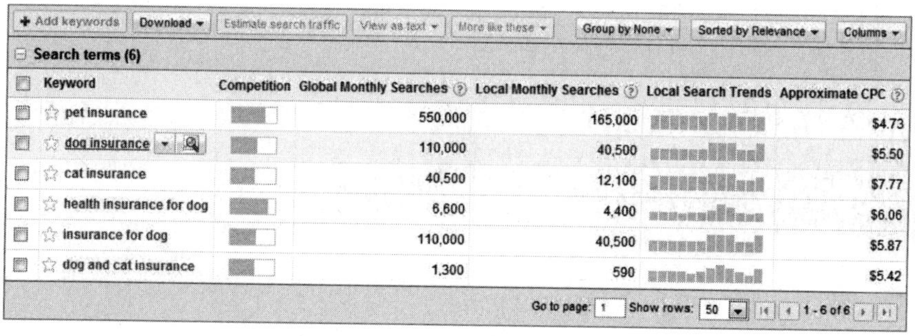

Keyword	Competition	Global Monthly Searches	Local Monthly Searches	Local Search Trends	Approximate CPC
☆ pet insurance		550,000	165,000		$4.73
☆ dog insurance		110,000	40,500		$5.50
☆ cat insurance		40,500	12,100		$7.77
☆ health insurance for dog		6,600	4,400		$6.06
☆ insurance for dog		110,000	40,500		$5.87
☆ dog and cat insurance		1,300	590		$5.42

Figure 3.23 Google Keyword results page

After you enter your keywords and get your results, you have the option to set your match type to either Broad, Exact, or Phrase. This is very helpful as you are narrowing your keywords by target audience. The keyword data you get is broken down into several categories:

- Competition
- Global Monthly Searches
- Local Monthly Searches
- Local Search Trends
- Estimated CPC

Competition

The Competition column provides insight into the number of advertisers that are bidding for your targeted search term. As you can see, it is represented as a bar graph. Each bar represents the amount of competition. A full bar would represent a keyword that is fully saturated with competitors. If you want to note the actual number you can export your keywords into a spreadsheet. In Table 3.2, you can see the actual competitive values with values that are similar to percentages. The keyword "pet insurance" is about 74 percent competitive, for example.

▶ **Table 3.2** Google Keyword Competition Index

Keyword	Competition
pet insurance	0.74
dog insurance	0.59
cat insurance	0.53
health insurance for dogs	0.85
insurance for dog	0.59
dog and cat insurance	0.56

Local Monthly Searches and Search Trends

The values in the Local Monthly Searches column represent the average number of user queries for the keywords specified within your language or country selection. If you are more interested in global searches, then you can uncheck this modifier in the advanced options section of the interface (shown previously in Figure 3.21).

The Local Search Trends column shows local traffic fluctuation for the past 12 months, with each bar representing a different month.

Approximate CPC

The approximate cost-per-click (CPC) is the cost you are likely to pay if you were to bid on this keyword, representing an average of all of your ad positions. This number can also give you some insight into how competitive your keywords are. A keyword with an approximate CPC of $.10 would be noncompetitive, while a keyword like "cat insurance" at $7.77 would represent a higher amount of competition.

Global Monthly Searches

The global monthly searches values represent fluctuations in search traffic globally over the past 12 months. With this information, you can get a glimpse of how well your keywords perform over a period of time. If you wish to get more details with a keyword, then move over to Google Insights or Google Trends, which I will touch on later in this chapter.

Traffic Estimator

The Traffic Estimator also appears within the Google AdWords Keyword Tool. Just look in the upper-left corner of the interface (refer back to Figure 3.21). I will not go into great detail about this tool except to say that you can learn a fair amount from specific keywords and how competitive they are by doing a search on estimated CPC, estimated position, estimated daily clicks, and estimated daily costs. This will also provide some insight into the size of an opportunity for how the keyword might perform.

The bottom line is that you will probably want the Google AdWords Keyword Tool in your arsenal. It provides a lot of great data with a nice interface. There are many options and filters to help you get the specifics you are looking for.

Google Insights for Search

Google Insights for Search (www.google.com/insights/search) is great tool for gathering keyword trends for past and forecasted performance. This tool provides trend analysis like that from the Google Keyword Tool, but takes it to a whole new level. Similarly, you need to be logged in to access the full results.

As you can see in Figure 3.24, you can add multiple keywords to compare one against another. You can filter by type (Web, images, news, products), region, time, and categories. Each of these filters will provide you with a unique insight into keyword performance.

Figure 3.24 Multiple search terms in Google Insights for Search

Because the data has been collected over a long period of time, Google Insights will also provide forecast numbers based on past trends to predict future performance. Similar to Google Trends, this tool will also attempt to display links to significant events that may have influenced keyword performance.

Please keep in mind that this tool uses data that has been aggregated over millions of users without any personal identifiable information and is powered by computer algorithms. Also, it shows results only for search terms that receive a large amount of traffic. So take the results with a grain of salt and be careful not to take the information too literally.

Google Trends

Google Trends (www.google.com/trends) is one of my favorite tools because it provides insight into keyword trends. Trends tell us so much more about what a keyword is or is not capable of. You can also learn a lot about keyword performance throughout the seasons during the 12 calendar months. As you examine these trends, you learn more about searcher behavior and the events that send more people to Google.

In the example in Figure 3.25, you will see the trending difference between the keywords "sofa" and "couch". Google Trends gives you insight into trends on these keywords not only for the last year but all the way back to 2004. This way, you can examine search patterns from year to year to see if there are any inconsistencies. The flags, labeled A, B, C, and so on, indicate significant news stories related to the keywords, which may give you additional insight into the rise or fall of search volumes. These annotations rarely provide the most relevant results, but it doesn't hurt to read through them.

Google Trends also breaks down the search patterns by region, cities, and languages. All in all, this tool provides a lot of interpretive data that can be useful.

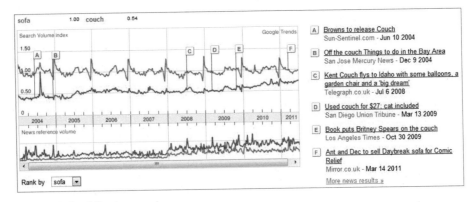

Figure 3.25 Google Trends

Microsoft Advertising Intelligence

Microsoft also has a set of tools to help you with keyword research; it's called Microsoft Advertising Intelligence (it used to be called Microsoft adCenter Add-in Beta for Excel). The tools are free, but to access them you need an adCenter account. These tools essentially add functionality to Microsoft Excel version 2007 or 2010, which is also required. You can download the plug-in from the Microsoft Advertising site (http://advertising .microsoft.com/small-business/adcenter-downloads/microsoft-advertising-intelligence) with the instructions for installation.

This plug-in tool will help you find and expand your keywords for your campaign. Like Google, this tool derives its data from Microsoft's own database, so keep this in mind when reviewing keyword performance and volume measurements.

As you can see from Figure 3.26, keyword wizards walk you through step-by-step to find and expand keywords with performance data. Along with keyword suggestions, there are tools to provide actionable data and insight into keywords that resonate will with your target audience. You can get data on the following topics:

- Demographics
- User location
- Top frequent search queries
- Traffic by month
- Traffic by day

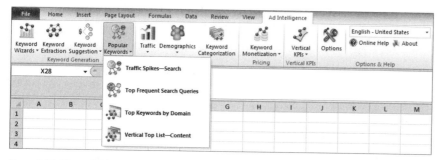

Figure 3.26 Microsoft Advertising Intelligence

  Another nice feature is the ability to help you with categorization or segmentation of your keywords, which I will discuss more in Chapter 5. Because it is a spreadsheet tool, you will need to have some familiarity with working with spreadsheets. The tool takes some getting used to, but there are written and video tutorials to help you get started.

Stage 3 and 4 Keyword Tools

I have covered tools that will help you with search stages 1 and 2 of the search funnel outlined in the beginning of the chapter. Now I will cover some of the tools in the last two stages, which I will call stage 3 and 4 keyword tools.

  Again, I do not have the room to cover them all, but there is a full list of keyword tools on www.keywordresearchbook.com. I will cover a couple of tools, those for competitive keyword research and those that offer insight into the conversion data in stage 4.

Keyword Competitive Analysis Tools

With more and more companies pursuing keywords for PPC, SEO, social networking, and so on, it is important to find (1) which keywords are the most competitive and (2) what your competition is doing with their keywords. Not only are these tools great for understanding the competition, they can be good general keyword research tools as well.

SpyFu

SpyFu is a feature-rich toolset that offers competitive insight into SEO and PPC campaigns as well as its own keyword research tool. The toolset includes the following tools:

- SpyFu Classic
- SpyFu Kombat
- SpyFu Keyword Smart Search
- Keyword Ad History
- Domain Ad History

SpyFu Classic is the main section that you will want to use specifically for competitive keyword research. You essentially enter a domain and are presented with a great deal of data, as seen in Figure 3.27:

- Daily AdWords PPC budget
- Average position of ads vs. the number of advertisers
- Estimated value of organic traffic
- Paid traffic compared with organic traffic
- Top ten (or more with subscription) paid and SEO keywords
- PPC and SEO competitors

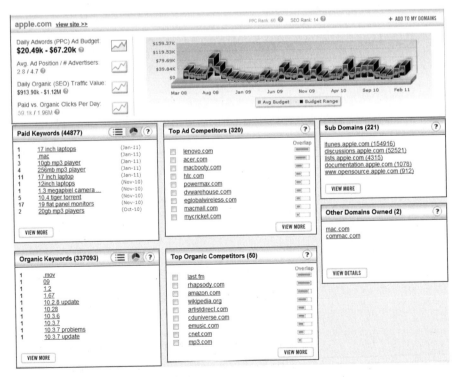

Figure 3.27 SpyFu competitive analysis

This provides a nice dashboard of information that is presented at your fingertips. You can gain full access to the tool for $79 per month or $499 for a 12-month subscription.

The other tools are nice and help provide more detailed information. SpyFu Kombat allows you to compare site-specific keywords for up to three websites. The keyword and domain ad history are also pretty straightforward tools for gaining insight into your competition's ad campaigns.

SpyFu's tools are great for competitive research, and if that is important to you, then this is a serious contender for your overall toolset.

KeywordSpy

KeywordSpy (www.keywordspy.com) is a feature-rich toolset that offers three types of subscriptions, depending on your needs: Research, Tracking, and Professional. This tool has similarities to the others and helps you keep track of the most profitable keywords. It can also provide insight on which ads are the most profitable, as well as CPC information. You can see from the tabs in Figure 3.28 that you can view the actual ads, PPC competitors, and organic competitors.

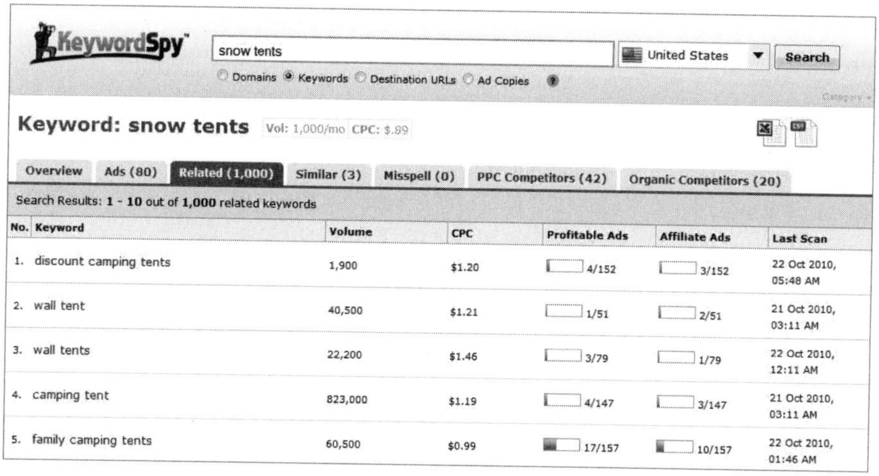

Figure 3.28 KeywordSpy

Keyword Spy also offers a keyword research tool that will help you build a list of search terms by looking at your completion as well as pulling from a large database of related terms. And there is an ROI indicator, which is a metric for pinpointing the profitable keyword and ad copy combinations of your competitors.

iSpionage

iSpionage a newer spy tool that is out on the market. It tends to be more PPC focused than SEO focused. The keyword and domain research tool helps you review your competitors' ads, their ad budgets, and the top-performing keywords. You can even do a keyword search instead of a domain search. Figure 3.29 shows snapshot of a search on the keyword "web hosting". You can view the top advertisers as well as the top keywords.

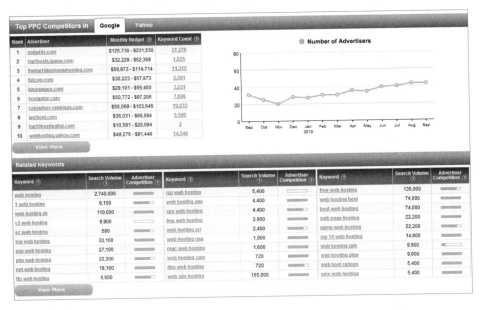

Figure 3.29 iSpionage

iSpionage seems to provide some great tools and features, and if you are focused on PPC rather than SEO, this might be the tool for you.

comScore Search Planner

The search offerings from comScore cover the full range of search funnel reporting, from searches and impressions to clicks and conversions.

Search Planner is an interactive search intelligence service that delivers direct insight into paid and organic search results, demographics of searchers by search term, and data on the broader online behaviors of those searchers. Search Planner provides online marketers with a single interface for the evaluation of key marketing data related to their online audiences and is part of comScore's suite of syndicated digital measurement services. Through an online dashboard, users have access to site profiles, search behavior, and the flow of traffic in and out of sites. In addition, Search Planner users can find where advertisers are running their paid search ads, which advertisers are placing paid search ads by term, and where advertisers are placing their non-search ads online.

Although comScore Search Planner offers competitive intelligence for each phase of the search funnel, the most popular reports tend to be the Competitive Intelligence reports related to paid and organic search click-throughs. While there are free and inexpensive tools in the marketplace to assist with general keyword discovery, these tools tend to lack critical components of the keyword discovery process, such as finding out which terms are working and which terms are relevant enough to drive click-throughs to websites. Just because a lot of searchers use a term does not mean that it necessarily delivers relevant results or drives search visits to particular websites. Understanding what is working for the competition inevitably impacts the value of your keyword list and can help streamline your focus.

Finally, as a result of comScore's panel-based measurement methodology, competitive conversion tracking is possible. This capability allows marketers to define and analyze a set of search terms and follow them all the way through to their intended impact, including both online and offline conversions. The analysis is able to include competitive conversion results for both in-session and latent session activity (that is, someone that searched on a term, visited a website, and returned at a later date to purchase).

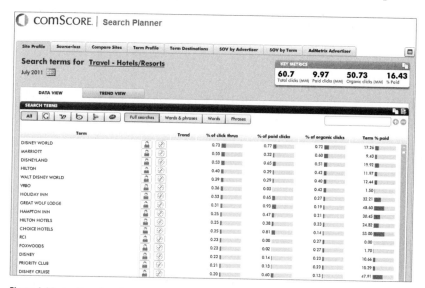

Figure 3.30 comScore Searcher

Hitwise Search Intelligence

Hitwise Search Intelligence is also an enterprise-level keyword research tool that provides extensive research on how people search for products and services in over 160 industries, across all major search engines.

Hitwise's primary data source for this information is user data collected anonymously though ISP network relationships. Search term data is calculated from the URL, including the query string. Hitwise then enhances the data with opt-in panels for demographic information like age and gender.

The keyword updates are available anywhere from 24 to 48 hours following the end of a weekly period. Data is not presented for a single week but as part of a rolling 4- or 12-week period.

Hitwise also presents actual keywords used. Clicks and success metrics are provided to show website visits that result from a keyword search. Additionally, Hitwise does not approximate click numbers in its reporting. Instead, it presents its findings as shares or a proportion of total. Demographics are available at the site level only.

The key benefit to using Hitwise is the speed at which the information becomes available. While other tools take some time for their results to populate, Hitwise can monitor movement and changes in a given market extremely fast. This can provide you with the information you need to make quick adjustments to beat out your competition.

Compete Pro Search Analytics

Compete is a company that provides many tools for helping big brands compete in their respective marketplaces. The tool we are interested in is Compete Pro Search Analytics. This tool provides keyword data for paid and natural search trends, historical search referral keyword data, and custom filtering capabilities that let you focus on the top-performing keywords and traffic of thousands of top name websites.

Compete's major data source is an online panel of Internet users who have opted in to be monitored. Data is obtained through the Compete toolbar and external ISP and ASP relationships. The data is then blended into panel multisourcing, falling somewhere between comScore Marketer's more panel-focused approach and Hitwise's ISP-centric approach, as shown in Figure 3.31. Compete currently claims a "dynamic" panel of 2 million.

Compete is a lower-cost solution than Hitwise or comScore. It even has a free version with limited features. Compete is a good complementary tool for keyword research, especially for small to medium-sized businesses with a limited budget.

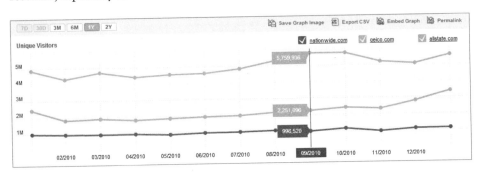

Figure 3.31 Compete

Summary

There are many keyword research tools out on the market and more are popping up. Work on getting a set of tools that works for you, whether you are a small business or a large enterprise. Using a few of these tools will provide clarity to the list of keywords you wish to grow. To help you keep up with current and new tools, please check out this book's site at www.keywordintelligencebook.com.

Finding Keywords

As you learned in Chapter 2, there are four phases to keyword research: Finding keywords, refine them, categorize them, and validate them. This chapter will focus on phase one, in which you are brainstorming to find new keywords.

Chapter Contents

Building Your Keyword Toolset and Methodology

Before we begin to identify new keywords, I want to discuss the tools you will use to help you in this process. I discussed specific tools in Chapter 3, but this is where you need to decide which of those tools to use for you and your organization. I recommended that you use more than one keyword tool; some tools are great for specific tasks.

As you get to know these keyword tools, you will find that most will export to a spreadsheet. Some tools will have built-in management systems to help you organize the keywords you find, but I have found that a simple spreadsheet is a great place to hold all of the keywords you find. The file format that is typically used is a comma-separated values file, or CVS file (the filename ends with .csv). This can be imported into any spreadsheet.

I prefer working with Microsoft Excel because its workbooks can contain multiple spreadsheets to hold working data, with each sheet tabbed and labeled for easy organization.

Computer Automated vs. Computer Aided

We live in a world of fast food and instant access. We thrive on gadgets and tools that save us time. That is no different when it comes to keyword research. If you have done keyword research before, you know that it can be rather tedious work. If you haven't, you will soon find out.

Keep in mind, though, that these keyword tools cannot do it all for you. There is no tool I know of that will do all of the research, rank and score your keywords, and tell you exactly which ones will bring you the most success. They are called keyword suggestion tools for a reason. They suggest.

You should not get into the mindset that tools will completely automate the keyword research process and do the work for you. This is a big mistake. They can certainly help you in the finding and refining process, but they will never be able to give you the exact keywords you need to succeed. For this to happen, you and your team need to get personally involved and get down in the trenches. That is the only way you will truly find what you are looking for.

The correct mindset for approaching tools is to think "computeraided," not "computerautomated." Keyword tools will help in the process and will shave off some time, but they cannot do it all. You will need to step in and provide human intervention by scrutinizing, studying, and considering all of your keyword choices.

Build into your keyword research process a qualitative assessment layer in which human decision making is required. For example, allow for time to study and interpret the keyword data and performance analytics. You and your team know your business better than the tools do and have to personally make decisions on the appropriateness of each keyword for your campaigns.

Brainstorming and Seed Keywords

As you learned in Chapter 2, there are four phases to keyword research:

1. Brainstorm

2. Refine

3. Categorize

4. Test

In the brainstorming phases, it is important that you open up your mind and not second-guess yourself as you find new keywords. You should rule nothing out. Save that for the next phase, and leave your mind unencumbered during this one. Instead, let the creative processes flow and focus on just finding. As you identify new keywords, just add them to your list and move on.

You might be surprised later as you and your team sit down and go through the keywords; some may spark an idea for new keywords that might be great performers. Whatever comes to you, whether it is through a keyword research tool, a dictionary, or other methodology, you should record it.

Brainstorming is the process in which you gather your brain's energies into a "storm," and you can transform these energies into recorded words or diagrams that will lead to identifying keywords ideas.

Seed Keywords

Seed keywords are the core words you begin with when you start researching. They are usually one or two word phrases that are less specific but represent a major theme or idea. For example, let's say that I am a personal fitness trainer and I have a site that outlines my services. As I begin my research, I will want to quickly identify seed keywords I can use to help generate more related keywords, like the "fitness".

If you type these seed words into a keyword suggestion tool, you will get a list of related keywords like this:

- fitness
- fitness center
- fitness equipment
- female fitness
- men's fitness
- fitness magazines
- physical fitness

Each of these keywords might be a niche for you and your business. You also might identify one or more of these keywords as a relevant term you wish to look into more deeply. So they become the new seed term.

Many keyword tools will allow you to search on a seed term and then click any of the results to drill down further for more specific terms. So in a sense, you are starting with a keyword and then moving to more specific keywords.

If you have a large project with many possibilities and you have a team of people to help you do the research, there is a nifty free tool that can help you brainstorm keyword ideas with the help of others. It is called Seed Keywords (www.seedkeywords.com).

You begin by creating a scenario for your search query, like "Faulty color printer and need it fixed". What would you search for? After you enter your scenario, a link appears. You then send this link to people who are helping you. They would be led to a page that looks like Figure 4.1, where they can enter search terms they might use for the scenario you came up with.

Figure 4.1 Seed Keywords tool

The recommendations from all your team members appear on another page, as shown in Figure 4.2, where you can conduct Google searches to check actual results.

Figure 4.2 Seed Keywords tool results page

What I like most about this tool is that it enables collaboration with team members and other helpers from anywhere in the world. You simply email or tweet the URL from seedkeywords.com and invite them to make suggestions. This is an excellent way to identify seed terms and scenarios to help you in categorization and in finding niche or seed keywords.

Mind Mapping

If you want to get a jump on the categorization phase, it might help to break your assignment down into multiple categories. Then brainstorm new keywords one level at a time. This may work especially well if you have a large or complex organization for which you need to come up with many and varied keywords.

Another way of looking at it is to create an outline, list the primary topics first, and then break those topics down into secondary topics. One way to do this effectively is through a process called mind mapping.

A mind map is a diagram you create that involves the use of words and drawings to outline your thoughts. Since most of us are marketers and marketers are visual, this is a process that usually works really well.

You start by choosing a seed term like "fitness". You simply write the keyword on a whiteboard or piece of paper and draw a circle around it. Now you are looking for keywords that are related to your seed term, like the ones I outlined earlier. Figure 4.3 shows a mind map using the seed term "fitness".

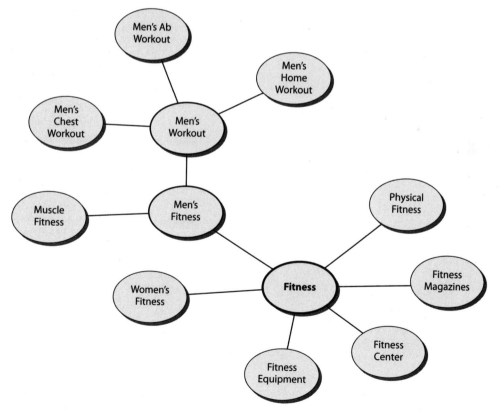

Figure 4.3 Mind map

You can see how the subcategories for "fitness" surround the main seed key-word "fitness". Then the branch "men's fitness" spawned "men's workout", which then branches off to more specific terms.

You can brainstorm as much as you like with this method because you can visually see the relationships between each group. It is usually good to have lots of room to work with. There are also several mind-mapping software programs on the market that will allow you to do this on a computer. However, I recommend a large whiteboard or several sheets of flipchart paper to start off with because they make the process easier and more fluid. Building a mind map on the computer might stifle the creative processes a little.

Google used to have a tool called the Google Wonder Wheel that would render related keywords into a visual mind map format. You can still gather the same data with Google's related searches as seen in Figure 4.4. To access this, you will need to click on the More Search Tools under All Results on the left side of the page. You won't get the visual mind map but you can click on the links to drill down for more detailed keywords.

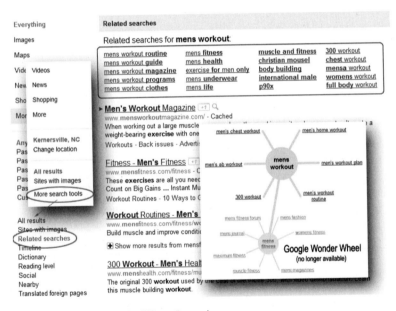

Figure 4.4 Google Wonder Wheel "fitness" example

These are just a few tools to help you in your brainstorming process. The main consideration is to come up with a process for you and your team that allows you to be creative and spontaneously come up with new keyword ideas. Try not to do things that will interfere with this process. You may even want to find a quiet place devoid of distractions.

Where to Find Good Keywords

As you begin your journey to identify new keywords, you'll want to follow a systematic approach. I recommend following a regimen of looking internally first and then looking externally. As you go through this chapter, you will follow the steps outlined in Figure 4.5 to search for new keywords.

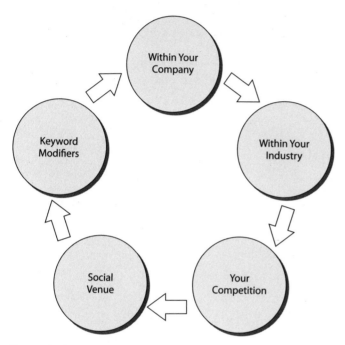

Figure 4.5 Where to look for keywords

Start, of course, with looking at your own organization and all of the data that is available. Much of the resource material needed to find new keywords already exists in various formats, like brochures, press releases, and web content, for example.

Once you have exhausted your search internally, take a step outside your organization and then move to your industry. You'll find many good sources for keywords as you read and absorb industry websites, magazines, and other media related to your industry.

Next, take a close look at those you compete with in your industry. Since your competition is probably engaged in many marketing channels, a quick study of keywords they use for these channels and how they perform can be quite enlightening.

Now we take a full step out of the industry and into the public eye. Social media has provided many great tools to tap into consumer thought and opinion. You may find keywords you have never thought of. Consumers usually don't know the right terminology to find what they are looking for, so they may begin searching by using their best guess. Using a crowd-source tool like seedkeywords.com, which I mentioned earlier, can be a big help in identifying words that consumers may use to begin their search process. The words they might use to find you can turn out to be high-performing keywords.

Finally, once you have a reasonable set of seed keywords, you can use various keyword tools to help you expand your set even further. This is where you consider misspellings, plural and singular forms of words, and other variations to squeeze out a final set of keyword ideas.

Within Your Company

As you start developing your keyword list, one of the first places to look is within your own company. You need to have a good understanding of what your company is all about and what you really want to be known for. Consider dusting off your mission and vision statements and looking for words that speak to who you are as a company or a brand. Look at your press releases for the past several years. Your current and past websites are also great places to mine excellent keywords.

Here is a list of places you might look within your organization to find keywords:

- Company statements, such as brand/positioning statements and mission and vision statements
- Press releases and news articles about you
- Product/service information and brochures
- Company websites, blogs, and social media sites

Company Statements

What about important statements that communicate what your company is all about, like tag lines and positioning and branding statements? These can be great places for mining new keywords. If the keywords get incorporated into your marketing campaigns, it can strengthen the statements even more. Consider some of these taglines/positioning statements:

- Professional money management services for discerning investors
- Factory direct, fine luxury furniture
- Oak furniture for every room in your house
- Low-cost vitamins for active seniors
- Equity strategies for low-risk investors

These statements are outward facing. They are statements that we as consumers remember. On the other hand, there are internal statements that are better known to employees. These are vision and mission statements and usually contain more content. Consider these vision/mission statements:

Heinz "Our VISION, quite simply, is to be 'THE WORLD'S PREMIER FOOD COMPANY, OFFERING NUTRITIOUS, SUPERIOR TASTING FOODS TO PEOPLE EVERYWHERE.' Being the premier food company does not mean being the biggest but it does mean being the best in terms of consumer value, customer service, employee talent, and consistent and predictable growth. We are well on our way to realizing this Vision but there is more we must do to fully achieve it."

Sears "To be the preferred and most trusted resource for the products and services that enhance home and family life."

Amazon.com "Our vision is to be earth's most customer centric company; to build a place where people can come to find and discover anything they might want to buy online."

Facebook "Facebook is a social utility that helps people communicate more efficiently with their friends, family and coworkers. The company develops technologies that facilitate the sharing of information through the social graph, the digital mapping of people's real-world social connections. Anyone can sign up for Facebook and interact with the people they know in a trusted environment."

Not only are they good sources for keywords, corporate mission statements also help you focus your research on the essence of what the company is all about. So take the time to look up your organization's various statements. If you don't have one, then plan to craft one *after* you do your keyword research so you can infuse them with your best, strongest core keywords if possible.

Press Releases and News Articles

Your company's press releases are another form of communication that is published out to the world. Even though they are often scrutinized and filtered internally by legal and other departments to make sure the company is portrayed correctly, they are usually still filled with words used to describe your products, services, and personnel changes and can be another fertile source for good keywords.

Many press releases are picked up by the media and other news publishers. Take the time to find what they are saying in response to the official release. They might put a different spin on the story, so pay attention to the keywords they use. They might use some keywords that you may not have considered. To learn more about writing press releases with your list of keywords, please refer to chapter 12.

Your Company's Website

Your company's website is probably the single most important place to look for keywords, mainly because this is where all outward-facing content is placed. Companies invest much thought and planning into developing a site. So why not pluck all of that low-hanging fruit like products and services information, press releases, and information about the company?

One thing I like about websites is that they are trackable. You have a wealth of information from which you can pull, and it's more than just information about your products and services. Some of that information is about how visitors have interacted with your website. This can be illustrated with two locations where you can strike gold:

- Site analytics
- Site search engine

The first one is site analytics. Ideally, you already have an analytics package such as Google Analytics installed on your site and you are already tracking information. Even if you don't have an analytics tool installed, it is still possible to gather some information through your site's web logs, but you will probably need to get the help of your IT person to get this data. It is important to understand that Google Analytics is a tag-based tool, meaning you have to embed tags into the files of your website in order for them to work, and they work only after the tag has been placed.

A log analyzer tool looks at your web server's log files and pulls analytics data from it. All web servers record these server log files. You simply need a software tool to make sense of the data. If you do not currently have an analytics tool, you may want to consider installing one. Here are some of the many web analytics tools that look at log files:

- Deep Software Log Analyzer (`www.deep-software.com`)
- Sawmill (`www.sawmill.net`)
- The Webalizer (`www.mrunix.net/webalizer/`)
- Mach5 FastStats Log Analyzer (`http://mach5.com/products/analyzer/index.php`)
- AWStats (`http://awstats.sourceforge.net`)

Analytics

Let's take a look at how an analytics tool can help you with your keyword research. In this case, I'll demonstrate how a free tool like Google Analytics can help expand your keyword list. Google Analytics needs to have been set up and tracking for a period of time before you can get any information of value. You cannot just install it and see the information you need. If you have another analytics tool, you will likely find a similar approach to gathering new keywords.

First, let's take a look at the keyword report in Google Analytics as seen in Figure 4.6. It can be found in the Traffic Sources section. Find the Site Usage tab. The keywords that show up under this tab are the keywords that have brought you traffic. Now look at the column that shows your bounce rate. The bounce rate is the percentage of visitors who came to your site and, for whatever reason, left immediately.

Figure 4.6 Google Analytics

A high bounce rate next to a keyword means that you pulled in traffic from that keyword, but those visitors weren't interested in what you had to offer or may not have seen what they were looking for on your site. Conversely, a low bounce rate next to your keywords would suggest that the visitors stayed long enough to look around. This can be a good indicator that these keywords may be good performers for you.

Now let's take this to the next level and try to identify the keywords that are already performing really well for you. At this point, you need to make sure you have some conversion goals set up correctly. To do this, identify what on your site might constitute a conversion. It is okay to have more than one conversion goal within your site. It might be a thank-you page that shows up after a customer purchases something or sends you a contact request. Once you have that figured out, click Goals in the list of links on the left side of the page. If you haven't already set up your goals, you will see something like Figure 4.7. Click the Set Up Goals and Funnels link at the bottom of the page.

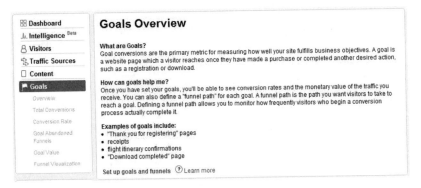

Figure 4.7 Setting up goals in Google Analytics

You will have the option of filling out up to four goals. These could be a URL destination, time on site, or pages per visit, as seen on Figure 4.8. Set one of your goals based on how you wish to measure success and then name the goal. If you have just set this up, you will need to wait for a period of time to start seeing results, but at least you have some conversion tracking set up.

More about how to use this tool can be found at www.google.com/support/analytics/bin/answer.py?hl=en&answer=55515.

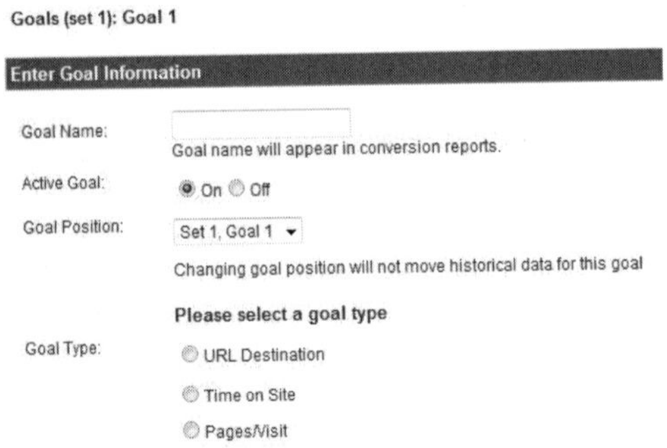

Goals (set 1): Goal 1

Enter Goal Information

Goal Name: _____
Goal name will appear in conversion reports.

Active Goal: ⦿ On ◯ Off

Goal Position: Set 1, Goal 1 ▾
Changing goal position will not move historical data for this goal

Please select a goal type

Goal Type: ◯ URL Destination
◯ Time on Site
◯ Pages/Visit

Figure 4.8 Enter your goal information.

Now go back and look at your keyword report as we did previously. Figure 4.6 shows a list of keywords that have brought traffic to your site. You will also notice a tab for goals. If you click this tab, you will get not only a list of user search queries that brought you traffic but also those that converted for you. These high-performing search queries are likely to be great performing keywords for you in the future.

As you deploy more keywords in your marketing campaigns, come back to this page within Google Analytics to identify even more search queries that are performing well, so you can continue to identify high-performing keywords.

Now, let's try expanding these "seed" keywords even more and see if you can find more keywords that are similar that will also perform. You can use the Google

Keyword Tool or any other keyword suggestion tool. (Keyword tools were covered in Chapter 3.) For this example, you will use the Google Keyword Tool. You will paste your set of keywords and the site URL into the appropriate fields.

Suggestions from this tool are particularly useful because they're specific to the site and keywords you define and are based on actual past queries. This is a nice tip to help you expand on a core set of keywords that you already know are performing well.

Website Search Engine

Search queries are as varied as the people who create them. The number of unique search terms created by Internet users makes it difficult to get a good idea of effective keywords potential visitors would use to get to your site. Recent studies are unique, which means the terms you come up with provide only an educated guess as to how you can attract customers to your site.

To help you get a more focused picture of what queries people are using to find information on your site, you can gather information from a site-search utility like the one on PETCO's site in Figure 4.9. A site search box gives you great information that will help strengthen your seed keyword list because it captures the exact words your site visitors use. It takes away the guesswork. You may need to get the help of your IT person or web developer to gather this information, especially if it has been stored in a database.

PETCO.com 10th Anniversary Sale! Ends March 10th
UP TO 40% Off Sitewide & FREE Shipping on $40

GET FREE SHIPPING
PROMOTION CODE ▶
Exclusions apply.

Search PETCO.com

DOG   CAT   FISH   SMALL ANIMAL   FERRET   REPTILE   BIRD   WILD BIRD   FLEA & TICK   SPRING APPAREL

Figure 4.9 Site search utility on petco.com

Pay special attention to the list of search queries that users typed into your site search box because it can give you deep insights into your visitors' intentions and expectations. For instance, if a certain keyword was used more than others, it doesn't necessarily mean the keyword was the most popular and will bring you more and more visitors. It might mean that you have some usability problems with your site and the only way visitors can find the content they are looking for is through your site search engine. It may also mean that search engines are sending visitors to your site on the "wrong" search terms, and if your paid search campaign is driving these visitors, then you may be able to fine-tune your paid search campaign by adding some negative keywords.

So look over the list of user queries from your site search engine and have your team check them over to understand, as much as you can, why visitors typed in these search terms. It could be that they know exactly what they are looking for, like a specific product or model number.

Specific queries like "Durango RD542 women's boots", as opposed to general search terms like "boots" they use before getting to your site, can yield new ideas for connecting people to your site content.

You may find that site search queries are very different, and often more specific, than the search queries people use to find your site via search engines. For instance, someone may have come to your site through a Google search for the term "personal injury lawyer". However, using the search box on your site, they refined their search by typing in "spinal injury attorney in Miami". Those are the kinds of long-tail search terms you can build a keyword campaign around.

Within Your Industry

Now that you have taken the time to look within your company, it is time take a step back and broaden your focus a little. If you have been around your industry for some time, you should be familiar with many good keywords already. Your industry is made up of many companies and websites that contain useful keyword choices.

What Is Your Niche?

One way to approach your research is to ask yourself what your place in the industry is, or in other words, what is your niche? You may have already done a competitive analysis and identified your niche.

Once you have determined this, you can mine new keywords based on a set of core keywords related to your niche or specialty. Let's say you are selling digital cameras. Try inserting this seed term into your keyword suggestion tool.

Your keyword tool will likely show you lots of variations and related terms that are derived from the terminology surrounding digital cameras. You can pick and choose which ones to focus on based on how close a fit they are for your business and how popular they are. It might make sense to target popular keywords that are closely related to your business. But keep in mind that if you sell expensive digital cameras, it makes no sense to target "cheap digital cameras" no matter how popular the term.

You'll likely do the same thing if you are in the legal industry specializing in personal injury or any other specialized field. For example, suppose your company sells legal counsel for personal injury cases. If you type "personal injury" into a keyword tool, you find a list of related keywords, such as "personal injury attorney" and "personal injury settlement" and "personal injury settlement". But you'd also find "car accident attorney" and "motorcycle attorney" and many other variations. Depending on what products or services your company sells, some of these are very close fits, and some are not.

The second approach is to find industry categories that will help you find industry themes or subjects that can be grouped together. You might use a tool like Keyword Discovery to help you find these themes. Just type in an industry keyword and then click the "industry" modifier and you will get a directory-like structure that shows various groupings. If you use the keyword "digital camera", you would get something like what you see in Figure 4.10.

Industry ?
/Shopping/Photography/Cameras_and_Camcorders/Cameras
/Kids_and_Teens/Arts/Photography/Cameras
/Home/Consumer_Information/Electronics/Photography/Digital_Cameras
/Computers/Hardware/Peripherals/Scanners
/Home/Consumer_Information/Electronics/Photography
/Shopping/Photography/Cameras_and_Camcorders
/Computers/Hardware/Systems/Notebooks_and_Laptops/Manufacturers/Sony
/Home/Homemaking/Frugality/Refunds_or_Rebates
/Arts/Photography/Techniques_and_Styles/Digital
/Home/Consumer_Information/Electronics

Figure 4.10 Category grouping

From there you can click a category for a list of related keywords. When doing this search, it is a good idea to start with broad keywords first.

There are other resources that will help you zero in on industry phrases and jargon. Most of these have both online and offline components and can be a great source of inspiration:

- Magazines and trade journals (online and in print)
- Membership organizations
- Trade organizations

Magazines and Trade Journals

Magazines are typically made up of writers and editors who are very close to the industry they write about. When they write, they will typically use industry terminology, which would include terms or keywords that businesses and consumers might use as they converse about products and services.

I'm a cyclist, and I enjoy reading magazines like *Bicycling* and *VeloNews*. Both are full of articles, ads, and information rich with cycling-related keywords. I used to have a subscription for the printed magazines and now I have opted for the iPad version so I don't have all of the clutter that comes with many magazines lying around. You can also access these publications online and read through the many articles, stories, and reviews. As you read this content, it will help you get into the right mind-set and to find the key terms that are used to help describe various aspects of the industry.

Membership Organizations

Administrators of membership organization are there to serve their members, who are professionals within a given industry. As such, they offer programming, events, and other content that provides value to the membership base. These programs and events are another great source of industry-related content.

One of the organizations I have had the privilege of working with is the America Outdoors Association. They provide annual events and other resources to help rafting companies, outfitters, and other outdoor-related businesses to learn more about the outdoor industry.

You may already be a member of such an organization. Look at what resources they offer and any materials they have. You might find economic, political, and other industry-related information that can be a source for great keywords.

Trade Organizations

Trade organizations are another great place to find industry-related keywords. Typically, a trade organization is an advocacy group that is designed to help perpetuate and elevate awareness of its respective industry. In my industry, that would be Search Engine Marketing Professional Organization (SEMPO). I have served as an officer and on the board of directors for that organization in the past.

SEMPO provides education, training, industry trends, and statistics, and net-working opportunities that serve the search industry. It even has local chapters where I can join other professionals in my area. It provides training and certification programs that help me in the field of Internet marketing. Throughout all of these programs and any websites or publications, you will find industry-related terminology that can be used as possible keywords. These organizations are usually made up of industry leaders and experts, so what they have to say should be viewed accordingly.

From Your Competition

After looking at your own company and the industry, you can pull out a little more and see what your competition is up to. Studying your competition is a must if you plan to stay competitive and increase your market share.

In Chapter 2, I spent some time discussing competitive keyword analysis and what you can learn from your competition. In this chapter, I would like to focus more on actually finding new keywords. You can use any of the handful of competitive research tools covered in Chapter 3 to help you mine new keywords as well.

It is very likely that your competition is or has engaged in Internet marketing, which means if you go to their site, you can see what keywords they are optimizing for. One way to do this is to use the method discussed in Chapter 2, looking at the key-word meta tag.

You can also just review their website and read over their content. You should start to get an idea what keywords are important to them. You may also discover that keywords you know they should be optimizing for are missing from their site. This can turn in to a great opportunity if you can find those keywords because they will be easier to rank for.

Just as you did for your own company, you should look at your competitors' branding statements and marketing materials. What is their core message? What is it they want to be known for? What is their value proposition? Take some time to get to know what their competitive advantage is. How can you be a little different? What differentiates you from your competition? What keywords can you use to make this distinction?

Taking the time for this kind of analysis can be enlightening and may even help you with more than just finding unique keywords. It may help you navigate a course that leads to your own distinctive value proposition and therefore helps you lead the charge in your respective niche.

From Social Media and Blogs

At this point, it's helpful to pull all the way out and look at the social venue to catch a glimpse of what the outside world thinks of your organization and your industry. With many new social media sites and tools that exist today and many more to come, we have plenty of resources to help us tap in to the collective banter at the virtual water cooler.

What is it that people are saying? What keywords are people using as they talk about your company or industry? This is a wonderful opportunity to dig in and identify keywords that you may never have thought of because you are so caught up in your own world.

Consumers are influenced by branding messages from many marketing channels. However, they still might not pick up on the right terminology as they consider what words to use in a Google search box. The words they use to describe you and your products can be found by using keyword tools. The problem is that you aren't visualizing those words with any context.

Social media provides that context and allows you to peek in and view whole sentences and paragraphs of dialog with comments and opinions about everything. Typing "ikea" in a Twitter search netted the discussion in Figure 4.11.

Figure 4.11 Twitter comments about IKEA

This is just a small sample, but you get the idea that IKEA's stores are huge and it's hard to find your way around. Take some time to read through these kinds of conversations and you'll start to get some ideas on consumer thought and, in many cases, mine some new keyword ideas.

Or you might decide to use some keywords that counteract any negative sentiment. You could build a campaign to push messages out through various marketing channels that get consumers thinking a different way.

Another way to find these kinds of conversations is by reading through blogs. Technorati (www.technorati.com) is a great source for finding blogs that may have conversational threads about topics related to your company, competitors, or industry. Simply type in a keyword and you'll see a list of discussion threads. Reading them provides an opportunity to learn more about, for example, slang terms that might be candidates for your list.

Focus Groups and Surveys

Focus groups have been the mainstay of traditional advertising for years. They give marketers a better understanding of their target audience and their needs, wants, and desires. Surveys have also been a long-standing tool for gathering the same kind of information. The information that can be derived from focus groups and surveys can often be found online, especially with some social media sites like Facebook. Focus group testing can simply be informally talking to targeted individuals with predefined questions. Or you can go all out and find a moderator and conduct a full-scale focus group.

Social media can be used to get feedback from your users. You can upload sample content and ask users for their feedback. In film production, for example, producers have used this technique by offering part of a film on YouTube and allowing users to comment.

The same can be said for conducting surveys. You can set up Facebook and Twitter polls and let users provide their input. Dell has taken this idea to the next level with its Idea Storm site (www.ideastorm.com), which allows users to submit product enhancement ideas and lets other users vote on their favorites. This allows Dell to see which enhancements are more popular than others.

So if you employ any of these kinds of tactics, make sure you scour the comments and feedback for keywords that seem to resonate with your audience.

Hashtags

You have probably seen the # next to words in Twitter as you have read tweets from those that you follow, such as #followfriday. These tags are called hashtags and they help to spread information on Twitter while also helping to organize it.

Using hashtags is also a favorite tool for those hosting events for conferences. They encourage Twitter users to use this tag in every tweet that is about the event. This way, people who want to follow the event can simply do a search on the hashtag keyword and read all of the thoughts and opinions.

So as you are going through your tweets looking for possible keyword phrases, notice the hashtags that are being used. They might lead to good keyword ideas. Once you find a hashtag, you can go to Hashtags.org (www.hashtags.org) and type in the keyword to get the latest chatter on the topic. You can also get some interesting stats, as seen in Figure 4.12 for the term "iPad 2".

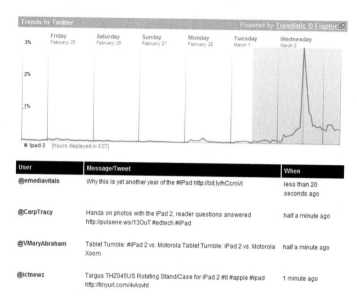

Figure 4.12 Hashtags.org

Social Tagging and Tag Clouds

Another form of tagging is called social tagging, as seen on social bookmark sites like Delicious (http://delicious.com/tag), StumbleUpon (www.stumbleupon.com/tag/), and Technorati (www.technorati.com/tag/), just to name a few. These sites allow users to organize and manage their bookmarks online. The bookmarks are then tallied and the more popular ones bubble up to the top of the charts.

They are also classified in the form of a tag cloud, as seen in Figure 4.13. The keywords that are larger and bolder are more popular.

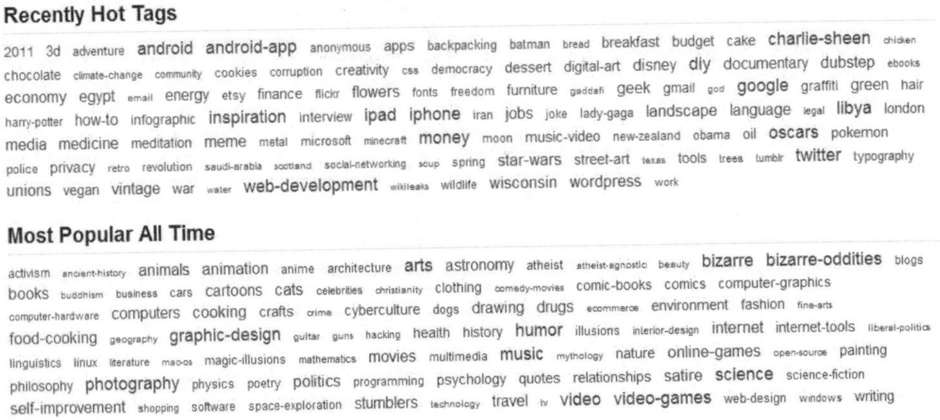

Recently Hot Tags

2011 3d adventure **android android-app** anonymous apps backpacking batman bread breakfast budget cake **charlie-sheen** chicken chocolate climate-change community cookies corruption creativity css democracy dessert digital-art disney **diy** documentary dubstep ebooks economy egypt email energy etsy finance flickr flowers fonts freedom furniture gaddafi geek gmail god **google** graffiti green hair harry-potter how-to infographic **inspiration** interview **ipad iphone** iran jobs joke lady-gaga landscape language legal **libya** london media medicine meditation meme metal microsoft minecraft **money** moon music-video new-zealand obama oil **oscars** pokemon police **privacy** retro revolution saudi-arabia scotland social-networking soup spring **star-wars** street-art texas tools trees tumblr **twitter** typography unions vegan vintage war water **web-development** wikileaks wildlife **wisconsin** wordpress work

Most Popular All Time

activism ancient-history **animals animation** anime architecture **arts astronomy** atheist atheist-agnostic beauty **bizarre bizarre-oddities** blogs **books** buddhism business cars **cartoons cats** celebrities christianity **clothing** comedy-movies comic-books comics computer-graphics computer-hardware computers **cooking** crafts crime **cyberculture** dogs **drawing drugs** ecommerce environment fashion fine-arts **food-cooking** geography **graphic-design** guitar guns hacking health history **humor** illusions interior-design **internet** internet-tools liberal-politics linguistics linux literature mac-os magic-illusions mathematics **movies** multimedia **music** mythology nature online-games open-source painting philosophy **photography** physics poetry **politics** programming psychology quotes relationships satire **science** science-fiction self-improvement shopping software space-exploration **stumblers** technology travel tv **video video-games** web-design windows writing

Figure 4.13 StumbleUpon tag cloud

The point here is that these tag clouds are great for finding new keywords, especially in real time. You can revisit these tags anytime and the keywords and their popularity will be different, based on the buzz of the day.

Blogs and Discussion Boards

The phraseology of the Internet can have a turnaround of weeks, if not days. The jargon of your target field is constantly evolving. Blogs and forums are major sources for monitoring these changes; blogs focus the collective voice of consumers and providers into an ever-moving entity of opinion, fact, and consumer thought.

To make sure you are constantly aware of what is going on in your industry (or that of your client), you must read blogs. And to make sure you get the most relevant information from the blogs, you need to remember three things: authority, frequency, and freshness. Authority means how popular the blog is, usually measured by how many sites link to it or reference it; frequency can be, for example, how many times a week a blogger posts; freshness is how recent the comments are. If 400 people link to a blog but the last post was three years ago, that is not a good sign.

Technorati (www.technorati.com) is the primary site for cataloging all of these things and rating their relative importance. This is not to say that smaller or less frequent blogs do not have relevance.

Discussion boards, also known as forums, are not dissimilar from blogs. You are looking for conversations (threads) that have frequent and fresh posts. You can also search ready-made communities that may engage in discussions relative to your topic. Google Groups (http://groups.google.com) and Yahoo Groups (http://groups.yahoo.com) are two popular bases for such searches.

So you've found relevant and interesting blogs and forums that are up-to-date and frequently visited. What do you do now? Read. Take notes. Buzzwords and common phrases are what you want to focus on. Remember, these are the people who may turn to your site one day to find what they're looking for. Make sure that when they search, you know what they're searching for.

Keyword Modification Techniques

Once you have a list of keywords, there are a couple of techniques you can use to expand the list even more. Some of these methods can be used with keyword tools and others can be employed manually. Take a look at each one so you can at least understand the process and how it works.

Thesaurus

Using a thesaurus is a very straightforward approach. If you will be researching keywords often, it's good to have a thesaurus handy. Granted, that might seem old-fashioned, but taking a few minutes to flip through a decent thesaurus can get ideas going as the words flash past your eyes. You can also try to find how to access the thesaurus in your word processing application. For Microsoft Word, right click on a word and select Synonyms. You will see a short list of terms related to the word as well as the option to open the thesaurus for more options.

I wish it was that simple for Microsoft Excel. The thesaurus is located under the Research tab. Once you select it, a windowpane opens on the right side and you can do lookups there.

Nostalgia over the printed version aside, Merriam-Webster has a good online thesaurus at www.m-w.com. Thesaurus.com, at www.thesaurus.com, is even better.

To illustrate, Table 4.1 shows the results you would get if you were to look up the word "jewelry" at Thesaurus.com.

▶ Table 4.1 Results from looking up "jewelry" on Thesaurus.com

adornment	charm	jewel	rosary
anklet	choker	junk	solitaire
band	cross	knickknack	sparkler
bangle	crown	lavaliere	stickpin
bauble	earring	locket	stone
beads	finery	necklace	tiara
bijou	frippery	ornament	tie pin
bracelet	gem	pendant	treasure
brass	gewgaw	pin	trinket
brooch	glass	regalia	gold
cameo	hardware	ring	diamonds
chain	ice	rock	silver

This is really pretty simple and straightforward. Your keyword tool will probably find some of these, but your thesaurus will often show you new possibilities.

Plural and Singular Forms

The next technique is to look at your list and simply add or delete the *s* for both a plural and singular form for each keyword. For example, "jeweler" can become "jewelers" and "jewelry store" can become "jewelry stores". It is amazing how just adding an *s* can make a difference. Depending on existing trends with the words you are using, you could double your exposure with this simple tip:

jeweler	jewelers
book	books
bike	bikes
computer	computers

Again, many of your keyword tools will help with plural and singular forms of words, but scan your list to see if any of them were missed.

Misspellings and Typos

Some words are easier to spell than others. As you review keywords that are derived from your product names, for instance, you might identify some that can be challenging to spell by your visitors.

The best way to handle this is to make the mistakes the way users would: Spell the word phonetically, add or remove (skip) letters, and look at the potential for typos on the QWERTY keyboard. Add the misspellings to your list. Here is a list of common misspellings for "mortgage": "mortgauge", "mortgage", "morgauge", "morgage", and "mortage". Using the word "jewelry", from our previous example, we can, by playing with the pronunciation of the word, come up with six common alternate spellings: "jewlry", "jewelry", "jewlrey", "jewelery", "jewelrey", and "jewelerey". Later in this chapter, I'll talk about prefixing and suffixing the word "jewelry" to create 50 new phrases. When we add in these misspellings, the list grows quickly from 50 to 350.

Even though your visitors might misspell your product name, the search engines use predictive models to attempt to serve you up the results you meant to find with misspelled words. They will even suggest the correct spelling and give you an opportunity to do the search again with the correct spelling. So this is something you don't have to worry about too much, but it is good to identify those keywords that you know are challenging to spell.

If you wish to look up common misspellings, there's a nifty little keyword typo generator www.seochat.com/seo-tools/keyword-typo-generator/ that will help you find misspellings from a seed keyword.

Prefixing

In the context of keyword searches, think of prefixes as "words that come before" (and suffixes as "words that come after") that you might use for a keyword. Imagine you are the person searching for "jewelry". What types of jewelry could you be searching for? For instance, you might add "best" or "inexpensive" or "fashion" in front of the term. Use these ideas as well: After choosing "expensive", for example, you can add "inexpensive". Again, think of the end user and what prefixes they might use to narrow their search query.

For this example, I'll do a quick brainstorming session, as seen in Table 4.2, on types of jewelry using prefixes.

▶ **Table 4.2** Prefixing the word "jewelry"

gold jewelry	quartz jewelry	sardonyx jewelry
silver jewelry	aquamarine jewelry	sapphire jewelry
platinum jewelry	bloodstone jewelry	lapis jewelry
diamond jewelry	rock crystal jewelry	opal jewelry
amethyst jewelry	emerald jewelry	tourmaline jewelry
moonstone jewelry	chrysoprase jewelry	topaz jewelry
mother of pearl jewelry	alexandrite jewelry	citrine jewelry
birthstone jewelry	pearl jewelry	tanzanite jewelry
(quick lookup of birthstones)	ruby jewelry	zircon jewelry
garnet jewelry	carnelion jewelry	turquoise jewelry
rose quartz jewelry	peridot jewelry	amber jewelry

This is a good example of how one idea can lead to a great many key phrases. While brainstorming, you might think "Ah, birthstones," and after a quick Google search, you have added over 20 phrases.

Suffixing

Now, we will do the same thing with suffixes, using our root word "jewelry" and adding to it by thinking of words that might come after. Table 4.3 shows the results.

▶ **Table 4.3** Suffixing the word "jewelry"

jewelry company	jewelry soldering	jewelry sellers
jewelry repair	jewelry store	jewelry shopping
jewelry cleaning	jewelry sales	jewelry wholesalers
jewelry design	jewelry deals	jewelry resellers
jewelry catalog	jewelry coupons	jewelry manufacturers
jewelry fixing	jewelry dealers	

You can figure it out from here. There are tools and techniques that you will use to grab other phrases, but nothing can take the place of a good brainstorming session to come up with original ideas and branches you may never have envisioned without some open, free thought.

Keyword Stemming

The idea behind keyword stemming is to return to the root of the word and start at the base. With a root word, you can expand it in either direction and even add words, increasing the number of variable options and the size of your keyword list.

For example, you are trying to grow a list around "technology management". "Technology" is the adjective in this case. Remove that and you are left with "management". The root of "management" is "manage".

How can we expand "manage"? It is limited only by your imagination. Obviously, "management" is what we started with, so you include that, then "managed", "managing", "manager", "managerial", "manageable", "unmanageable", "unmanaged", "unmanagerial". This is the brainstorming part. Don't be critical of yourself or teammates, but try to keep it to real words.

Now you need to take the words you have put together and combine them with other keywords to create useful and specific phrases. Using just the word "manager" will be too broad since you are specifically targeting "technology" as well. Let's combine the "management" words with "technology":

- technology management
- technology managed
- technology managing
- technology manager
- technology managerial
- technology manageable
- technology unmanageable
- technology unmanaged
- technology unmanagerial

How reasonable you want to be is up to you. In this case, some of these do not make sense, so mark them out:

- technology management
- technology managed
- technology managing
- technology manager

- ~~technology managerial~~
- ~~technology manageable~~
- ~~technology unmanageable~~
- technology unmanaged
- ~~technology unmanagerial~~

Because of differences in phrasing, you can also switch these words around:

- management technology
- managed technology
- managing technology
- manager technology
- managerial technology
- manageable technology
- unmanageable technology
- unmanaged technology
- unmanagerial technology

Finally, you can use all these phrases again with "tech" instead of "technology", effectively turning "technology management" into the terms seen in Table 4.4.

▶ **Table 4.4** Example of keyword stemming

technology management	manageable technology	managed tech
technology managed	unmanageable technology	managing tech
technology managing	unmanaged technology	manager tech
technology manager	unmanagerial technology	managerial tech
technology unmanaged	tech management	manageable tech
management technology	tech managed	unmanageable tech
managed technology	tech managing	unmanaged tech
managing technology	tech manager	unmanagerial tech
manager technology	tech unmanaged	
managerial technology	management tech	

Depending on your specific aim or goal, some of these phrases may need to be removed.

With the example word "jewelry", your root word is "jewel" and you can expand with endings like "jeweler(s)", "jewelry shop(s)", "jewelry store(s)", and so on. Another example is the root word "fashion", which could be stemmed to be "fashioned", "fashioning", and "fashionable". The possibilities in growing your list are endless.

Summary

At this point, you have discovered many places to find new keyword ideas. Remember to record all of the keywords you can find, and don't hold back and stifle your creativity. Use a good old spreadsheet to document your list. You are going to need it for the next chapter as you start filtering out the keywords and identifying those that are likely to perform well for your campaign.

CHAPTER 4: FINDING KEYWORDS ■

Refine Your Initial List of Keywords in Seven Steps

You have built a set of keywords by using many different methods you learned about in Chapter 4. Now it is time to do a little analysis and learn what you can about these keywords and how effective they might be for your campaign. This chapter will focus on a seven-step process for organizing, analyzing, and sorting your new keywords.

Chapter Contents

The Keyword Refinement Process

You now take off your brainstorming hat and put on your sorting hat. It would be nice to have a magical hat like the one in *Harry Potter*, but you are left to your own skills and resources. You have all of these great keywords; you now need to organize and prioritize them into meaningful groups and then sort them in order of those most likely to succeed.

Categorization and Audience Segmentation The first step will be to categorize your keywords using an Excel spreadsheet. Create tabs at the bottom of the spreadsheet for each of your categories. It is a good idea to keep one tab reserved for your original master set of keywords. This is so you can refer back to them when you conduct you keyword research every 6 to 12 months, which is recommended.

Scoring for Relevance You'll learn about gauging the relevance of each keyword to your category lists by analyzing how relevant they are to your business, your products, and your service offerings.

Scoring for Specificity You'll learn how to refine your category keyword lists to ensure the "right" level of specifics—neither too broad nor too narrow—and score them based on actual search data.

Scoring for Competition We'll look at how much competition there is for each keyword so you can determine how easy or hard it will be to achieve the results you are looking for.

Scoring for Popularity We'll cover the methods of measuring the real-world popularity of your keywords using keyword tools to rank and score your keywords from most to least popular.

Keyword performance score We'll look at methods to pull together an aggregate score for each keyword that blends together the scores for relevance, specificity, competitiveness, and popularity. Then you will sort your keyword list based on that overall score so you can view the top potential performers first.

Keyword Interpretation Finally, we will look at methods to "interpret" keyword potential and then choose your keywords for individual campaigns.

To keep things consistent for each refinement step, we will use a scoring system of 1 to 10, with 10 being the highest score and 0 the lowest score. So create a new spreadsheet and set it up to look like the one in Figure 5.1.

You can see I have one tab called Initial List, which represents the master set of keywords, and then three category tabs, which you will define next in the categorization step. You can also see the columns at the top for each of the refinements. I have added the notation of our scoring system from 1 to 10 for clarity.

You will learn how to convert actual data from keyword tools into a number from 1 to 10 so you can keep everything consistent. This helps when trying to calculate the overall score.

	Keyword List	Relevance Score	Specificity Score	Competiveness Score	Popularity Score	Overall Score		Annual Searches	Competition Index
1									
2	Formula	1 - 10 (10 best)	1 - 10 (10 best)	1 - 10 (10 best)	1 - 10 (10 best)	Avg (B + C + D + E)			
3									
4	bicycle								
5	mountain bike								
6	bike								
7	bike shop								
8	bike shops								
9	bike shop dallas								
10	road bike								
11	trek madone ssl								

Initial List **Category 1** Category 2 Category 3

Figure 5.1 Spreadsheet framework

This is the fundamental layout we will use. For each step, you will build on this structure and add formulas to help in the refinement process. When you are done, you will have a full spreadsheet with formulas that will help you see your list of keywords in a whole different light.

Step 1: Categorization and Audience Segmentation

Categorization is one of the most important steps in the refining process. In fact, if you have a good idea of what your categories are, you might have set them up ahead of time. I have done this step before and after the brainstorming phase. You might find it easier to cover this step even before you start looking for your initial keywords and then place your newfound keywords into one of your defined categories. If you have done so, then you are a step ahead. If you haven't grouped your keywords by category yet, no problem; we will cover that now.

Audience Segmentation

One of the key aspects to deciding which keywords to keep and which to discard is to have organized groups of buckets in which to place keywords. This can easily be done by first knowing your target audience. Your target audience comprises the people to whom you are marketing your products and services.

Traditionally, most people think of their target audience in demographic terms like age, ethnicity, gender, household income, and education. For the online community, those things are still significant, but even more important are statistics about searcher intent. I prefer thinking of my target audience in terms of a persona instead of demographics.

By definition, a persona is an archetypal user or searcher that represents the needs of larger groups of users, in terms of their goals and personal characteristics. They act as "stand-ins" for real users and help guide decisions about website functionality and behavioral site design.

In Chapter 10, I will go into a more extensive outline of personas and how they can be used for structuring your website. As you structure your website into logical segments for your audience or personas, you will find that each of these segments is a type of categorization. Many of these buckets might resemble your sitemap or top navigation. Each one can be a bucket where you can develop a logical grouping of keywords.

Another way of looking at categorization is through audience segmentation. This is a process of studying the keywords and then determining who the audience is. For instance, you would know that a person using "cloud computing deployment" was an IT manager, but someone using "cloud computing cost benefits" or "cloud computing strategy" would be a CIO or CTO, depending on their specific roles.

Audience segmentation can be done here at the beginning of your process as you study your master list of keywords and then break them down into logical segments. Or you can do the segmentation at the end after you have gone through the next few steps. Either way, it helps to provide greater insight into user intent and can also help in the information design process I will discuss in Chapter 10, "Keywords and Site Architecture."

Another way to help you in this categorization process is to break your keywords down into groups that mimic the organization of information on your current website. Although I highly recommend the persona design approach, you may have a site that is already fixed and difficult to change for a number of reasons.

Remember, the key is to have relevant destination content on your landing pages. If your site is already set up with the right "content" or landing pages for specific keywords, then you can use that as a basis for categorization. The most common overall site organization centers on company divisions, products, and services.

If your website is organized around company divisions, then this would be a logical way to categorize your keywords. So start creating a list of categories for each division. Do the same thing for any product and services categories you create.

Step 2: Scoring for Relevance

Now that you have a handle on your categories, you can start applying scores for the other steps. The first step is relevance.

Relevance is often overlooked by many people who focus exclusively on high search volume keywords and use this as their only criteria for determining which keywords to use. Evaluating keywords by search volume only is by far the wrong approach.

Relevance is the most important primary factor to consider because it speaks directly to what you and your organization are all about. Keyword research tools cannot provide this kind of insight because they do not know your business or industry.

Let's look at an example. Let's say you are a personal injury attorney who focuses only on accident cases in Florida. You might have a set of keywords from your initial list that include "divorce attorney", "criminal lawyer", or even "personal injury lawyer in Mexico". These keywords are related somewhat but are not relevant. So you should eliminate these kinds of keywords or just give them a low score, like maybe a 0 or 1.

The principle is this: If a keyword is highly relevant to a specific page on your website, you will have a better chance of gaining a higher ranking with that page than you will with keywords of lower relevance. Furthermore, you will achieve a higher conversion rate. It is not useful to have "divorce attorney" content on a personal injury attorney website. I guess if it is an ugly divorce it may turn to personal injury, but that is beside the point.

Unfortunately this is one of those tasks that cannot easily be delegated to a keyword tool. It has to involve a human being that can make a judgment on how relevant the keyword is to you and your business. Some keyword tools do allow you to find related keywords around a seed keyword. These tools make come in handy for assisting in this process, but ultimately it will come down to human filtering.

So take a look at Figure 5.2 and see how my spreadsheet will shape up as I add relevance scores.

	A	B
1	Keyword List	Relevance Score
2	Formula	1 - 10 (10 best)
3		
4	bike	9
5	bicycle	9
6	bike rack	1
7	mountain bike	8
8	bicycle parts	8
9	road bike	9
10	bike parts	7
11	bike shop	10
12	bike shops	10
13	road bicycle	8
14	bike accessories	7
15	trek bicycle	6
16	trek bike	7
17	bike helmet	7
18	folding bike	5
19	tandem bicycle	4
20	recumbent bicycle	4
21	bicycle wheels	6
22	trek mountain bike	7
23	folding bicycle	5
24	mountain bicycle	6
25	bicycle store	10
26	bike frame	8

Initial List Category 1 Category 2 Categ

Figure 5.2 Relevance scoring

In this example, I have a set of keywords for a bike shop that sells and repairs road bikes and some mountain bikes. Notice that I give higher scores to "bike", "bicycle", and "mountain bike", but I give a 1 to "bike rack". If I do not sell bike racks or have content on my site supporting bike racks, then it is not relevant to my business.

Keywords like this will have the effect of attracting the wrong customers and web traffic. Bringing them to my site will just disappoint them and increase my bounce rate and lower my conversion rate.

Because relevance scoring is somewhat subjective, you should not worry too much about the difference between a 7 and an 8. If you have to think for more than a couple of seconds for each keyword, you are thinking too hard. Another way to look at scoring might be to create a scale like the following:

- Not relevant at all (0)
- Very little relevancy (1–3)
- Average relevance (4–6)
- Very relevant (7–9)
- This is exactly what we do, or perfect relevance (10)

Thinking of it this way may help you in your scoring process and reduce some of the ambiguity.

Step 3: Scoring for Specificity

Now let's move on to the next step in refining the refining process. The matter of specificity goes back to our discussion in Chapter 2 about the broad versus narrow principle. If you recall, we looked at two different strategies, a branding strategy and a conversion strategy. If your campaign is all about branding and you are mostly interested in impressions, then you would focus on broader keywords. On the other hand, if your strategy is focused on conversion and lead generation, then specific or long-tail keyword phrases will be more important to you.

So as you analyze your keywords, how do you determine what is too broad or too narrow? Let's try an experiment to illustrate the point.

In this example, we'll state that our company sells music boxes. That would define one of our root terms (remember those from keyword stemming?) as "box". Let's assume that single words are going to be too broad, and long chains of words may end up too narrow.

Our primary question: Is "box" too broad? For the answer, let's search with Google.

A Google search for "box" returns 2.6 billion pages. The first page of the SERP contains no music boxes but does list for "box": Box.net, a trading symbol, of course a *Wikipedia* definition, a movie, and so on.

This result is enormous and deals mostly with companies who have spent a great deal of money branding themselves with the word "box". If your company is called Music Box World, you would probably still work in the word "box" in conjunction with the other words. This is a clear case of a broad, single word being way too broad.

On the other hand, you can be too narrow by including too many terms in your search phrase. Be aware that most words, even when combined with others, will still generate results on Google because the engine conducts a broad search. So to get a true result, you should use quotation marks.

For example, "velvet elvis pink ballerina music box" as a search phrase (without the quotes) still returns 1 million results. But if you put the entire search phrase in quotes, you get nothing. In fact, most people searching for this type of item will probably be searching "ballerina music box" or "velvet elvis music box" or some other combination of those words. Thus, "velvet elvis pink ballerina music box" is too narrow, showing no SERP results on Google. That phrase needs to be broadened—it needs to lose a couple words—to actually be effective. This is the right level of specificity.

For this section, you need to score each keyword with a specificity score. As we did previously with keyword relevancy scoring, we will use a system of 1 to 10, with 10 being the highest (most effective level of specificity) and 1 being the lowest (least effective specificity as either too broad or too narrow), as seen in Figure 5.3.

	A	B	C
1	Keyword List	Relevance Score	Specificity Score
2	Formula	1 - 10 (10 best)	1 - 10 (10 best)
3			
4	bike	9	2
5	bicycle	9	3
6	bike rack	1	4
7	mountain bike	8	5
8	bicycle parts	8	5
9	road bike	9	5
10	bike parts	7	5
11	bike shop	10	5
12	bike shops	10	5
13	road bicycle	8	5
14	bike accessories	7	5
15	trek bicycle	6	6
16	trek bike	7	6
17	bike helmet	7	5
18	folding bike	5	6
19	tandem bicycle	4	6
20	recumbent bicycle	4	6
21	bicycle wheels	6	5
22	trek mountain bike	7	7
23	folding bicycle	5	6
24	mountain bicycle	6	6
25	bicycle store	10	5
26	bike frame	8	5

Initial List / Category 1 | Category 2 | Category 3

Figure 5.3 Specificity scoring

One way is to assign the highest score to keywords that have at least three or more words. If someone is typing more than three or four words into a search bar, then it is likely that the person knows exactly what they are interested in and that the search is highly specific. Using a general rule of thumb, keywords that have one word in the phrase should rank a 1, 2, or 3 on your specificity scoring spreadsheet. Keywords that have two or more words become more specific and should have a score from a 4 on up. Sometimes you need to look at the keyword itself to judge the words specificity. For example, medical terms like "coumadin" and "anticoagulant medication" are rather specific even though they are a one- and two-word search term.

Now, if your strategy is impression based for branding rather than conversion, you would do just the opposite and award the higher scores to those keywords that are broader in nature and lower scores to specific or long-tail keywords. So you really need to make sure you understand your strategy before you apply your specificity scores.

Step 4: Scoring for Competitiion

Next is to analyze how competitive each keyword is. This can be another overlooked factor in scoring keywords. The principle is if a keyword has a lot of competition, then the keyword will be more challenging to use. You need to understand how competitive each keyword is so you can decide if it is worth it or not to optimize for that particular keyword. If a keyword is not competitive, then you have a much greater opportunity for that keyword to work for you.

There are two types of competition. One is for search engine optimization (SEO) and the other is for pay-per-click (PPC). You need to distinguish between the two so you have a better understanding of what type of competition you are talking about.

If a keyword is highly competitive for SEO, you will have a harder time ranking naturally for that keyword. It may take you much longer to achieve the first page ranking you desire. If this is the case, you should decide if it is worth it in terms of time and money. A more competitive term will take more time and thus more money.

For PPC, a highly competitive keyword simply means more money. If a keyword's maximum CPC (cost per click) is $.05, then that would suggest it is not competitive and you could pick up that keyword for very little cost. Alternatively, if the keyword is $3.50 or more, it can become a very expensive proposition, especially if the keyword has high search volume.

Therefore, it is a good idea to understand and discern between both PPC and SEO competitiveness. So how do we find these numbers? There are a couple of ways. The easiest is to use the Google Keyword Tool, which will provide a small visual index of competitiveness. This is only showing PPC competitiveness, not SEO competitiveness, although they are probably somewhat closely related. Any other keyword tool that uses the Google API will likely give you this number.

If you want to get the actual index number rather than a visual, you will need to export your keyword list, which will provide you with a specific number like .56 or .93. The best way to interpret these numbers is to think of them as a percentage. A keyword with a .93 is like saying it is 93 percent competitive. Or in other words, the competition level is pretty saturated. You can also eyeball the approximate number by looking at the index visual. For instance, in Figure 5.4 "mountain bike clothing" is roughly 90 percent.

Download ▾ | View as text ▾ | More like these ▾

☐	Keyword	Competition	Global Monthly Searches ⓘ
☐	☆ mountain bike tours	▬	9,900
☐	☆ mountain bike tires	▬	27,100
☐	☆ mountain bike racks	▬	2,400
☐	☆ mountain biking gloves	▬	3,600
☐	☆ northwave mountain bike shoes	▬	480
☐	☆ mountain bike protective gear	▬	390
☐	☆ mountain bike shorts	▬	8,100
☐	☆ mountain bike magazine	▬	14,800
☐	☆ gt mountain bike sale	▬	480
☐	☆ padded mountain bike shorts	▬	590
☐	☆ iron horse mountain bike	▬	2,400
☐	☆ mountain bike trainer	▬	1,600
☐	☆ mountain bike jerseys	▬	3,600
☐	☆ mountain bike clothing	▬	4,400
☐	☆ mountain biking magazine	▬	14,800

Figure 5.4 Google competitive index

Now let's look at SEO competitiveness. In this case, your intention is to learn about the number of websites that are optimizing for your targeted keyword. One of the best ways to get this number is to do a search for sites that use the keyword in a URL string or in a <title> tag. If there are keywords here, that would suggest those site owners are optimizing for those keywords.

To find this, let's say we are looking for sites that are optimizing around the keyword "mountain bike clothing". I would go a Google search with the following:

Title: "mountain bike clothing"

This would tell the search engine I am looking for only keywords that are in a title tag for the specific term "mountain bike clothing", as you can see in Figure 5.5. If I wanted a broader search, I could lose the quotation marks.

Figure 5.5 Title tag search

Notice that the search found 95,800 results. This also works if you substitute the word "URL" for "Title". If you use "URL", you get results based on how many people have your keyword somewhere in their URL.

Wordtracker actually can provide this number for you if you use its tool. Its competition IAAT (In Anchor and Title) filter will list this information for each keyword, as seen in Figure 5.6. It tells you for how many pages the keyword appears in both the title tag and the anchor text of a backlink.

Keyword (?) (8)	Searches (?) (3,622)	Competition (IAAT) ▼ (?)
1 ☑ bicycle (search)	1,515	471,000
2 ☑ mountain bike (search)	525	128,000
3 ☑ road bike (search)	96	29,100
4 ☑ bike shop (search)	48	25,500
5 ☑ bicycle parts (search)	1,411	6,180
6 ☑ bike frame (search)	25	4,170
7 ☑ trek madone 6.9 (search)	1	241
8 ☑ cervelo bicycle (search)	1	3

Figure 5.6 Wordtracker competitive search

Wordtracker data is not shown on the spreadsheet, but you could add a column and load the competition data for each keyword. Then you would score it as you would for popularity scoring, which I outline in the next step.

Now that we have this information in hand, let's return to our spreadsheet and look at how we can make sense of scoring for competitiveness. The first thing is to decide if you want to score for just PPC or just SEO or both. For our purposes, we will keep this simple and add the competition numbers from the Google Keyword tool as seen in Figure 5.7.

	A	B	C	D	E	F	G	H	I
1	Keyword List	Relevance Score	Specificity Score	Competitiveness Score			Search Volume	PPC Compeition	Avg CPC
2	Formula	1 - 10 (10 best)	1 - 10 (10 best)	1 - 10 (10 best)				-((x*10)-(10))	
3									
4	bike	9	2	6.5				0.35	$0.73
5	bicycle	9	3	6.1				0.39	$0.74
6	bike rack	1	4	2.8				0.72	$1.23
7	mountain bike	8	5	6				0.4	$0.57
8	bicycle parts	8	5	2.6				0.74	$0.49
9	road bike	9	5	5.9				0.41	$0.75
10	bike parts	7	5	3.2				0.68	$0.65
11	bike shop	10	5	8.4				0.16	$0.58
12	bike shops	10	5	7.4				0.26	$0.55
13	road bicycle	8	5	5.1				0.49	$0.63
14	bike accessories	7	5	2.5				0.75	$0.70
15	trek bicycle	6	6	4.6				0.54	$0.38
16	trek bike	7	6	5.6				0.44	$0.40
17	bike helmet	7	5	3.9				0.61	$0.67
18	folding bike	5	6	2.4				0.76	$0.69
19	tandem bicycle	4	6	4.5				0.55	$0.57
20	recumbent bicycle	4	6	2.9				0.71	$0.69
21	bicycle wheels	6	5	3.5				0.65	$0.59
22	trek mountain bike	7	7	5.4				0.46	$0.39
23	folding bicycle	5	6	2.2				0.78	$0.72
24	mountain bicycle	6	6	5.3				0.47	$0.53
25	bicycle store	10	5	6.6				0.34	$0.56
26	bike frame	8	5	7.3				0.27	$0.61

Initial List | Category 1 | **Category 2** | Category 3 | Category 4 | Category 5

Figure 5.7 Competitiveness scoring

You will also notice that I added CPC numbers as in column J. I do not include them in the calculation but they are good to reference since a high CPC usually means the keywords are competitive where low CPC usually means they are not. You can also add a column for SEO and create a formula to calculate a weighted overall score for competition if you like. Again, for this example I will just use the PPC competition score from the Google Keyword Tool.

To get the numbers I have from Google translated into a number on a scale from 1 to 10, I use the following formula, where X = the Google Competition number, in this case cells in column H:

$$-((X*10)-(10))$$

So for cell D4, I place the following formula:

$$=-((H3*10)-(10))$$

Then I copy this formula all the way down column D. This is a quick way to convert the numbers.

Now, it is important to know what I did here. I am awarding high points to keywords that have a low competition number because there is a better opportunity to pursue that keyword because there is less competition. So I am essentially flip-flopping the number from .35 to .65 and moving the decimal point over one place to get 6.5.

Again, this is just one way to handle this. If you have access to a math major, you can create your own formulas to calculate these results quickly, which will provide some level of automation so you aren't pulling your hair out, manually scoring these keywords.

Step 5: Scoring for Popularity

This next step is one that most people are familiar with and that is popularity, or search volume. Popularity in keyword discovery means the same thing it did back in high school: Who's getting the most attention?

We can determine exactly who is getting the most attention by using some of the tools we have already discussed. This part of the refining process will result in a popularity score that, in turn, you can use in relation to relevance and specificity and competitiveness.

The best way to get popularity numbers is to use a keyword research tool. For this example, let's take a look at eight keywords using three keyword tools. We will use Keyword Discovery, Wordtracker, and the Google AdWords Keyword Tool. We will look at popularity numbers for the keywords found in Table 5.1.

▶ Table 5.1 Looking at search volume with three Keyword Tools

Keywords	Keyword Discovery	Wordtracker	Google Keyword Tool
bicycle	12,136	1,515	5,000,000
mountain bike	8,013	525	2,2240,00
road bike	3,724	96	673,000
bicycle parts	1,334	1,411	90,500
trek madone 6.9	12	1	9,900
bike shop	83	48	673,000
cervelo bicycle	97	1	1,000
bike frame	205	25	165,000

Remember that different keyword tools will give you different results because of how they get their data and then how their algorithm is set up to parse the data into what you and I see as the results. So as you can see in Table 5.1, we have different results for each of the eight keywords.

This may seem confusing, and it is important to understand that keyword tools will not be exact, but they should be close to each other in relative terms. So even though Google is reporting a whole lot more searches than Keyword Discover and Wordtracker, they are at least "relatively" the same in most cases. This is why you should use more than one tool to help get a clearer picture of what the data is telling you.

As you attempt to score for popularity, you can either pick one tool's results or you can combine two or three and then take the average if you want. It is up to you. For our purposes, we will just use one set of numbers and import them into our spreadsheet.

It should now look like Figure 5.8.

	A	B	C	D	E	F	G	H	I
1	Keyword List	Relevance Score	Specificity Score	Competitiveness Score	Popularity Score		Search Volume	PPC Compeition	Avg CPC
2	*Formula*	*1 - 10 (10 best)*	*1 - 10 (10 best)*	*1 - 10 (10 best)*	*1 - 10 (10 best)*			*-((x*10) -(10))*	
3									
4	bike	9	2	6.5	10		716,107	0.35	$0.73
5	bicycle	9	3	6.1	10		651,465	0.39	$0.74
6	bike rack	1	4	2.8	9		340,448	0.72	$1.23
7	mountain bike	8	5	6	9		254,883	0.4	$0.57
8	bicycle parts	8	5	2.6	6		93,894	0.74	$0.49
9	road bike	9	5	5.9	6		65,238	0.41	$0.75
10	bike parts	7	5	3.2	6		52,280	0.68	$0.65
11	bike shop	10	5	8.4	6		34,601	0.16	$0.58
12	bike shops	10	5	7.4	6		32,523	0.26	$0.55
13	road bicycle	8	5	5.1	6		32,410	0.49	$0.63
14	bike accessories	7	5	2.5	6		26,491	0.75	$0.70
15	trek bicycle	6	6	4.6	6		21,273	0.54	$0.38
16	trek bike	7	6	5.6	6		20,544	0.44	$0.40
17	bike helmet	7	5	3.9	5		19,640	0.61	$0.67
18	folding bike	5	6	2.4	5		13,934	0.76	$0.69
19	tandem bicycle	4	6	4.5	5		13,274	0.55	$0.57
20	recumbent bicycle	4	6	2.9	5		12,631	0.71	$0.69
21	bicycle wheels	6	5	3.5	5		11,883	0.65	$0.59
22	trek mountain bike	7	7	5.4	5		10,506	0.46	$0.39
23	folding bicycle	5	6	2.2	5		10,420	0.78	$0.72
24	mountain bicycle	6	6	5.3	4		7,681	0.47	$0.53
25	bicycle store	10	5	6.6	4		7,586	0.34	$0.56
26	bike frame	8	5	7.3	4		7,318	0.27	$0.61

Initial List / Category 1 / **Category 2** / Category 3 / Category 4 / Category 5

Figure 5.8 Popularity scoring

To score this section of your spreadsheet, you will need to get a little creative. The first thing you need to do is to create a *ceiling number*. In Figure 5.8, you see that "bike" garnered about 716,107 searches per year. So, for these terms to be accurately scored for popularity, the keyword with the highest number would equal a 10 (highest), and all other keywords would score relative to that number.

One way to do this is to set up a table that associates the global search number with a 1–10 score as shown in Table 5.2.

▶ **Table 5.2** Global formula

Threshold Number	1–10 Score
300	1
600	2
2000	3
5000	4
10000	5
30000	6
50000	7
75000	8
75001	9

Once this is done, you can use the following formula in your spreadsheet to convert any number that fits within these ranges into a number from 1 to 10. For this formula, A = the popularity number, B = the threshold number, and C = the 1–10 score. The general syntax of the formula is a nested loop where

```
IF(logical test, [value if true], [value if false])
```

```
=IF(A<B$3,C$3,IF(A3<B$4,C$4,IF(A3<B$5,C$5,IF(A3<B$6,C$6,IF(A3<B$7,C$7,
IF(A3<B$8,C$8,IF(A3<B$9,C$9,IF(A3<B$10,C$10,IF(A3>B$11,C$11)))))))))
```

Once you have this formula in one cell, you can copy and paste it throughout the whole column. The $ symbol next to B and C anchors them so that they do not shift when you paste the formula. Modify this in any way you want for your own needs, but this will allow you to automate this process and score this column rather quickly.

We do this because we are grading on a 1–10 scale and we need to score all keywords on this scale or we will not be able to get the overall score calculated correctly. Assuming you want to score this way in the future you can easily develop a formula that will automatically assign a number from 1–10 based on numbers from a keyword tool to help automate the process.

Step 6: Overall Scoring and Prioritization

Now that you have all of the data you need, add up the scores for each of the four scores (relevance, specificity, competitiveness, and popularity) by keyword and divide that total by 4 to get the average, or overall, score as shown in Figure 5.9. This resulting average number represents the overall score for each keyword. Here is the simple formula I used:

$$= (B3+C3+D3+E3)/4$$

If you feel you would like to give precedence to one column over another, you can weigh the formula accordingly. For instance, say you felt that a higher popularity score is worth more overall points. You could use the following formula to get those results:

$$= ((B3*1) + (C3*1) + (D3*1) + (E3*1.5)) /4$$

This will effectively increase the numbers for popularity by 50 percent, giving those keywords that are more popular a higher score overall. You can decrease the weight from one of the other columns by using a number lower than 1 to deemphasize that column's ranking impact. It is up to you.

Remember that you will need to do this average scoring for each category tab that you have set up in your spreadsheets.

	A	B	C	D	E	F	G	H	I	J
1	Keyword List	Relevance Score	Specificity Score	Competitiveness Score	Popularity Score	Overall Score		Search Volume	PPC Compeition	Max CPC
2	Formula	1 - 10 (10 best)	1 - 10 (10 best)	1 - 10 (10 best)	1 - 10 (10 best)	Avg (B+C+D+E)			-((x*10) -(10))	
3										
4	bike	9	2	6.5	10	6.88		716,107	0.35	$0.73
5	bicycle	9	3	6.1	10	7.03		651,465	0.39	$0.74
6	bike rack	1	4	2.8	9	4.20		340,448	0.72	$1.23
7	mountain bike	8	5	6	9	7.00		254,883	0.4	$0.57
8	bicycle parts	8	5	2.6	6	5.40		93,894	0.74	$0.49
9	road bike	9	5	5.9	6	6.48		65,238	0.41	$0.75
10	bike parts	7	5	3.2	6	5.30		52,280	0.68	$0.65
11	bike shop	10	5	8.4	6	7.35		34,601	0.16	$0.58
12	bike shops	10	5	7.4	6	7.10		32,523	0.26	$0.55
13	road bicycle	8	5	5.1	6	6.03		32,410	0.49	$0.63
14	bike accessories	7	5	2.5	6	5.13		26,491	0.75	$0.70
15	trek bicycle	6	6	4.6	6	5.65		21,273	0.54	$0.38
16	trek bike	7	6	5.6	6	6.15		20,544	0.44	$0.40
17	bike helmet	7	5	3.9	5	5.23		19,640	0.61	$0.67
18	folding bike	5	6	2.4	5	4.60		13,934	0.76	$0.69
19	tandem bicycle	4	6	4.5	5	4.88		13,274	0.55	$0.57
20	recumbent bicycle	4	6	2.9	5	4.48		12,631	0.71	$0.69
21	bicycle wheels	6	5	3.5	5	4.88		11,883	0.65	$0.59
22	trek mountain bike	7	7	5.4	5	6.10		10,506	0.46	$0.39
23	folding bicycle	5	6	2.2	5	4.55		10,420	0.78	$0.72
24	mountain bicycle	6	6	5.3	4	5.33		7,681	0.47	$0.53
25	bicycle store	10	5	6.6	4	6.40		7,586	0.34	$0.56
26	bike frame	8	5	7.3	4	6.08		7,318	0.27	$0.61

Initial List / Category 1 / **Category 2** / Category 3 / Category 4 / Category 5

Figure 5.9 Overall score

Now that you have an overall score for each keyword, you need to sort your spreadsheet on this column. In my example, it is column F. Next, select just the entire row of keywords, including the scoring and keyword data. Only the cells you select will be sorted, so you do not need to select the headings. Then, assuming you are using Microsoft Excel 2010, you would click the Data tab at the top and click the sort icon. Next you will see a window like the one in Figure 5.10 that shows three ways to sort.

You want to sort by column, so choose column F (or the column that has your overall score) from the Column drop-down menu.

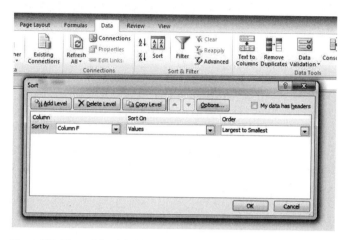

Figure 5.10 Microsoft Excel data sort

Notice in Figure 5.11 that the keywords are now in order from the highest score to the lowest score. This will give you an objective view on which keywords might provide you with the best value.

	A	B	C	D	E	F	G	H	I	J
1	Keyword List	Relevance Score	Specificity Score	Competitiveness Score	Popularity Score	Overall Score		Search Volume	PPC Compeition	Max CPC
2	Formula	1 - 10 (10 best)	1 - 10 (10 best)	1 - 10 (10 best)	1 - 10 (10 best)	Avg (B+C+D+E)			-((x*10)-(10))	
3										
4	bike shop	10	5	8.4	6	7.35		34,601	0.16	$0.58
5	bike shops	10	5	7.4	6	7.10		32,523	0.26	$0.55
6	bicycle	9	3	6.1	10	7.03		651,465	0.39	$0.74
7	mountain bike	8	5	6	9	7.00		254,883	0.4	$0.57
8	bike	9	2	6.5	10	6.88		716,107	0.35	$0.73
9	road bike	9	5	5.9	6	6.48		65,238	0.41	$0.75
10	bicycle store	10	5	6.6	4	6.40		7,586	0.34	$0.56
11	trek bike	7	6	5.6	6	6.15		20,544	0.44	$0.40
12	trek mountain bike	7	7	5.4	5	6.10		10,506	0.46	$0.39
13	bike frame	8	5	7.3	4	6.08		7,318	0.27	$0.61
14	road bicycle	8	5	5.1	6	6.03		32,410	0.49	$0.63
15	trek bicycle	6	6	4.6	6	5.65		21,273	0.54	$0.38
16	bicycle parts	8	5	2.6	6	5.40		93,894	0.74	$0.49
17	mountain bicycle	6	6	5.3	4	5.33		7,681	0.47	$0.53
18	bike parts	7	5	3.2	6	5.30		52,280	0.68	$0.65
19	bike helmet	7	5	3.9	5	5.23		19,640	0.61	$0.67
20	bike accessories	7	5	2.5	6	5.13		26,491	0.75	$0.70
21	tandem bicycle	4	6	4.5	5	4.88		13,274	0.55	$0.57
22	bicycle wheels	6	5	3.5	5	4.88		11,883	0.65	$0.59
23	folding bike	5	6	2.4	5	4.60		13,934	0.76	$0.69
24	folding bicycle	5	6	2.2	5	4.55		10,420	0.78	$0.72
25	recumbent bicycle	4	6	2.9	5	4.48		12,631	0.71	$0.69
26	bike rack	1	4	2.8	9	4.20		340,448	0.72	$1.23

Initial List   Category 1   **Category 2**   Category 3   Category 4   Category 5

Figure 5.11 Sorted spreadsheet

Again, you can add more columns for other ranking factors you wish to use to help add more granularity. That is just a matter of creating the right formulas and retrieving the right data from keyword tools. But at this point you should have a good idea of how the process works. Remember that you will customize this to suit your own situation. Be creative and look at different angles to find what works best for your situation.

Step 7: Keyword Interpretation

Now that you have a list of keywords that have been sorted and organized by category, you need to start looking over your list and interpreting what the data suggests. This is where I would get the entire team involved again.

I want to emphasize a very important point.

This scoring system is designed to help you move your potentially higher-scoring keywords to the top and your lower ones to the bottom. This is not foolproof, and it needs personal attention. Don't just assume these keywords are all perfect and start using them in your campaign.

You need to scrutinize them. Look at the top potential keywords for each category and make sure they make sense. Maybe you flubbed up your formula or copy and pasted from a keyword tool incorrectly. Or maybe the numbers just don't make sense for a given keyword.

You will have to make manual adjustments to get the keywords prioritized properly. I recommend that, knowing you can set your sights on the top performers, you take some time to do some deeper analysis on each keyword to further validate that it has the potential to perform.

Instead of doing a deep analysis on all of the keywords you initially found, you have essentially isolated the top performers. Now you have a much smaller list of keywords to inspect rather than a larger list. This will save you time and effort.

I will now run through some other factors that will help you scrutinize your new sorted list of keywords to narrow them down even further and then prioritize them accordingly.

You now have a sorted list of keywords that have been ranked and sorted. Depending on the size of your lists or the number of keywords, you can now scrutinize the top 10 or 20 or even 50. This is where your qualitative process needs to come into play. You should make sure your team reviews these top keywords and makes some judgment calls as to their validity. In most cases, the top-performing keywords are likely to be at the top, but not always. So far we have used tools and formulas to "automate" this process. Now the human assignment is to find any flaws and make the necessary adjustments.

If you have many categories that match up to your landing pages, then you should look at the top keywords within each category to use for SEO purposes. The remaining keywords can be used in a PPC campaign because they will align quite nicely with the way you set up your ad groups.

Once all of this has been done, you will be ready to start using them in various media campaigns.

There are two filters I would like bring to your attention that will help as you continue to refine and prioritize your keywords: seasonality and ambiguity. We will not rank these in the spreadsheet, but I wish to discuss them here. As you go through your list of keywords, you should consider how seasonality and ambiguity might impact their performance.

Seasonality of Keyword Usage

Seasonality is a little tricky because a keyword may be relevant during one season but not as relevant during another. It is more about watching your keyword list in reference to different cycles than permanently deleting words that don't fall in a particular season.

Holidays are a seasonal factor that influence searching and shopping. If holidays did not have this effect on search and shopping behaviors, the malls wouldn't be clogged with people the day after Thanksgiving, shopping for Christmas and Hanukah. Candy sells at Easter and Halloween. Champagne and exercise equipment sell well around New Year's Day. Take a careful look at what you are promoting and where on the holiday calendar it fits with people's motivations and actions.

The Summer Olympics, US presidential elections, and leap years occur every four years (and always on the same four-year cycles). The census in the United States is conducted every decade. There are cycles that cover more than one year. Do these cyclic events affect your product or service?

An excellent tool from Google will show you what search trends look like over time. You simply visit the Google Trends site at http://trends.google.com as seen in Figure 5.12. Then separate your phrases by commas and "let 'er rip." Remember that this is used mainly for very general searches.

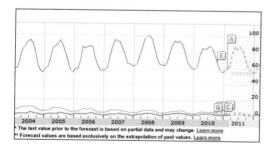

Figure 5.12 Google Trends

The report (Figure 5.13) shows a comparison of the keywords "bike", "road bike", and "mountain bike". You can see that "bike" is searched on much more than the other two. You can also see the seasonality of each keyword and how it has trended over the years. I like this tool because it shows multiple years and historical data. Another great tool that is similar is Google Insights for Search, at www.google.com/insights/search. This tool not only shows trends, it will forecast for the next year what might likely occur based on the past trend.

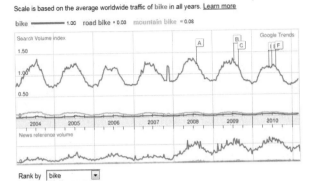

Scale is based on the average worldwide traffic of bike in all years. Learn more

bike ———— 1.00   road bike • 0.03   mountain bike = 0.08

Figure 5.13 Google Insights

Notice the projected forecast for these three terms for the year 2011. Both of these tools provide information regionally and will provide possible categories for the keywords. The more you know about the seasonality of your keywords the better you will be equipped to use them properly and in their proper time.

Understanding Ambiguity

Another consideration in refining your keywords is to remove ambiguity. Some keywords can have more than one meaning, but when you are targeting terms, you want to ensure that you are targeting the right audience with the right meaning. So you will need to remove or modify terms to make them as relevant and specific as possible.

One example of removing ambiguity is working on keywords that are more relevant to a business to consumer (B2C) audience than a business to business (B2B) target audience. The audience is different, and the words you use should cater to the right audience.

Other layers of ambiguity lie entirely in linguistics.

Homonyms

Homonyms are words that have more than one meaning. Some homonyms are spelled the same, and some are pronounced the same. All of them work to make your list more complicated than it has to be.

Homophones

A homophone is a word that sounds the same as another word but is spelled differently. Excellent examples of homophones in the English language are *to*, *too*, and *two* and *sent*, *scent*, and *cent*. Because homophones are spelled differently, they are not your main concern in keyword discovery and refinement.

It is advisable, however, to pay attention to homophones' potential for misinterpretations. If you're selling a book titled *Read, I See*, it would be a shame if half your target audience searched for "Red Eye Sea".

Homographs

Homograph is the linguistic term for two words that are spelled the same but have two or more distinct meanings. For example, a *fly* can be a small, annoying insect; a method of fishing; or a mode of transportation for a bird. Because the words are spelled the same, these alternative meanings need to be your main consideration.

Do you have any keywords in your list that could be pronounced differently? Do any of them have multiple meanings? Is someone playing a *bass* or fishing for *bass*? Does he *bow* before a hunt or does he hunt for *does* with a *bow*?

Correcting Homographs

Mainly, homographs become an issue only in broad or single terms, like *bass*. Changing your broad, ambiguous words into narrower, more specific phrases by adding another word, you can avoid this pitfall. For example, change *bass* to *bass fishing*.

Heteronyms

A heteronym is just like a homonym, but the meanings *and* pronunciations are different with heteronyms. In this case, follow the advice offered in the preceding section, "Correcting Homographs."

Capitonyms

A capitonym is a word that has a different meaning (and sometimes different pronunciation) when it is capitalized. Examples of capitonyms include *polish* and *Polish and* a baby's *mobile*, a *mobile* phone, and *Mobile*, Alabama.

Since capitalization is marginally important to search engines, keep an eye out for capitonyms and make any adjustment in the way they have been sorted in your spreadsheet.

Slang

What's wrong with these phrases?

Don't be a tool.

Put on your thinking cap and give it a minute to sink in.

Take your ride for a spin to the bell if you need a break.

Surf the web and chill for a sec.

Brilliant!

Remember, before using any of these, or other English slang phrases, that the Brits and Irish and Aussies and Kiwis are in on the English slang game too.

I don't want you walking on eggshells, but joeys and bonnets could come round to box your ears.

Language may have many facets, but our laziness and propensity for doing things and saying things the way we want to has *not* helped to refine the language. Our slang adds dimension and character, but it also adds confusion, especially when you remember that a search engine does *not* hit on context, only the *order* of the letters and the *order* of the words.

Scan your list. Are any of your terms ambiguous because they are common slang? Can you refine the phrase to be more specific and less dependent on the current *hip*, *phat*, or *bad* slang terms?

Branding

Branding, as a keyword ambiguity issue, ties back into those fancy capitonyms. When a word is capitalized, it may pertain to the name of a person, place, or thing. For example, look at *Coke* and *coke*: *Coke* is a cola drink, but *coke* is coal residue (the process of turning coal into coke); *coke* with no capital letter is also slang for the illegal amphetamine cocaine.

Branding can turn a Greek goddess into a shoe (*Nike*), a barren land into a well-stocked oasis (*Outback*), and—returning to one of our previous examples—both a guitar and a fish into a refreshing drink: ale (*Bass*). Branding has taken words from the esoteric and is made up into the world of plain old nouns.

Correcting Branding Confusion

Again, you want to focus on narrowing your results by adding more words to your key phrase. *Outback Steakhouse* is one example. Make sure you are specifying *granny smith apples* to prevent false hits on computers from *Granny*, everyone named *Smith*, and any proper nouns using those words. This is not about your brand so much as avoiding other brands.

We have now covered the ambiguity-refining process. The basics of language can be deceptive, and we can make it even more complicated by adding slang and branded terms. By keeping the key phrases definitive, you can avoid false positives and focus your results.

Summary

With these organizational skills and filtering steps, you are now ready to start using your keywords in media campaigns. It is advisable to redo this process at least every 6 to 12 months to see if any keyword data has changed, especially for your top-performing keywords.

In the next few chapters you will learn how to use these new keywords specifically for SEO, PPC, social media marketing, and other channels in upcoming chapters. This now will form the basis for which you can build as you approach different channel campaigns.

Using Keywords for SEO

Now that you have identified, categorized, and refined your list of keywords, you need to use them appropriately and optimize your landing pages to get the best results. This chapter deals with using your targeted keywords to specifically optimize your website for search engine optimization (SEO). You will also learn about exciting uses of keywords in video and images and how to optimize for these important media elements.

Keywords and Their Role in SEO

Search engine optimization (SEO), sometimes known as organic or natural search, is a discipline that has been around since the beginning of the Internet. This topic is huge, and there are many books on the subject. For in-depth study on this topic, let me point you to a few excellent resources (although there are many, many more to choose from):

- *SEO for Dummies* by Bruce Clay (Wiley Publishing, 2009)
- *Internet Marketing: An Hour a Day* by Matt Bailey (Sybex, 2011)
- *Search Engine Optimization: An Hour a Day, Third Edition* by Jennifer Grappone and Gradiva Couzin (Sybex, 2011)
- "Periodic Table of SEO Ranking Factors," a great online resource from Search Engine Land at `http://searchengineland.com/seotable/`

I would also like to point out that even though most of this chapter focuses on the "tactical" aspects of SEO, it is important that SEO be thought of more as a strategic component of your marketing campaign. It is clear that Google and other search engines are putting a lot of stock into providing searchers with an excellent user experience. That has manifested itself in the recent Panda updates by Google. Some see these updates as mere algorithm changes, but in reality it is changing the philosophical way those who concern themselves with SEO need to think about optimizing their sites. It is more about tying into Google's vision of driving searchers to the right content quickly and efficiently. If you play along and provide content worthy of this vision, you will be rewarded. Ignore it and you will be passed up. I will discuss this more in Chapter 11.

For our purposes, we will explore only the aspects of SEO that focus on the use of keywords. I have always broken down SEO into three distinctive groups, or as I like to call them, the three pillars of SEO:

- Search-engine-friendly design
- Keyword optimization
- Link building

Search-engine-friendly design is all about designing and developing your site so that the search engines can visit and index every part of it that you wish them to index. By indexing, I mean record all of the information about your site the search bot can find and then deposit that information into a database so that you and I can find it.

Many people think that when they type a search phrase into Google, they are actually searching the entire Internet. That is not the case. Google (and other search engines) have developed a small program called a search bot (sometimes called a spider or crawler) to follow all the links it can find and then visit the resulting pages, as seen in Figure 6.1. Once the Google bot lands on a page, it reads all of the information it can see and deposits it into Google's database. Then when you and I do a search, we are searching the database, which has the latest information the bot has collected.

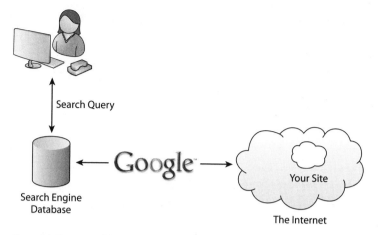

Figure 6.1 How a search bot works

Sometimes bots will travel to one of your website pages and get stuck and be unable to follow the links to other pages on your site. Links contained in Flash, JavaScript, and other programming barriers that the bots cannot read can get in their way. If the bots cannot read the link information, they cannot reach the pages behind them and those pages will not get indexed. If they are not indexed, you and I will never find them using a search engine.

So the idea of search-engine-friendly design is constructing your site in such a way that search engine bots reach all of your pages.

Once your site design accommodates visits from the bots, the next step is to place your targeted keywords into all aspects of your site to help both visitors and search engines come away with a solid understanding of what each page is about and, more specifically, what keywords best describe those pages. The process is called *keyword optimization*.

The next pillar is *link building* for both internal and external links. The best way to understand the importance of links is to think of them as votes. The more votes your site has, the more popular it is. Search engines believe that the more popular a site is, the more relevant it is to more users, and so they want to rank you higher than less-popular sites. When someone creates a link to your site, they are essentially saying that this is a great place to visit because it relates to a specific topic. That topic can usually be summed up in a keyword phrase.

We will be spending most of our time in this chapter on keyword optimization and keyword linking because they are foundational to your SEO efforts. But first before we jump in, let me address an important question that I get asked a lot.

How Many Keywords Should I Use for SEO?

To answer this very important question, you need to first think of your website as many individual pages. Instead of thinking about optimizing your website as a whole, think instead about optimizing the individual pages, including your home page.

Although many people consider their home page to be the most important page and the "front door" through which all visitors enter, the truth is that many visitors arrive at pages other than your home page. In fact, many visitors never actually see your home page because they followed a link that led to another page on your site. Therefore, each page of your site needs to stand on its own and be optimized accordingly.

With this concept in mind, I recommend optimizing each page for no more than three keywords. The more keywords you attempt to optimize for, the more diluted and generic your page theme becomes. When a visitor lands on one of your pages, they are going to make a split-second decision as to whether or not they have arrived at the right place and if your page content is relevant to their search. If your content and targeted keywords have razor-sharp focus, then your visitors can quickly understand what the page is about. When your page is relevant and includes keywords related to the search query that brought them to you, they are likely to stay on your site longer. The longer they stay, the better chance their visit will result in a conversion.

Now, with this in mind you can begin learning about where and how to place these one to three keywords throughout each page on your website.

Keyword Optimization

In the following sections, I will tell you how and where to place your target keywords for each page for this keyword optimization process. We will explore the use of keywords in the following areas:

- Domain names
- URL string and file structure
- Anchors and tags
- Site content

Keywords in Domain Names

It has been debated for some time how much weight you should put into having keywords in your domain name. Is it optimal to have keywords in your domain or should you have a domain like www.carpet-cleaning-boston.com or even a more brand-focused domain like www.target.com?

The answer seems be that the value of keywords in domain names has diminished over time. The latest study by SEOMoz, the results of which are shown on its 2011 Search Engine Ranking Factors page (www.seomoz.org/article/search-ranking-factors#predictions-4), shows that exact keyword matches in domain names isn't going to be as important. Other ranking factors will also come about as a result of the latest Panda updates that reward high-quality sites that have excellent content over other factors.

You do not have to have a keyword in your domain name to succeed. Think of Amazon, Google, IKEA, and Zappos. They do not have keyword-laden domain names, yet they are known for their brands.

However, if you can intelligently and creatively include a keyword in your domain name *and* have great content, you can come out on top.

Keywords in URLs and File Structures

Many of us work for organizations that already have an established domain name, so creating a new one with targeted keywords is out of our control. Fortunately there is something you can control, and that is the file structure of your site, which can help you get keywords in the URL string:

```
http://www.yourdomain.com/your-targeted-keyword/
```

To accomplish this, you will need to look under the hood of your site and examine your file structure. For small sites, this should be rather straightforward, but for larger sites or sites built on top of a content management tool, it might be a bit of a challenge.

The basic idea is to "silo" your content within your website to mimic your site structure. If you look at Figure 6.2, you will see the root folder that contains all of the files and folders for this book's website. The root folder represents the domain for a site. So for instance, the domain for this book's site is `www.keywordintelligencebook.com`. Notice that there is a subfolder under the root called `keyword-research-tips` and then another folder within that one called `for-seo`.

Figure 6.2 Website directory structure

By siloing these folders this way, it not only helps me to keep track of content on the site, it also gets the folder names into the URL string, as seen in Figure 6.3.

Figure 6.3 Website URL string

When you place your targeted keywords into folder and filenames, those keyword will display within the URL. This has the twofold benefit of helping both visitors and the search engines better understand the focus of page content.

When you use more than one word per keyword phrase, like "keyword-research-tips", make sure you use a dash (-) and not an underscore (_) to separate the words. Search engines see the dash as a space separating the words and therefore interpret each word individually. It also makes your URL string easier for people to read and understand. When using this technique, you do not need to include words like *and*, *the*, *too*, and so on. These are ignored by search engines and do not help your optimization in any way. You can use this method for any of your site files and folders, including those for press releases, documents, product pages, and even image and video files, which we will discuss further later in this chapter.

If you have a website that is dynamic, meaning much of the content and HTML is generated by a database, then the process is a little more complex. To achieve these same results, you may need to employ (Internet Server application programming interface [ISAPI] rewrites that convert the dynamically generated URLs that contain a bunch of unintelligible characters into a static, more easily interpreted URL that contains your target keywords. You may need to consult your web developer to better understand the technical nature of ISAPI rewrites and what your options are because they vary from platform to platform.

In this example, see how the Lowes site renders the URL string for "premium plywood underlayment" in Figure 6.4. You can see that it is rather unintelligible to the reader.

http://www.lowes.com/pd_80246-99999-LBR80246_4294815996_4294937087_?productId=3177699&Ns=p_product_prd_lis_ord_nbr|0||p_product_qty_sales_dollar|1&pl=1&currentURL=%2Fpl_Plywood_‹

Figure 6.4 Lowes URL string

Now look at how Amazon addresses this issue in Figure 6.5. Amazon.com is a pretty complex site, but they still manage to get keywords into the URL string after the root domain. There are still some database characters after the keyword "breakfast-foods-grocery". It would be optimal to lose this string of characters, but at least their keywords are displayed as close to the root as possible.

http://www.amazon.com/Breakfast-Foods-Grocery/b/ref=sv_gro_1?ie=UTF8&node=16310251

Figure 6.5 Amazon URL string

If you are looking at redesigning your website, it is important that you conduct a keyword research study prior to any development. Once you have your targeted keywords in hand, you should pass them on to your developers, who can make sure they architect the site in this siloing method and use keywords for folder and filenames from the beginning. It is a whole lot easier to do this on the front end than to apply this technique on an existing site.

Keywords in HTML and Tags

There are other important places to inset your targeted keywords within each page of your website. Remember that you want to keep a balance between satisfying the search engines and satisfying your human visitors. You don't want to overuse your keywords in your site content to the point that it is obvious. If your visitors see your keyword in every other sentence, and we have all seen it, you will lose your credibility and probably your visitors.

Within each page of your site, you should add your keywords to the following specific areas:

- Page title
- Meta description
- Meta keywords
- Headings
- Body copy

Page Title

Your page title is one of the most important places to insert targeted keywords. If you look at the title bar at the very top of your browser window, you will see the title of the page you are currently viewing. Notice the title for this book's home page, "Keyword Intelligence - Keyword Research for Search, Social and Beyond" as seen in the Firefox browser in Figure 6.6.

Figure 6.6 Page title in web browser

To create a unique title tag for each page on your site, modify the `<title>` tag for each page. The title tag is at the very beginning of your HTML source code, as shown in the heading like in Figure 6.7.

```
<!DOCTYPE html PUBLIC "-//W3C//DTD XHTML 1.0 Transitional//EN"
"http://www.w3.org/TR/xhtml1/DTD/xhtml1-transitional.dtd">
<html xmlns="http://www.w3.org/1999/xhtml">
<head>

<title>Keyword Intelligence - Keyword Research for Search, Social and
  Beyond</title>

<meta name="Description" content="Keyword Intelligence Book - Keyword
  Research for Search Social and Beyond. Learn about valuable keyword
research techniques, keyword research tools and how to deploy them
with SEO, PPC, Social Media and other marketing channels" />
<meta name="Keywords" content="Keyword Research, Keyword
Intelligence, Keyword Research Tools" />
<meta http-equiv="Content-Type" content="text/html; charset=utf-8" />
```

Figure 6.7 Title tag example

Notice the phrase in between the `<title>` and `</title>` tags? This is where you should place keywords that are important to the page you are optimizing for. As you are developing the title, you need to consider the following guidelines:

- Keep your title to approximately 70 characters in length. It is okay to occasionally make it longer (in a press release, for instance), but many browsers (and search engines) will only display the first 70 to 72 characters of the title.

- Be sure to use your most important keywords up front and less important ones toward the end. If your company name is in the title and it doesn't contain targeted keywords, you might want to have it on the end of the phrase instead of the beginning.

- Use no more than two to three unique keywords. If you feel the need to use more, maybe you need to split the page content into two more specific pages and keyword content.

Meta Description

The meta description tag is another area to insert keywords for each page of your site. This will help you get your descriptions correct within the search engine results page (SERP). Notice back in Figure 6.7, right below the page title, a phrase preceded by `<meta name="description"...>`. This is the description that the search engines pick up to describe your site within the SERP.

As you can see in Figure 6.8, the phrase that appears in Figure 6.7 also appears in the description. This description acts as an ad for your page. But you need to be careful that you keep it short and to the point. Notice that my description is too long and is cut off after the phrase "keyword research tools". At the very least you should make sure you have your keywords within the first 170 characters to ensure that they will show up for searchers to find.

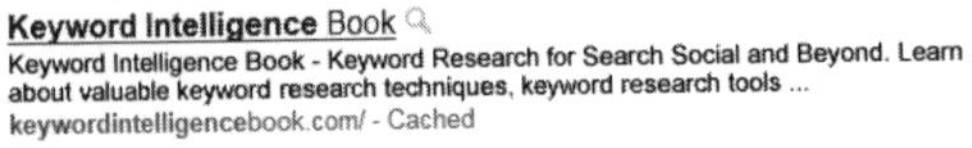

Keyword Intelligence Book
Keyword Intelligence Book - Keyword Research for Search Social and Beyond. Learn about valuable keyword research techniques, keyword research tools ...
keywordintelligencebook.com/ - Cached

Figure 6.8 Meta description example

Remember the importance of relevancy. If a searcher types in a keyword and then sees that keyword in the descriptive text in the SERPs, then they are more likely to click that link and visit your site. This will help you increase your click-through rate (CTR).

Meta Keywords

Under the meta description tag in Figure 6.7 is the `<meta name="keywords"..>` tag. The meta keywords tag carries little to no weight anymore for achieving higher keyword ranking because it was taken advantage of in the past. However, it does not hurt to place targeted keywords here; it is up to you. Let me put it this way: After you have finished with all of the other optimization practices and link building and find you have more time on your hands, then by all means add your keywords here, but please don't waste a lot of your up-front time on placing keywords in your meta keyword tags.

Headings

Inserting your keywords into page headings is another important SEO best practice. Search engines and visitors alike will look at headings to get a clue as to the page content. When your visitors see prominent keywords on your page that match their original search phrase, they are likely to stick around. If they can't easily find words they searched on, they are more likely to hit the back button and continue searching for a more relevant site. Additionally, the search engines will derive page-relevant content based on keywords that are included in your headings. Keywords in H1 tags are not as important as they are in title tags as a ranking factor, but they will help you capture your readers' attention and engage them. See Chapter 11 for more about the power of writing great headlines.

In HTML, headings are created by placing your keyword-rich description between `<H1>Your Heading</H1>` tag. Headings are denoted with different levels of emphasis. H1 is the most important, H2 is less important, and so on. The H1 heading carries the most weight, so it is a good idea to place your keywords here first. Those of you who read newspapers can see this illustrated by the use of headings, subheadings, and sub-subheadings to create an information hierarchy.

Body Copy

Now that you have the most important tags set up, you can look at the body copy that makes up the majority of your page content. You need to be careful that you think again in terms of your visitors and the text, image, and video content they will see. You should develop your page content first around your readers and then consider the search engines.

Now look at your keyword list. If you categorized your keywords, you should have a list of terms that you can use for each page of your site. Look for those that ranked highest and place those in the tags just mentioned. Then you will use those terms in the body of your page. This will strengthen the core meaning of each page for the reader and the search engines. Be consistent with your use of these keywords, not only on this page but also on other pages of your site.

Even if you already have an established site, you can read through the copy and find opportunities to replace some phrases with the one to three keywords you are optimizing for each page. Just a few tweaks here and there can make a big difference. If you have an outside party generating content for you, like an agency or a public relations firm, you should equip them with your keyword list so they uniformly use those keywords when possible as they write.

To further increase the prominence of your target keywords, you can format them as bold, italicized, or underlined. Do this as it makes sense for the readers' benefit and as it helps you to emphasize your point. Be careful not to do this too often because it will appear as if you are just trying to please the search engines.

Keyword Density, Frequency, and Prominence

So how often should you use these keywords on your web pages? How much is too much? One method to use is to evaluate the keyword density of each page. Keyword density measures the number of times a keyword phrase appears on a web page relative to the total number of words on that page. It is one of the factors search engines use to determine relevance to search queries.

To see how this works, let's say you have a page that has 800 words. Within those words your keyword appears 17 times. This includes keywords in all of your anchor text as well as in body copy. To determine the keyword density, you simply divide the number of keywords (17) by the total number of words (800) to end up with 2.13 percent.

Another factor search engines use to determine relevancy is keyword frequency. Keyword frequency is simply the number of times a keyword appears on a page. Together, keyword density and keyword frequency are used by search engines to establish a keyword's relevancy for a given search query.

A word on your web page is generally considered by search engines as a relevant keyword if it is used at least twice. So if you have words that appear more than once and they are not targeted keywords, you may want to find alternatives so you can focus the attention on those that are. The keyword density for any keyword phrase generally should not be more than 5 percent. Going beyond this amount can make your copy appear unnatural to the reader and spammy to the search engines. Again, the goal is to find the balance of natural, quality content that emphasizes the theme and message of your page without overdoing it.

One final aspect to consider is keyword distribution. This measures whether the keyword is distributed evenly throughout the page and the site. As long as you have your keywords in the right places—title, URL, heading, and so on—then I recommend that your keywords are distributed evenly so your content reads and flows naturally.

For a landing page with 750 words, I recommend the following distribution of keywords:

- Once in the title tag
- Once or twice in the meta description tag
- Once or twice in the meta keywords tag
- Once in the heading H1 tag
- Twice in the first 200 to 300 words of readable text in the body copy
- Once in all paragraphs

Again, use your judgment and see how your document reads. If it sounds like you are using a keyword phrase too often, then back off and delete some of them so your page sounds natural to the reader.

Keywords and Link Building

Another way to emphasize keywords on a page is by turning them into links to other relevant content, either on your site or away from your site. This leads to the next pillar of SEO, the overall topic of link building. This topic needs a lot of attention to fully understand its importance to SEO and to keyword use.

Let's start by first defining some terms. Link popularity is a measurement of all the links coming into your site, also known as *backlinks* or *inbound links*, and the quality of those links. Basically, search engines reason that if your site is any good, other sites will link to it. If few other sites link to your site, then it is considered less relevant than other similar sites that have lots of inbound links and search volume. The more links leading to your site, the more "votes" you have and the more relevant search engines think you are. Before I begin with this topic, I need to stress a very important point: You should identify the keywords you want to be ranked for and use those keywords in your links and *anchor text*, which is the clickable text in a hyperlink. How many of you have used this phrase: "To learn more about Acme Widgets, click here," where the link is on the word "here". If "Acme Widgets" is the keyword phrase you want to optimize, then make sure that phrase has the link.

Internal Links

The place to start is on your own site and its internal linking structure. This concept of creating backlinks from one internal page to another is sometimes overshadowed by efforts to acquire backlinks from external pages. While external link optimization plays a larger role when it comes to gaining higher rankings and natural organic traffic, you can still see 20 to 30 percent boosts in rankings by properly optimizing links within your own site.

The general idea is to first build an internal linking structure, which can be done with a well-thought-out site map that shows relationships between content within your site, as seen in Figure 6.9. This is a simplified illustration, but you can outline where the dependencies are and which content will link to which pages as you build out your sitemap.

As you can see, this linking structure is made up of your targeted keywords. If you have done your categorization properly, then this structure can mimic that grouping. As you can see, you can start with your core grouping as your main subpages, and as you go deeper, you can use more specific keywords. Then as you place these keywords on other pages, make sure they link to the landing pages you just created or identified. By doing this simple task, you can pass on "link juice" to those pages and strengthen their authority. I will cover site architecture in more detail in Chapter 10.

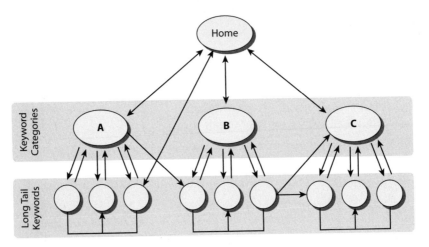

Figure 6.9 Simple site linking structure

Contextual Link Building

If you are an authority or have a passion for what you do, consider writing an article about a specific topic you have on your site. By doing so, you will have the opportunity to place a quality, relevant link back to your site.

If you or your PR agency writes press releases, make sure you get those releases submitted online. There are still a number of companies that send them out via fax, so try to avoid this method, or at least use it in conjunction with online submissions. By releasing them online, you can create wonderful keyword link opportunities that will pay great dividends. Once the articles are written and submitted, they are distributed to various feeds and eventually get picked up by news sources. When they do, most editors will copy content directly from your release, which has the keywords already linked up to the appropriate landing pages.

Try to find sites like PR Newswire (`www.prnewswire.com`) that let you submit your article with links back to your site. Once your release goes out, it will be picked up by other feeds and will land on other news sites, thus netting you more links.

One of the first principles to understand is that while the quantity of inbound links is important, the quality is much more so. Links from sites that are topically or contextually related to your site carry much more weight than links from unrelated sites. In addition, links from sites that are considered authorities for a specific topic (that is, they rank high on organic search results for a given topic) are of much higher value than those from unpopular or obscure sites.

One positive aspect of contextual link building is that it is a stable and ethical way of building links. Additionally, since the links from contextual sites are relevant to the content on your site, you will likely have a higher conversion rate from this targeted traffic. Visitors from these related sites will already be in the right mindset to review what you have to offer, which makes conversions easier for you.

Links from Press Releases and Other PR Sources

One of the most productive link-building strategies is to leverage an SEO consultant's expertise for the mechanics of contextual link building in addition to gaining an understanding of how to leverage what corporate communications, PR, HR, Marketing, Sales, and even Investor Relations are already doing within a company that could result in relevant inbound links. This two-prong approach is very effective and leverages existing content and communications in a way that drives the building of incoming links.

Here are a few examples:

Public Relations Links can be included in press releases, an online newsroom, within email pitches to journalists and bloggers, in PDF documents of case studies, with media coverage, and so on. Also, here's one of the best tips: When a journalist confirms they're running a story citing your company, *ask them for a link.*

Human Resources Job listings and open house events are good opportunities for links when promoted on aggregation sites for jobs and events. Optimize the job and event listing titles and always add a link back to an optimized web page for more information. In some cases, paid job listings will include a link, but one that gets redirected by ad tracking software. *Ask for a direct link* when possible.

Marketing Companies partner with other companies, join associations and often produce microsites, buy ads, sponsor events/conferences/causes, and engage in many other off-corporate-site communications. All of those present some type of link opportunity. You get visibility via email distribution, and when the HTML version of the newsletter is published online, there's a link back to your site. Charitable giving often involves a website that lists donors, so ask for a link back to your site in such cases.

Local Newspapers Developing relationships with local newspaper writers and always making yourself available for comments on news stories that involve your industry is a great way to build awareness about your company and get links back to your website (if the newspaper is published online).

Press Releases Writing press releases and submitting them to places like PR Web or Web Wire is a great way to generate interest and buzz about your business and also to get links back to your website. This method of link building is a little more difficult than other methods for getting links for your website. Writing a press release requires skill—a skill that the average person does not have. Press releases have certain requirements that must be met and a certain format that must be followed, and in most cases, they need to be super interesting. Not having any of these elements can almost guarantee that your press release will either be rejected outright or not distributed to other news-related websites.

Directory Submissions

Anyone studying SEO will find ample information about submitting websites to directories on the Internet. Before you go crazy and start submitting to thousands of directories, seek out local directories and directories that are specific to your business/industry. Submit to these first, and take your time filling out all of the information that they ask for. These will be some of your most valuable links since they are so relevant to your website and business.

If you submit your site to good (quality) directories and in appropriate categories/areas, then the link back to your site from the directory can be considered a quality backlink. One nice thing about directory submission is that it will give you one-way links. Here are a few things to consider when submitting to directories:

Use of Anchor Text You can usually use your desired keyword in your site title/description. Therefore, a directory pointed to your site with a particular keyword will give you a good anchor text backlink.

Niche Directory Submission Niche directories are focused directories that have specific categories for niche topics only. Submitting the site to those directories will give you quality contextual backlinks. Niche directories will usually send you better-targeted traffic too.

Deeplink Directory Submission Deep linking involves submitting your website's inner pages rather than the home page only. It can be beneficial to spend some time finding directories that allow deep linking and submitting your inner pages to those directories.

Local Organizations

Just about every city in the country has a local chamber of commerce. Joining a chamber of commerce will not only get you a very good link back to your website, it also provides networking opportunities with other local businesses. Look for other local organizations with online sites that provide links as well. Most of the time, depending on your business, you can generate new leads rather easily by getting to know other individuals and businesses in your area.

You might be surprised how many nonprofit organizations are operating in your city and your state. I guarantee that there is a nonprofit organization that could use your help, whether it is designing their website or painting the conference room of their new office building. If you offer yourself and your services freely, you can most likely ask for and get a link to your website from theirs.

There are many other ways to gain backlinks from a website. You can offer valuable information on something that an end user finds useful, such as a map to or from a destination, a tool such as a mortgage calculator, or even a coupon or shopping tips. This is the way the search engines want backlinks to occur—a visitor to your website finds something that they feel is useful and they create their own link to it. Some experts suggest the idea of dropping the term *link building* because it implies quantity over quality. I agree. It's important to focus instead on the idea of reaching out to others and building quality connections that make sense. Concentrate on offering something of value to the online community/industry to demonstrate why they should pay your site a visit. Keep this in mind as you read these other link-building ideas.

Write an Insightful Article

Writing articles and submitting them to article directories can be a great way to get links back to your website. Identify something you can contribute of value for your industry, write a detailed article, and submit it to a few article directories like Ezine Articles, Article City, and Go Articles. The opportunity to get backlinks comes from the author bio that goes with the article, so when writing your bio, don't forget to add keyword-rich anchor text links pointing back to your website.

Link Building with Social Media

With the growing popularity of social media there comes a new opportunity for building links. Social media sites can be a good source for developing good-quality links. As you participate in the many conversations that are happening online, you have the opportunity to place links in appropriate places. Here are a few places that offer link juice to stories that are submitted:

Twitter – Your tweets can include links back to your site, and often these links are picked up and added to sites that monitor Twitter conversations. (More about Twitter in the next section.)

Digg – Digg includes links to sites featured in its stories. If you end up on a top page, the link to your site will be considered higher quality (i.e., more link juice).

Reddit – Reddit is one of the most popular social media sites that will provide links back to your site. Again, if you make it to the top pages, you'll get a great boost to your incoming link power.

Generating Links with Twitter

I'll elaborate a little more on Twitter because of its popularity and potential for building quality links. This may not be the first thing you think of when you think about Twitter, but it can be one of the best tools to gain targeted, relevant, and natural links to your site. However, like any link-building strategy, it must be done properly or you will end up wasting a lot of time with poor results. Here are some general guidelines for building quality links with Twitter:

- Build a Twitter profile around a specific topic and stick to it. The more focused your profile is, the better your chances of attracting relevant followers and links.

- Provide relevant, focused, and valuable tweets. Focus on news, content, and links that are of high interest to your intended audience. The more valuable the information/link is to the reader, the more likely they are to follow you and ultimately provide you with links from their own blogs/sites. Avoid too many tweets about your personal life or other content unrelated to your specific niche.

- Tweet often and consistently. Be consistent in your use of Twitter. The more active you are in the conversations pertaining to a specific topic, the better your results will be.

- Identify the major players in your topic/industry. Twitter is a great resource for identifying the heavy hitters around a specific topic. A simple Twitter search on targeted keywords will reveal the movers and shakers of a specific niche. Once you've identified these people, network with them via Twitter and through other channels if appropriate.

- Integrate Twitter into your website. This will greatly improve your chances of finding good, targeted followers. A simple Follow Me on Twitter link/button can be added to your site quite easily. More advanced options include Twitter widgets that will show your latest tweets and your followers on your site.

Again, I would like to reiterate that if you think of link building as more about making quality connections rather than just placing links, you will come out stronger in the long run. Also remember to think in terms of offering something of value to others.

Just as with internal linking, it is optimal to get your keywords into the linked text. So as you establish external links that point to landing pages on your website, make sure the keywords are in the linked text. Many times you have little to no control over how links are set up on other sites. I recommend emailing them samples or even have a place on your site where they can copy and paste your links into their HTML. The easier you make it, the higher the likelihood it will work in your favor. Now let's look at some places where you can place links. With most of these places, you do have some control over the link placement.

Optimizing Image and Video Assets with Keywords

Search engine optimization used to be straightforward, but in today's world it has become more complex. With the emergence of image search, blended search, and universal search, preparing images for SEO has become more important.

As a result, many people are starting to see the value of quality video, audio, and images. These engagement objects help visitors develop a deeper understanding of what your site is all about. They also help to keep your visitors on the site longer, which reduces your site's bounce rate. This is becoming a very important metric for measuring visitor engagement. A *bounce rate* is the percentage of people who get to your site and then quickly leave, suggesting they did not see anything of interest.

The fact that search engines like Google are studying bounce rates on your site suggests you should be looking at it as well. They will award sites with lower bounce rates because it suggests that visitors found what they were looking for and stay longer. Let's look at the specifics for each media type.

For Images

Remember that search engines cannot see keywords that are integrated in video, audio, and images. So, for instance, if you use Photoshop or some other graphics program to place text into your images, the search engines cannot decipher those words. If you have targeted keywords you wish to be integrated and associated with those images, you need to *tag* the images with the keywords. The search engines can see the tags.

The same goes for video and audio files. However, search engines have made some great strides in being able to convert audio speech to text and then index the text, which is amazing.

Use Descriptive Image and Folder Names

First make sure you have your targeted keywords handy. Once you have your keywords ready, you will need to use them as file and folder names.

Digital cameras label pictures with names like `_DSC368.jpg`, and if you use those filenames on your website, you really can't expect search engines or visitors to easily identify what the image is about. A much better idea is to rename them with more descriptive and keyword-rich filenames.

For instance, if your image is about white-water rafting in California, you might rename the file `california-white-water-rafting.jpg`.

Notice I used dashes to separate each word in the phrase, not underscores. Search engines interpret underscores as alpha characters, while dashes are interpreted as spaces, meaning they can develop a context around each of the words—"california", "white", "water", and "rafting"—and take those words into account for indexing and relevance ranking purposes.

You can take this a step further by creating a descriptive folder name in which these images will be stored, such as white-water rafting. This gives search engines even more cues to develop a context for your images and results in a wonderfully keyword-rich URL string for the image that looks like this:

`yoursite.com/white-water-rafting/california-white-water-rafting.jpg`

Use Descriptive Alt and Title Attributes

Another way to help search engines learn what your images are about is to use descriptive alt and title attributes. You do this in the HTML code that tags the image with a description. The text contained within the alt attribute is used to specify alternative information that should be shown if an image is inaccessible. So this text is typically shown to visitors if an image is missing or cannot be downloaded. It is also shown to people who have disabled images in their browsers. If you have not specified alt text, a missing image is displayed as a blank or empty box or icon, depending on your browser. Additionally, alt text is typically shown when users hover their mouse pointer over an image.

The text contained within the title attribute is used to display additional information. This attribute is primarily important to users. When you hover over an image with title text, the data contained within this attribute pops up.

The alt attribute is most important to search engines and should always include your targeted keywords. The title attribute is optional but can be part of a good user experience to help describe images.

The important part is to make sure you use a description about the image, not just random keywords. Look at the image in Figure 6.10 of an ocean kayak trip in Dominica. When tagging an image, you should use a description rather than just keywords, like alt="Malibu Ocean Kayaking near Dominica in the Southern Caribbean".

Figure 6.10 Image file tagging

Each image should be unique and no more than a dozen words should be used in the alt attribute. For instance, instead of using alt="Ocean Kayaking", you should use a little more detail, like alt=" Malibu Ocean Kayaking near Dominica in the Southern Caribbean", which is better. Additionally you will want to place your images as close to any text content that is contextual and relevant to them. This helps to associate the image with descriptive text to help the search engines and visitors have a better understanding what your image and web page are all about.

Use Descriptive Anchor Text

Let's take it a step further. If you are linking to or from an image using text, you should also use descriptive anchor text that includes keywords and helps to describe the image. Remember, anchor text is underlined text that is hyperlinked to other content. As with the alt attribute, use good anchor text that describes the contents of the image. This may be similar to descriptive text you have used in image filenames and alt attributes, as in the following two examples:

alt=" Malibu Ocean Kayaking near Dominica in the Southern Caribbean

For more information on <u>Ocean Kayaking in the Southern Caribbean</u> click here.

Using these steps will help you make the most of the images you use on your website and optimize their value to both the search engines and your visitors, not to mention that the use of alt attributes is helpful to visitors with disabilities.

Optimize Image File Size for Faster Load Times

From a usability perspective, you want to make sure your images are optimized for the Web. Even though we live in a world with plenty of bandwidth, I have seen web pages slowly build because the images on the site were too large. One of the main culprits is using images formatted for print, usually 300 dpi. You can fix this by reducing from 300 dpi to 72 dpi using a program like Adobe Photoshop (see Figure 6.11). You can also adjust your quality settings when you save your image. Usually the highest quality setting isn't necessary, but somewhere between medium to medium high is about right. Remember, the higher the setting, the larger the file size.

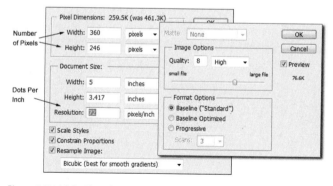

Figure 6.11 Adobe Photoshop

Images and Social Media

Social media has opened up new channels to market our products and services. Many sites that let you upload images, such as Facebook and Flickr, let you tag the images with keywords and descriptions. Make sure you take advantage of this. When you post images to these sites, use the target keywords you used in your image titles, attributes, and descriptions. Then make sure you link to targeted, relevant pages on your website. If you have your images properly tagged, you will likely find new visitors from these social sites.

For Video

Video is one of the fastest growing media types on the Internet. Back in late 2010, comScore named YouTube the second largest search engine with over 2 billion videos viewed each day, and it is projected to increase rapidly in the next few years. Marketers hoping to leverage this new medium can improve their "findability" by revisiting and updating their strategies to improve search visibility as well.

With Internet video on the rise and the search engines looking more favorably on video content, there is an opportunity to use this medium for your SEO efforts. Additionally, for the keywords with which you've been trying to achieve high rankings, you could use YouTube and quite possibly get even better placement in search engine results.

Just as with image optimization, there are several tips for optimizing video for not only for SEO but for a better user experience:

- Use keywords in your video transcripts
- Video production
- Landing pages
- Uploading and optimizing videos
- Tracking/analytics

Use Keywords in Your Video Transcripts

Your targeted keywords should be embedded into your video transcript, if there is one. Some search engines have the capability to convert speech to text and then index the results. Your keywords should be infused within the title, the description, and even the filename and URL where possible. With video, it is best to go for the long-tail keywords. The more specific the keywords, the better.

Video Production

The first step in optimizing for video is creating the video. You can either hire someone to do it for you or do it yourself. If you decide to hire someone, your choices range from a college student to a fully fledged production company. Think about your audience. Some might expect a high-quality production, but some might be fine if your video isn't too polished. There is something to be said about producing a video that is not quite perfect. It seems more down to earth and genuine and that can be a plus—not to mention that it's usually cheaper to produce. On the other hand, a nice, clean, well-done video can be a great showpiece for your brand.

So how long should your video be? A good rule of thumb is anywhere from 30 seconds to 3 minutes. Again, think about your audience and ask yourself how much they will be able to handle. You need enough time to get across your point with a call to action, but you don't want to make it so long that it will bore them to death.

Another thing to consider in producing your video is to be creative and find ways to make it unique. With so many videos out there, how will yours stand out and be memorable and cause people to tell their friends about it. Consider the folks at Will It Blend (www.willitblend.com). To illustrate the power behind their blenders, they produce videos that show their product blending things like an iPod and glowsticks. Not only is this demonstrating the product's capabilities, it is also entertaining and more likely to go viral.

Landing Pages

Before you are ready to upload and distribute your video, you need to decide where you want to direct people who see it. Suppose your video has a call to action that motivates the viewer to learn more about your product or service. You will need to designate a *landing page* that will provide that detail. Remember to use the keywords with which you tagged your video on these pages. This will help transfer the keyword relevance to your landing page.

The landing pages you use can be a Facebook page, a blog, a website, or a business page in a directory. You will also want to tag that landing page for analytics purposes. This will help you see how many people acted on your video and wanted to learn more.

Once a prospect views your video, they have begun a journey that will ultimately lead them to a mutual goal or a conversion for you. It is your job to lead them one step at a time: Engage them with your video, get them to your landing page, and then motivate them to make a purchase or complete some other type of conversion.

Uploading and Optimizing Videos

Some of the most notable video sharing sites are YouTube (www.youtube.com), Metacafe (www.metacafe.com), Viddler (www.viddler.com), and Vimeo (www.vimeo.com), just to name a few. TubeMogul (www.tubemogul.com), however, makes uploading to multiple video sites a simple process. You will need to set up the initial accounts on each video site first, of course. TubeMogul also features a large number of tracking options that will let you follow your videos wherever they end up.

The video search engines out there are: blinkx (www.blinkx.com), Google Video (http://video.google.com), Singing Fish (AOL Video, http://video.aol.com), CastTV (www.casttv.com), and VideoSurf (www.videosurf.com).

As you upload your video, you will have the option to add your keyword phrases into the title, description, and tags for each site. Here are some guidelines for each:

Titles Your title should act as a headline for your video. It is sometimes the only way for people to know what your video is about. It should be anywhere from 75 to 120 characters. The lowest common denominator is 75 characters, but some sites will give you more room. Make sure it is readable by humans. A title that is simply a list of keywords will appear to be spam. Also, if you want to include your brand name in the title, it should be last. You want the emphasis on what the video is about first.

Description The description should be detailed and utilize your set of top keywords while still being human readable. You have about 200 characters, so you have a little more room for more detail. A good tip is to include your landing page URL as the first thing in your description and be sure to include the `http://` because most of the sites you submit your video to will include your description, which will include the URL. As a bonus, many of the sites will automatically convert the URL into a link.

Tags Again, be as detailed as possible when utilizing top keywords. You may also include your brand, city, and topics to add further context.

Tracking/Analytics

Tracking and analytics are always of the highest importance because they provide the statistics that tell you what works and what doesn't. As previously stated, it is important that you tag your landing pages and other pages a visitor might view on their journey to a final goal. The same basic principles apply for other landing page optimization. Switch out different pages or parts of pages, and use A/B testing and multivariate testing to shake things up and see if you achieve better results.

Video advertising can be effective for large and small businesses. Try it, test the results, and then modify your plan accordingly. There is still an opportunity to benefit not only for video search but also for leveraging it for universal search.

According to a recent Nielsen study called the Three Screen Report (`http://blog.nielsen.com/nielsenwire/nielsen-news/americans-watching-more-tv-than-ever/`), video usage is up by 53 percent from last year. The *Three* stands for TV, Internet, and mobile. I will focus on reaching the Internet and mobile audience and how to optimize for video search.

Many search technologies are based on reading text and HTML, so how can you reach the video viewing audience? There are two methods to use:

Video Search Engine Optimization (VSEO) The optimization of any video asset to lift organic search listing results in order to increase views and findability of your content

Video Search Engine Marketing (VSEM) Targeting video content, on any site with indexed video, by the selection of paid keywords pertaining to what you are marketing, with video ads and/or accompanying banners

VSEO Basics

Every marketer should use VSEO to ensure that content can be found and watched.

VSEO is directly comparable to standard site SEO. Both are done to improve the visibility and relevancy of your content. Video can live on multiple indexed pages, where each one can appear as a separate result, increasing your results page share.

How does one practice VSEO? Once again, it can be compared to standard SEO, with a few major differences.

Here are the key elements of VSEO, which should be used with any and all videos you distribute on the Web to gain visibility and relevancy:

Meta Tags As with a web page, these are keywords associated with your video, built into the coding of both the video and on the page where it lives.

Context The contents of any page surrounding a video will be indexed to help find relevancy to some broader keywords.

Unique URL Every video should have its own URL to ensure that all contextual and metadata indexing is as relevant as possible.

Format Knowing your content and potential viewers can determine the most appropriate format. For some viewers, HD is very important. For others, fast downloads is the priority.

Seeding The more places a video is available for viewing, the higher your page share with any video search engine results can be.

Deciding what you want out of your video will help focus your VSEO efforts appropriately. The two options are promotional video, where the video is the message and is geared toward distribution and seeding efforts, and stationary video, where the video is used to draw traffic to a specific site, creating inventory that can be monetized.

Promotional Meta tags and format are crucial for indexing your video because you must rely on only what is packaged with the video and not necessarily the surrounding content as it is shared.

Stationary Format, context, and unique pages are all important because these will allow publishers to most effectively monetize content for VSEM purposes.

What Opportunities Do VSEO Efforts Create?

The monetization opportunities for VSEO lie with both advertisers and publishers. For advertisers, it's the promotional videos. For publishers, it's mostly with the stationary videos, though the distribution of content can be monetized for publishers as well.

Advertiser monetization of VSEO practices falls into a totally new category. Though it could rely on some paid media to help seed and push the content, the core is video distribution. Systems to monetize VSEO are based on number of videos distributed, number of sites distributed to, and how deep each individual video should be tracked.

Publisher monetization, around stationary content video, is best thought of as creating relevant, targeted video inventory. The targeted inventory could then be sold in the form of pre-, mid- or post-roll or through the banners accompanying a video. The value of this inventory is increased when it can be targeted by keyword rather than by channel or bucket. Publishers can take steps either to make the video sharable, and potentially further increase value to advertisers if a pre-roll or other unit is embedded with a video, or to prevent the video from being shared in order to retain the ad inventory for content on your page.

Video distribution through companies like TubeMogul have made the process of uploading to multiple video share/hosting sites a one-step process (after the initial accounts on each site are set up). They also feature a large number of tracking options that will let you follow your videos wherever they end up.

Summary

Keyword research has naturally been tied with SEO and will continue to be in the foreseeable future. You cannot ignore the power of using targeted keywords on your site, landing pages, or blog. It is essential.

By using your keyword list and placing keywords into the specific areas mentioned in this chapter, you will be well on your way to providing clarity and focus to the content on your site. This is important not just for the search engines but also to your visitors.

Keep in mind the new and exciting medium of video and images and don't overlook their potential to not only engage your visitors more fully but also to provide new ways to be found on the Web; more and more people prefer to watch a video than to read a bunch of text.

Using Keywords
for PPC

The connection between keywords and pay-per-click (PPC) advertising goes back a long way. In fact, when they hear about keyword research, many people naturally think of PPC. Since PPC is mostly text-based, keyword research provides valuable insight into your prospective customers and the behavior that led or will lead them to you.

Chapter Contents

Keywords and Their Role in PPC

Many people learned the hard way not to be too hasty in setting up a PPC campaign. Throwing a few seed keywords in a keyword tool and then adding any and all keywords that shows up into an ad group is not the right approach. It takes a methodical process and a healthy amount of time to harvest the best keywords, the ones that will perform optimally for your campaign.

By conducting keyword research ahead of time, you should have already learned some valuable information. If you took the time to categorize your keywords into meaningful categories, you have already formed the framework for a great PPC campaign.

Keyword Categories and Ad Groups

To begin let's draw some comparisons between your keyword lists and ad groups. You can see the levels of a PPC campaign in Figure 7.1

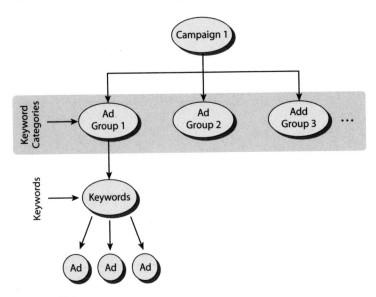

Figure 7.1 PPC structure

You begin with a campaign that has multiple ad groups. These ad groups should mimic the keyword categories you have already created. Each ad group will have a list of keywords that should consist of the same keywords you have in each category.

To illustrate how this might work, let's look at a fictitious company called Carbonville Mountain Bikes. We will start with list of keywords. I will keep the list short and simple:

mountain biking

mountain bikes

mountain bike parts

mountain bike trails

mountain bike for sale

discount mountain bikes

new mountain bikes

mountain bike reviews

mountain bike shop

best mountain bikes

mountain bike frames

mountain bike store

full suspension mountain bikes

From these keywords, I will create a few logical categories:

mountain bikes

mountain bike parts

full suspension mountain bikes

mountain bike frames

Each category could have its own landing page loaded with great relevant content. As such, each should also have its own ad group. Now let's build out some of these with their keywords:

Ad Group 1: Mountain Bikes

mountain bike

mountain bikes

buy mountain bikes

new mountain bikes

discount mountain bikes

best mountain bikes

Ad Group 2: Carbonville Mountain Bikes

carbonville mountain bike

carbonville mountain bikes

buy carbonville mountain bikes

new carbonville mountain bikes

Ad Group 3: Full Suspension

full suspension mountain bikes

full suspension mountain bike

best full suspension mountain bike

carbonville full suspension mountain bike

Notice that in the second group I inserted a branded term for those who might be searching on the brand keywords. As you can see, there are very few keywords per ad group and they are very closely associated with one another. This makes it easier to create your text ads so they can be highly relevant to your keywords. You can have multiple ads that are slightly different but are still relevant.

Can you see the resemblance between your keyword categorization and ad groups? If you have already built out your categorizations then you are that much closer to having your ad groups built out for a PPC campaign.

SEO and PPC Keywords

It is important to point out here the differences between SEO and PPC keywords. Your core keywords are used for SEO because you really want to be known for those keywords. It is up to you whether or not you also want to include them in your PPC campaign. It is a powerful statement when your listings come up in both organic and PPC results. However, this can be an expensive prospect depending on how competitive your keywords are. Most tend to place the specific, or long-tail, keywords into a PPC campaign and their core keywords in their SEO campaign.

So identify which strategy is best for you and choose your keywords accordingly. Another strategy that works well if you are doing a combination of SEO and PPC campaigns is to start off with a strong PPC campaign to get you into the game early, and when your SEO efforts achieve the desired visibility, you can then back off on your PPC campaign to save money. A representation of this strategy is shown in the graph in Figure 7.2.

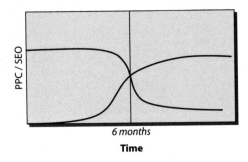

Figure 7.2 PPC/SEO campaign strategy

As you move down to the ad group level in Figure 7.1 you will see the ads. One of the most important factors of a successful PPC campaign is writing relevant and engaging ad copy for each ad in each ad group. With small, tightly organized ad groups, you will find it much easier to write better, more focused ads. If you spend a good deal of time on other aspects of your campaign but skimp on the ad copy, you might not get the results you are looking for. I will review several tips for crafting high-performing ad copy and methods for testing its effectiveness.

Ads and Searcher Behavior

I discussed in Chapter 2 the importance of gauging user expectations and matching those expectations to your ads and landing pages. Before a user begins their search, they have an expectation or even a mental image of what it is they hope to find. When they approach a search engine, they have to put that mental image into a search query with the hope that their search query will net them relevant results. The first thing they will see is the organic listings, blended search results, and PPC ads.

They quickly look over the elements of the SERP for listings that not only confirm their search query but will lead them to the content they envisioned. Since this chapter is on PPC, we will focus on the PPC ads that show up. One of the best ways to call attention to your ad is to include a keyword that matches the user search query somewhere in your ad. This will help them zero in on the ad for a bit more detail that might lead them to the actual content they are looking for. The more relevant the ad to the search term, the better.

Once they decide to click on your ad, they will end up on your landing page, which again should be rich in relevant content that meets their expectations and includes any promises you made in the ad.

You will not only have met the user's expectations, you will likely get them to act. More-relevant ads translate to a higher click-through rate (CTR) and relevant landing pages translate to higher conversion rates (CVRs). More-relevant ad copy and higher CTR also lead to higher-quality scores. The benefits of a higher-quality score are higher ad rankings and a lower cost per click (CPC). I will cover keywords and quality score later on in the chapter.

So the challenge is to divide up your keywords into smaller ad groups with fewer keywords that are centered on a strong theme. This will help you write your ads so they are relevant to your keywords. Many people create only one or two ad groups and put hundreds or thousands of keywords in them. With this scenario, is it difficult to write effective ad copy that is relevant to each of those keywords. This will force you to write generic ad copy that will not stand out and will get lost among all of the competing ads.

Ads and Ad Groups

To create your first ad group and ads, you should have two things in mind: relevancy and action. Your ad group should contain keywords that are relevant to each other and to your ads. Your ads should link to a page that is just as relevant. A strong, effective call to action will generate higher CTRs. You will find that these two principles will greatly increase your campaign effectiveness and your quality score.

Google offers an offline tool that allows you to download your campaign and make all the changes you want and then upload the changes back into AdWords. It is the AdWords Editor (`www.google.com/intl/en/adwordseditor/`), and as most tools from Google, it is free. It is much easier to group your keywords with the AdWords Editor than to do it online with AdWords. I really love this tool. So find the tool and start segmenting your large list of keywords into the categories you came up with earlier.

By the way, if you are looking for a good keyword tool and a way to help you manage your PPC campaign, I also recommend WordStream for PPC (`www.wordstream.com/wordstream-for-ppc`), which was covered in Chapter 3. This tool will help you to identify great keywords, organize them and group them into meaningful ad groups, and make changes as needed. This is mainly because it is directly linked to your Google AdWords account.

I recommend adding at least two ads per ad group if not more. To ensure relevancy, each ad should have the core, or theme, keyword in it. Keywords can go into the title, description, display URL, and even the destination URL. Keywords in the destination URL are not visible to searchers until they actually click your ad, but if you are using dynamic landing pages, the keywords in the destination URL can display on your landing pages. And finally, pick the most relevant page for your destination URL. Don't just send your potential customers to your home page.

Because you have only a limited amount of space for your ads, you need to make each character count. You have only 25 characters for your headline and 70 characters for ad copy. Let's start with tips for writing a good headline. This is where you can have the most impact.

Using Keywords in your Headlines

Including your keywords in your ad headlines is widely considered a best practice for PPC, and it is a very good way to ensure that your ad is relevant to the user's search query. People are more likely to click a headline that closely reflects what they were searching for. So if a searcher typed in "Carbonville Mountain Bike" as a search query, a great headline for the ad would be Carbonville Mountain Bike. Notice also that as an added benefit to your keyword research, when words in your ad match the user search query, these words are bolded in your ad wherever they appear, which draws more attention to your ads.

As discussed earlier, this is an easier task to set up if you have an ad group that contains a smaller set of keywords and that are very similar to your headline. Here is an example of using a headline from the ad group #2 for the Carbonville Mountain Bikes example at the beginning of the chapter.

Carbonville Mountain Bikes
www.EZMountainBikes.com
Your Best Price & Value Guaranteed!
Suspension Mt **Bike** from Top Brands.

Dynamic Keyword Insertion

Another way to ensure that your keywords are used in your ad within Google AdWords is to use a technique called *dynamic keyword insertion (DKI)*. This is an advanced method that allows you to dynamically insert a keyword from your ad group into your ad copy when triggered from a search query. Essentially, you place a short piece of code into your ad text. Each time the ad shows, the code will be replaced by the keyword that triggered the ad. You can use DKI to insert keywords into the title, description, display URL, and destination URL.

To use dynamic keyword insertion, you insert the following code at any part of your ad text

```
{keyword: default text}
```

If the keyword is too long and exceeds the maximum character count, the default text will be used instead.

Let's say you have an ad group called Jewelry. In this ad group you have three keywords: "fashion rings", "fashion necklaces", and "diamond stud earrings". You then create the following ad using the keyword insertion code:

Buy {keyword:Jewelry}
www.*yourwebsite*.com
From Top Name Brands
Satisfaction Guaranteed!
Destination URL: `http://www.acmejewelry.com/?kw={keyword:nil}`

When Google matches search queries for those three keywords, your ads will show up in one of the following ways, respectively:

Buy Fashion Rings
www.*yourwebsite*.com
From Top Name Brands
Satisfaction Guaranteed!
Destination URL: `http://www.acmejewelry.com/?kw=fashion%20rings`

Buy Fashion Necklaces
www.*yourwebsite*.com
From Top Name Brands
Satisfaction Guaranteed!
Destination URL: `http://www.acmejewelry.com/?kw=fashion%20necklaces`

Buy Jewelry
www.*yourwebsite*.com
From Top Name Brands
Satisfaction Guaranteed!
Destination URL: `http://www.acmejewelry.com/?kw=diamond%20stud%20earrings`

Notice that for the last ad, the keyword "diamond stud earrings" does not fit in the ad title, so the default keyword "buy jewelry" is used instead. However, the destination URL will take people to the diamond stud earring landing page as long as the destination URL does not exceed 1,024 characters.

You need to be very careful when using this method because it can get you into trouble if you use it incorrectly. One of the main ways of misusing it is to have one large ad group with hundreds of keywords and using DKI to just insert the keywords as they are triggered. Indiscriminate use of DKI results in ad copy that is worded for the "common denominator" of the keyword set, with diluted messages that fail to exactly match the searcher's intent or need, as I explained earlier. So having small ad groups with fewer keywords is highly recommended to ensure the relevant use of the keyword in the ad copy.

Ask the Question

Another way to set up your headline is to simply ask a question that gets the searcher thinking. You might be surprised if you ask a compelling question and then follow up in your description with some compelling answers. This can also help make your headline stick out, especially if your competition is employing the dynamic keyword insertion method.

Need a New **Mountain Bike?**
www.EZMountainBikes.com
Your Best Price & Value Guaranteed!
Suspension Mt Bike From Top Brands

Mountain Bike Cheap
www.acmebikeshop.com/**Bikes**
Save on **Mountain Bikes** Cheap
Compare Prices. Save up to 60%!

Descriptions

The keyword insertion method will also work for your descriptions. You have a little more room with the character limit of 2 lines with 35 characters each. Notice in the previous ads where "Mountain Bikes" is bold in the description. This is to draw the searchers' attention to those keywords.

Now, if the headline is used more or less to capture the attention of the searcher, the purpose of the ad description is to provide enough detail to help convert your searcher into a visitor. You should put yourself in their shoes and try to discern their needs and intent. For each keyword in your ad group, imagine what information might get you to click the ad to learn more.

Call to Action

Promotions and sales have a way of capturing people's attention. If you have a give-away or a product that is on sale, put that in your ad. If you use this method, be sure people are sent to a page that actually has the promotion or the sale.

Qualifications and Guarantees

Another way to help your searchers feel a little more comfortable about clicking your ad is to state any qualifications or guarantees you have. Are you a certified professional? Are you an award winner? Do you offer a money back guarantee? Answering these questions might be enough to get a click.

Display URLs

The display URL is the URL shown in the ad, as seen in Figure 7.3. In this example, you can see that the URL is right under the headline. This isn't the exact URL that leads to the landing page, but it gives the searcher a clue as to where the landing page is. In this example, you can see that you will be to www.bikebling.com/Pinarello. The overall effect is that this helps to increase CTR, especially if the content of the display URL is the same as or similar to the ad.

2011 **Pinarello** Bike Deals
www.bikebling.com/Pinarello
Deals on 2010 **Pinarello** Bikes
Large Selection - Discount Codes

Figure 7.3 Display URL example

It is obviously helpful if your display URL also contains your keyword. If the keyword is embedded in the domain name, that is great. This is not always the case, so you can set up a landing page that includes your keyword. In the example in Figure 7.3 the keyword is "Pinarello".

Qualify Your Traffic

One thing your ads need to do is to qualify your traffic. You will be wasting your money if you drive the wrong traffic to your site. If you are a high-end mountain bike dealer that caters only to the wealthy, then you don't need words like "cheap" or "bargain" in your ads. Write your ads to help set the right expectations. Using negative keywords in your campaign will help with this. More on negative keywords later in the chapter.

Remember that your ultimate goal is to get searchers to your site and then convert them into customers. Your job is not over after you have them on your site—you still need to deliver on what you promised in your ads.

Launch Campaign—Measure and Tweak

As you prepare to launch your paid search ad campaigns, make sure to check that your web analytics is working and verify that your landing pages are live and functional so you can measure your results immediately. As you monitor your campaigns, you will undoubtedly find spots that need tweaking. Expand your keyword list if necessary, add more ad groups with relevant keywords, monitor your quality score, and check your conversion rates. After all, you are going through all of this trouble to get people to your site for a reason, right?

Once you feel you have your campaigns running smoothly, you can duplicate it and place it on other PPC networks. Other networks provide different features, so make sure you take advantage of those that are important to you. Also, as I stated at the beginning of this chapter, be aware of the strengths of the other search networks you choose to use and measure accordingly. What works on one network might not work the same on the other, so test to make sure you are achieving the correct results.

Setting up a PPC campaign the right way can be a fun and rewarding journey. Following these steps has worked for me and for other professionals. There will always be new tools and new tips that will become available. Make sure you play it smart and test and make sure it works for you. Don't be afraid to try something different to see if it will make an improvement. PPC management is all about dialing it in and then making small, methodical course corrections to squeeze out a little more performance when you can.

Keywords and Quality Score

Early pay-per-click advertising networks were based on price auctions where whoever bid the highest got the top spot. However, this model did not work well for up-and-coming search engines such as Google. Remember that search engines are in the business of trust. If you and I use a search engine and we are consistently taken to relevant landing pages, then we are likely come back and use that search engine again. They are constantly looking for ways to increase the user experience and lead people to the right content. The problem with the auction model is that just because you have the most money doesn't mean you have the most relevant campaign. Your ad text and keywords and landing pages may not be relevant to the users' search queries.

Now most search engines use a hybrid auction that takes both price and ad relevance (also known as quality score) into account to determine which ads show and the order in which they get shown. In addition to the price you are willing to bid to show your ad, Google takes into account the quality score of your keywords.

In AdWords, the quality score is a dynamic value that is assigned to each keyword in your PPC campaign and indicates how relevant and competitive your keywords and ads combinations are relative to other advertisers competing for the same keywords; it is mostly based on the click-through rate of your ads. A high quality score will positively influence your ad position and effectively decrease your minimum cost per click for your keywords. So if you're the underdog and aren't as rich as your competition, you have a chance to get the top spot with less money. To explore this topic in more detail, see the new book written and published by Craig Danuloff called *Quality Score in High Resolution* (2011).

Before the quality score was introduced, the primary means for achieving a high ranking was to have the highest bid for your target keyword. Search engines learned that those that had the most money didn't necessarily provide the best ads or destination sites. So they introduced the quality score as another criterion for determining ad placement. By incentivizing advertisers to create high-quality and relevant PPC campaigns, search engines benefit by providing searchers with a better experience, thus ensuring their brand loyalty. So basically they reward advertisers that have a higher quality score. Searchers then have a better experience and search engines keep market share. Win-win-win.

Quality Score Factors

So how does this work? What are the factors that influence your quality score (QS)? One key factor is the relevance of your keyword to your ads in the ad group. The most important factor is the click-through rate of your keywords and your ads in combination.

There are other factors, but suffice it to say your goal is to make sure your keywords are very closely related to your ads. The landing page for each ad should contain content that correlates closely to your ad and its message.

As you can probably tell by now, relevance is key. When a searcher steps up to a search engine, they already have an expectation what they are looking for. They then type in a search query that best represents that expectation and are presented with a page of ads. When they see an ad that either has the keyword in it or is very closely related to the keyword that matches their expectation, they are more likely to click on that ad. Your goal is to deliver on that expectation by taking them to a landing page that contains the content they are looking for.

Steps to Achieve a High Quality Score

Now let's develop a PPC campaign using the principles discussed so far. Here are the steps:

1. Identify campaign strategy and goals.
2. Organize a campaign structure.
3. Identify keywords and relevant ad copy.
4. Ensure landing page quality.
5. Measure performance.

Strategy and Goals

With any campaign it is always good to identify your strategy and goals. Is your campaign designed more for branding or is it a lead generation strategy? With that in mind, start conducting your keyword research and identify those phrases that will help drive the right traffic to your site.

Campaign Structure

I suggest you organize your keywords into themes. Keywords that are very closely related should be grouped together. By doing this you are beginning to develop ad groups, which is the next step in forming a good campaign structure. I have seen people create one ad group and dump hundreds or even thousands of keywords into it. Your goal is to create many ad groups that contain keywords that are very closely related to each other. This is a harder task, but it is well worth it.

Ad Copy

For each ad group, you need to develop ad copy that incorporates your keywords or is very closely related to your keywords. When a searcher sees an ad that is closely associated with their keyword, they are more likely to click the ad. The more clicks, the higher your CTR, which is one of the primary quality score factors.

Landing Page Quality

The next step is to identify or develop landing pages for each ad group. The searcher has an expectation for each ad group and is looking for a message to meet that expectation. Make sure each landing page contains content that will deliver on the ad's message or promise. This of course will lead to a higher conversion rate for you.

Performance Measurement

The final step is to measure. The key measurement to look at is your CTR. As I said before, CTR is a primary factor of achieving a high quality score. Of course, you also need to keep an eye on your quality score. You will probably see a close correlation between a high CTR and high QS. If you consistently have keywords or ads that are not performing, you should delete them.

By performing these steps, you will be on your way to achieving a higher quality score for your PPC campaigns, which in turn means higher ad placement and lower costs for you.

Quality Score Case Study

To illustrate how this can work, I will share with you a case study on how to optimize campaigns using quality score. I had a client with a campaign that seemed to be stagnant and wasn't going anywhere. The client's representatives couldn't seem to make any positive improvements.

They were spending on average about $.42 per click across five ad groups. Each ad group had about 150 plus keywords. Seventy-two percent of their keywords had a "poor" quality score. They were also using broad match for all of their keywords. They were not aware of what their quality score was or how it could be used to help them make improvements.

After reviewing the account, we made the following adjustments:

- We split keywords into smaller, more targeted ad groups. We expanded the 5 ad groups to 17. We had no more than 15 keywords in each ad group to keep the relevancy high.

- Then we adjusted the ad copy for each ad group to be more relevant to the keywords in each group. This was a lot easier since we had only 15 or fewer keywords per ad group instead of 150.

- We added and refined creative by testing four different ads and used the Display Campaign Optimizer to rotate the ads so that the best-performing ads were shown more of the time. Then we discarded the ads that did not perform well.

Then we moved on to the landing page and applied SEO best practices:

- We optimized the landing pages with top-performing keywords from the campaign into copy and HTML tags.

- Then we optimized the landing pages with multivariate testing to determine the best organization of content for optimal conversion.

- Finally, we checked the pages with the Google Keyword Tool by entering the landing page URL and making sure the keywords Google saw as top keywords were the ones we were targeting.

The result of this exercise was a noticeable improvement from how it was set-up previously:

- The average minimum CPC went from $.37 to $.09 cents.

- The CTR increased by 11 percent.

- Their conversion rates went from 2.6 percent to 4.8 percent. Some went as high as 8 percent.

- Within two weeks, the quality score for 58 percent of the keywords went from poor to great. All keywords that still had a poor quality score after a month were deleted from the campaign.

Most B2B search marketers spend the majority of their time analyzing conversion data within their PPC campaigns. They adjust budgets and bids to ensure adequate funding of the top-converting keywords (i.e., keywords that record a conversion, at an acceptable cost, within the 30-day tracking window, based on user cookies).

While this approach is logical and typical, it may not be the most effective. Savvy B2B marketers look outside the "conversion box," understand their prospects' search process, and optimize campaigns based on ROI (not just immediate conversions).

Using Negative Keywords

You may have spent countless hours and money setting up your targeted keywords, text ads, and landing pages, but if you have not employed a negative keyword list then you are missing out on a big opportunity to further refine and target your keywords to reach the right audience.

Here are some reasons you might want to consider using negative keywords:

- You have zero conversions.

- You have expensive conversions.

- You have a limited budget.

- You experience bad brand association.

- You seek quality improvements.

- You would like to lower your PPC costs.

Negative keywords are essentially filtering keywords. If a keyword in your negative keyword list appears in a searcher's query, it will prevent your ad from being displayed on that search result. So, for example, let's say you sell luxury designer handbags and "handbags" is one of your keywords. When a searcher types in "cheap handbags", "imitation handbag", or *any brand you do not sell* handbag", then your ad could be triggered and show up in the search results.

However, someone searching using these search terms may not be your best target audience. Unless you have a negative keyword list to filter out these searchers, you will be paying to drive the wrong audience to your site. They will likely leave your site instantly once they discover it doesn't have what they are looking for.

Using this simple list of negative keywords in your campaign will ensure that your ads are not triggered for these searches:

- cheap

- imitation

- free

- Burberry (and other brands you don't carry)

This is really a win-win situation because you don't want those visitors and they don't want to land on your site. As noted, negative keywords will help you increase your CTR, your conversion rates, and your CPC. So if you do not have tracking set up for these specific metrics, it is important that you do so. Let's look at why:

Click-through rate (CTR) The relevance of the searcher's keyword and your ad text is very closely related, so they are likely to click through to your landing page. Without a negative keyword list, you would have ads that trigger that are not relevant to your search, thus producing a lower CTR.

Conversion rate (CVR) Again, because your ads are now more precise by stopping ads that are not relevant *and* your landing page also has relevant content, searchers are more likely to convert because their expectations are being met.

Cost per conversion (CPC) Because your ads show up only for relevant searches, you are not paying for ads that would otherwise be triggered without a negative keyword list. So you are not wasting money on inappropriate ads and you are achieving a higher CTR and conversion rate.

These are factors you need to be monitoring as you employ a negative keyword list. If these factors are not improving, you should revisit your list and look for the culprits and eliminate them.

Which Matching Type Should You Use?

First let's talk about the four other match types that you have an option of using with your PPC campaign:

- Broad match

- Broad match modifier

- Phrase match

- Exact match

Broad match is designed to be a catchall for any search queries that are remotely related to your keywords. The algorithm looks for any of the words in your keyword and displays all results that have any relationship for any of those words. For example, if I used the keyword term "tennis racket", my ad would show up for any of these search queries:

- tennis
- racket
- buy tennis racket
- racquet ball rackets
- tennis racket photos
- tennis balls

Broad match modifier is a relatively new targeting feature that gives you a little more control than broad match. To use broad match modifier, you simply place a plus sign (+) in front of the one or more broad match keywords. This means that any word preceded by a plus sign must be present in the searcher's query exactly (or it could be a close variant). This includes misspellings, singular/plural forms, closely stemmed forms, and some abbreviations. This does not include synonyms. So for our keyword "+tennis racket" we would get the following results:

- tennis rackets
- tennis racket
- buy tennis rackets

Phrase match allows you to tighten the net even more by allowing ads to trigger only if the keyword phrase plus a word appears before or after the keyword. It also covers plurals. So for "tennis racket", your ad would trigger for any of these keyword phrases:

- graphite tennis racket
- tennis rackets
- tennis racket supplies

Exact match is where you have the most control because your ads will not trigger for a search unless it is the exact keyword you are targeting. So for "[tennis racket]", your ad gets triggered for someone who searches on "tennis racket" only.

When to Use Negative Keywords

Now that you understand the various match types, let's look at when and how to use negative keywords. If your strategy is more for branding and you wish to get as much exposure and impressions as possible, then you might not want to use negative keywords. However, you may want to find any keywords that might associate you with a negative image.

If you are focused on a conversion strategy, you definitely want to use negative keywords because, as I have already pointed out, they will increase your conversion rates.

If you are using broad, broad match modifier, or phrase match, you also should use negative keywords to help weed out any unwanted visitors. If you are using exact match, then you really do not need to use negative keywords because you have very tight control.

Benefits of a Negative Keyword List

As you initiate a negative keyword list for your campaigns, you will find many benefits in areas like conversion and leads and even user experience.

Conversion/Leads

- Conversion rate will increase.
- Qualified leads will increase.
- Cost per conversion will decrease.
- Profits and ROI will increase.

Visitor Experience

- Relevancy will increase.
- Bounce rate will decrease.
- Brand association will increase.
- Conversion rate will increase.

How to Find Negative Keywords

There are several ways to identify negative keywords that you can use in your campaigns. You can use the Google AdWords Keyword Tool (`https://adwords.google.com/select/KeywordToolExternal`) or other keyword tools to find synonyms or related keywords. This will help you find all of the variations that might appear for a search on your targeted keyword. You can also consult a thesaurus to accomplish the same task.

If you are using the Google AdWords Keyword Tool, you can paste your page URL into the Website Content box and the tool will show you keywords it sees on your page. With this you can make adjustments to not only your negative keyword list but also your landing page.

WordStream has a negative keyword tool (`http://www.wordstream.com/negative keywords`) that I would also recommend. Just type in a seed keyword and it will display possible negative keywords. If you are using the paid version of WordStream for PPC, you will be able to add these negative keyword to your ad groups instantly because this tool actually links up to your campaign and helps you manage it directly.

Google Analytics or other analytics tools will help you identify search queries and keywords that are driving traffic to your site. Which of those keywords are driving the wrong traffic? Check the bounce rate for each keyword. This will suggest that the visitor did or did not find what they were looking for. If keywords have a high bounce rate and/or a low conversion rate, then consider adding them to your negative keyword list.

There are a couple of places on the Internet where people have posted large lists of negative keywords:

- The 200+ B2B negative keyword list from Komarketing Associates (`www.komarketing associates.com/blog/200-plus-negative-keywords-to-consider-for-b2b-ppc/`)

- A large list of negative keywords from Clix Marketing (`www.clixmarketing.com/blog/wp-content/uploads/2008/02/worlds-biggest-negative-keyword-list.txt`)

Remember that when you look at these lists, they are mainly to help you generate ideas. You do not want to copy and paste them into your own lists because that might eliminate very good candidates.

Search Funnels

As marketers, it is always important to find ways to better understand our target audience and the behavior they exhibit online. We relish any tool that can provide insights into their decision-making paradigms. As we gain insight, we can better anticipate their needs and wants and provide a superior user experience. In early 2010, Google provided a new tool for PPC advertisers that helps provide some useful statistics into search behavior throughout the buying process. It is important to point out that these statistics represent PPC activity and not organic.

Typically conversions are attributed to the last ad clicked in a PPC campaign. The idea of search funnels is to observe all of the ads that were viewed or clicked prior to the conversion taking place. So essentially this tool helps you understand how your keywords, ads, and campaigns work together to create sales and conversions.

The search funnel reports are generated from conversion paths and the sequence of ad clicks and impressions that lead to conversions. For example, looking at Figure 7.4, let's say that I am searching for a new road bike and I use the broad keyword "road bike" as I begin my search. As I do so, I see an ad. Maybe I click it; maybe I don't. As I continue my search, I use more-specific keywords and see more ads in the process. Finally, I narrow down my choice and click an ad that catches my attention, visit the site, and convert. In each case the ad was either viewed or clicked. The last phrase resulted in an ad that was clicked and ultimately converted.

Let's start by taking a look at the Reporting And Tools tab within Google AdWords, shown in Figure 7.5. To locate your search funnel reports, you need to click the Reporting And Tools tab and then select Conversions. You will see on the left side a Search Funnels link. To see any conversion data, you will need to have already set up conversion tracking (`http://adwords.google.com/support/aw/bin/answer.py?hl=en&answer=115794`).

Once you click on the Search Funnels link, you will see a list of eight reports to view PPC conversion data and searcher activity, as seen in Figure 7.6. I will not go through them all, but I do want to outline five behavioral insights that you will find useful.

road bike	✓ saw ad (*impression*)
road bike reviews	✓ clicked ad
road bike store	✓ saw ad (*impression*)
trek madone 6 series reviews	✓ clicked ad
trek madone 6.9 ssl	✓ saw ad (*impression*)
trek madone 6.9 ssl price	✓ **clicked ad and converted**

Figure 7.4 Keywords that trigger ads

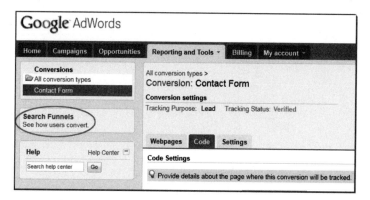

Figure 7.5 Reporting And Tools tab in Google AdWords

Figure 7.6 Search funnel options

How Many Ads Do Your Users View Before They Convert?

I remember seeing the Tootsie Pop commercial "How many licks does it take to get to the center of a lollipop?" when I was growing up. The Path Length report answers a similar question. How many ads does it take to get to a conversion? Good question—we usually don't think about the many ads that may have assisted in the conversion process.

In the example in Figure 7.7, you can see the percentage of searchers that converted after the first ad. In this case, there were 34.79 percent of users that had to see two or more ads before they converted. So if one of your conversion points is a contact form, then you would know that 34.79 percent of your visitors generally need to see more than one ad before they are ready to fill out the form.

This will provide some insight into conversion behavior but not conversions. It is up to your website, its content, and user experience to lead people to a conversion. Ads in and of themselves do not convert but can aid in the conversion process by setting the proper expectation.

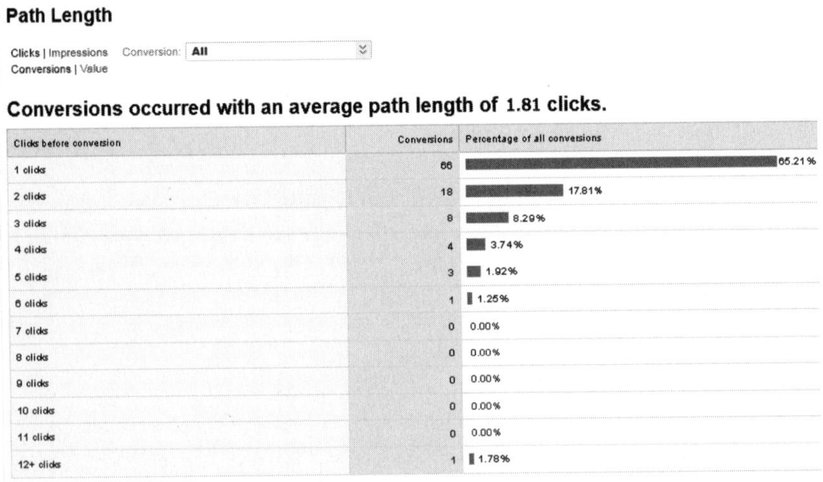

Path Length

Clicks | Impressions   Conversion: **All**
Conversions | Value

Conversions occurred with an average path length of 1.81 clicks.

Clicks before conversion	Conversions	Percentage of all conversions
1 clicks	66	65.21%
2 clicks	18	17.81%
3 clicks	8	8.29%
4 clicks	4	3.74%
5 clicks	3	1.92%
6 clicks	1	1.25%
7 clicks	0	0.00%
8 clicks	0	0.00%
9 clicks	0	0.00%
10 clicks	0	0.00%
11 clicks	0	0.00%
12+ clicks	1	1.78%

Figure 7.7 Path Length report

How Long Does It Take Before Users Convert?

Next, look at the Time Lag report, which provides data on the average amount of time it takes for users to convert. In Figure 7.8, you can see that on average, users converted within the first three days after clicking the first ad. About 69 percent converted within one day of clicking the ad.

See how this measures up to the buying cycle for your product or service. Is the click path and time length a typical conversion for your customers? Maybe it takes about three days from the time people start their research to the time a purchase decision is made. If you are not sure about this information, having this knowledge is a great place to start.

Now, if your conversion point is just a simple contact form and it takes on average three days for a conversion, then you might have a problem engaging users when they first land on your site. In this case, you should take some action to shorten the time frame.

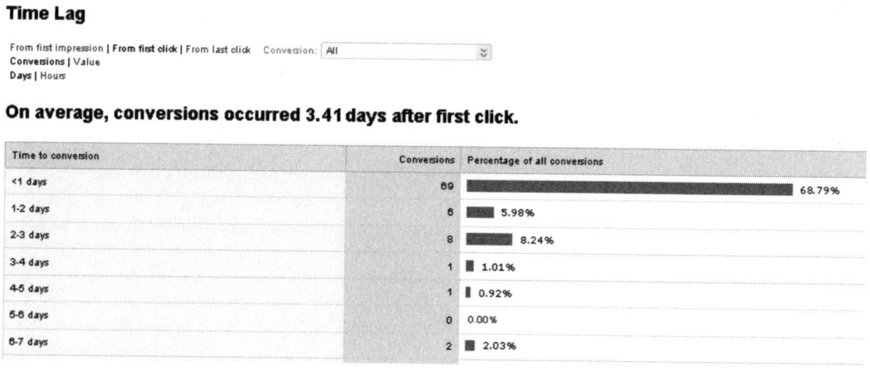

Time Lag

From first impression | **From first click** | From last click   Conversion: All ⌄
Conversions | Value
Days | Hours

On average, conversions occurred 3.41 days after first click.

Time to conversion	Conversions	Percentage of all conversions
<1 days	69	68.79%
1-2 days	6	5.98%
2-3 days	8	8.24%
3-4 days	1	1.01%
4-5 days	1	0.92%
5-6 days	0	0.00%
6-7 days	2	2.03%

Figure 7.8 Time Lag report

This information can help you better understand your buying cycle. Recall that in Chapter 2 I discussed the type of keywords that are used in each phase of the buying cycle.

What Is Your Customer's Search Process?

Tracking the actual search path your users take before a conversion can help you to learn more about your customers. For example, you can learn which keywords they used and which ads they did or did not click on. To understand this better, let's define some roles:

- The *last click* is the search and click that immediately precedes the conversion.
- An *assist* click is a search and click that precedes the last click.
- An *assist impression* is any time your ad is displayed but not clicked.

In the Assisted Conversions report (Figure 7.9), you can see the keywords and the number of last-click conversions and their associated value. It also shows you assisted conversions and their values. The assisted conversions/last-click conversion analysis gives you an indication of whether or not the keyword was more of a last-click conversion or an assisted conversion. A value closer to zero would suggest it is closer to a last-click conversion. A higher value might suggest it is closer to an assist click. This report will display both last-click and assisted conversions for each campaign, ad group, and keyword.

The insight gleaned from this report will help you understand what prospects search for before they convert. If multiple impressions and clicks are required before the desired online action is taken, then it is important to understand searchers' preconversion search process and fund the keywords that support and enable conversions.

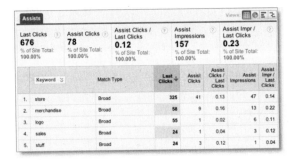

Figure 7.9 Assisted Conversions report

What Are the Most Common Paths Your Users Take to Convert?

The Top Paths report will show you how your campaigns, ad groups, and keywords work together to create conversions. If you choose Keyword in the drop-down box, you will see the most common path for keywords. If the same keyword is repeated, it represents two clicks for that keyword that then lead to a conversion. Additionally, you can view data on the campaign and ad group level. If you select keyword path or impressions, you will see the sequence of keywords that showed your ads, regardless of whether the ads were clicked or not. This data closely represents the breadth of related keywords people are searching for prior to converting.

What Are the Enabling Keywords that Support Your Conversions?

Specifically, look for keywords that assist with conversions but may not convert themselves. Without the benefit of the search funnel reports, you might neglect these keywords and underfund them because you don't know how they impact overall conversions.

In addition to using your top converting keywords, focusing on keywords and phrases that assist with conversions can differentiate your PPC strategy and provide a strategic advantage.

In many industries, these less-obvious words are much less expensive than the well-known top converting words.

As with any report, I recommend scheduling a consistent time at least once a month to review these reports so you can take advantage of the insight they bring. To review:

- Understand your customers' search process.
- Identify conversion-enabling keywords and fund appropriately.
- Reduce overall click costs from PPC campaigns.
- Get an edge on the competition.
- Learn about all of the factors that contribute to ROI, not just last click (or immediate) conversions.

Summary

As with SEO, keyword research has been closely tied to building PPC campaigns and is a critical tool in helping you find the right terms to make your campaign a success. With your list of keywords that have been categorized and segmented, you are well on your way to developing highly relevant ad groups and text ads that are associated with your keywords.

By using the tips in this chapter, you can build a solid, effective campaign that will bring you results. Additionally, search funnel and other reports can offer valuable insight into searcher behavior and the necessary information you need to make the right adjustments, which will lead to an even better campaign.

Using Keywords for Social Media

8

In this chapter you will learn about developing a social media strategy that incorporates your targeted keywords. You will also learn how to find keywords and use them for many social media sites, including YouTube, Twitter, Facebook, and blogs.

Chapter Contents

Role of Keywords and Social Media

Many people will agree that keyword research is important for SEO and PPC, but many fail to recognize that it can be highly effective for social media marketing as well. I established in Chapter 4 that social media can be a tool for finding keywords your audience is using. Before you actively participate in social media conversations, you should understand more about your audience and the keywords they are using.

Keyword research will specifically help you learn more about the needs and wants of social communities in several ways:

- Gauging interest for products and services
- Gaining better insight of user intent
- Tracking relevant topics that are trending
- Discovering which keywords are used most often
- Learning relevant points of engagement
- Understanding the sentiment of keywords

Social media is all about the message or conversation. The insights gained from keyword research will help you construct and communicate your message more effectively. Applying this insight to your social media campaigns and optimization efforts will greatly enhance your performance whether you are tagging, tweeting, or bookmarking.

One thing to understand is that the keyword research you have done for SEO and PPC might not translate directly to your social media marketing efforts. There are some differences you need to be aware of:

Behavioral differences Search queries on social media sites are different from search engines like Google and Bing. In fact, there are even differences among social media sites. Searcher behavior on photo sharing sites is going to be different from searches on Twitter, for example, partly because of the medium. Photo sharing sites are visual, while tweets are short, concise micro-statements.

Search query variances Just because your keyword has a high search volume on Google doesn't mean it has the same volume on Facebook. Each social media site will likely have a different volume of popular search terms.

Query and conversations We are accustomed to using a search query with search engines, but social media is more conversational. Users make their queries in a more conversational way, like asking a question. Learn to find these conversational queries. This will help you better develop your message to meet user expectations.

With that said, your approach to keyword research for social media needs to be slightly different, even from one social media site to another. Before I get into methods for performing keyword research for social media, I will define what it is and how to build a solid strategy. This will help put keyword research for social media into better context.

What Is Social Media?

With a plethora of social media sites coming and going, it is hard to put your finger on just what social media is. I define it as groups of online media sites where people are talking, participating, sharing, networking, and bookmarking. Most social media sites encourage discussion, feedback, voting, comments, and the sharing of information from all interested parties. It is a two-way conversation rather than the one-way broadcast of traditional media. Another unique aspect of social media is the idea of staying connected or linked to other sites, resources, and people.

It used to be that companies and organizations controlled the message they conveyed. With social media, control has shifted to the masses. Remember reading on product packages, "If you have any questions or concerns, please send a letter with a self-addressed envelope to…" We wouldn't dream of doing that today with all of the social media tools that are available. We now have a voice to express ourselves and our comments and opinions.

Organizations have to be on their guard and increase customer support. I have heard many stories of companies under fire because they did not support their customers well and they were slammed on social media sites. The viral effect of this medium acted as judge, jury, and executioner for businesses who failed to meet customers' needs.

Social media essentially takes the water cooler conversations that have already been going on for ages and puts them online for everyone to read and react to. Tapping into this massive conversation and leveraging it for your organization is imperative for success in today's world. Even if you don't actively participate in the conversation, you should at least use social media to "listen in" to what people are saying about you and your company.

So what are all of these social media sites and how does it all work? Many social media sites come in the form of a blog, microblog, podcast, videocast, forum, wiki, or some kind of content community. To help you understand social media better, I will break them down into four basic groups: social news, social sharing, social networks, and social bookmarking.

Social News

Sites like Digg (http://digg.com), Sphinn (www.sphinn.com), and Newsvine (www.newsvine.com) let you read about news topics and then vote and/or comment on the articles. The articles with the most votes get promoted to a prominent position.

In the past, we would read news articles and simply take them at face value. We may have commented on the article with others offline, but social media has changed the rules. No longer are we subjected to just the authors' opinions and views; with social media, the readers can participate and chime in with their thoughts and comments.

Many of these articles are centered on a theme or keyword phrases that are popular one day and old news the next. You may see what are known as *tag clouds* that emphasize keywords that are trending upward and other phrases that are being discussed but may not be as popular. Figure 8.1 shows a simple tag cloud that displays the top 50 trends of all time from TweetStats. You may also have noticed the tag cloud on the cover of this book. Examining a tag cloud can quickly help you know what keyword phrases are more popular than others at the moment. Most sites will allow you to click a keyword within the tag cloud to see tweets and posts related to it.

Top 50 Trends of All Time

Adam Lambert American Idol Apple AT&T Avatar Christmas Easter #ff Follow Friday #followfriday #Gaza Glee Goodnight Google Wave H1N1 Haiti Halloween Harry Potter #iDoit2 Inception iPhone #iranelection Jay-Z Justin Bieber McCain Michael Jackson #mm #musicmonday New Moon #nowplaying Obama #omgfacts Paranormal Activity Rebecca Black Santa Sarah Palin Shorty Award SNL Snow Leopard Star Trek Susan Boyle Swine Flu #SxSW #tcot TGIF Thanksgiving Tweetdeck Twilight #worldcup Xmas

Figure 8.1 Tag cloud

Social Sharing

Sites like Flikr (www.flickr.com), Snapfish (www.snapfish.com), YouTube (www.youtube.com), and Metacafe (www.metacafe.com) let you create, upload, and share content with others. Most of this shared content is either photos or video.

People love to see images and video, and these engagement objects are extremely viral in nature. Because it is not as straightforward to derive any keywords from these two media, it is imperative that images and video are tagged properly with descriptive keywords. This will help them be indexed and then found by others. Most social sharing sites offer methods to tag your media with relevant keywords. Make sure you use them.

Some sites, such as YouTube, even provide keyword tools to help you learn what keywords people are using to find video and images. I will discuss this tool later on in the chapter.

Social Networks

Sites like Facebook (www.facebook.com), LinkedIn (www.linkedin.com), Twitter (www.twitter.com), and Google+ allow you to find and link to other people. You can follow and be followed. Once you're linked to a person, you can keep up-to-date with that person's contact info, interests, posts, and so on. Many people are reconnecting with friends and business associates with whom they have fallen out of touch.

Facebook is more of a general social network used for sharing with friends and family. It is finding its way into business relationships as well. LinkedIn is primarily for business connections and for following other companies. The new kid on the block is Google+, which launched early in 2011. Its unique offering is to allow you to make connections and label them as friend, business, or family or use another label, which is a truly innovative idea.

The number of conversations taking place on these platforms is growing exponentially as more and more people are becoming involved. One of the greatest aspects of social networks is the ability to monitor the interactions and conversations. Many of these platforms have search functionality that allows you to isolate specific posts or conversations in real time.

Also, many people tag their conversations with keywords to help readers focus in on the core idea of their message. I will discuss this more in the section on Twitter.

Social Bookmarking

Sites like Delicious (www.delicious.com), Faves (http://faves.com), StumbleUpon (www.stumbleupon.com), and Diigo (www.diigo.com) allow you to find and bookmark sites and information of interest. You can save your bookmarks online and access them from anywhere or share them with others.

Sometimes you may be interested in or may be looking for something and you just cannot think of the right search query to use on a search engine. By following others with interests similar to yours, you may run into content that you otherwise would not easily find.

Social bookmarking sites are great for following people who resemble members of your target audience so you can gain insight into their needs and wants and what interests them. These sites can also be helpful sites as you research personas.

New social media sites are springing up every day, and breaking them down into these categories will help you understand how they fit into your social media marketing plans.

Benefits of Social Media

Let's first look at the general scope of the social media universe. Did you know that out of the top ten fastest-growing web brands, five of them are user-generated content sites? Also, 67 percent of consumers say that the best source for advice on products and services are other consumers. Forty-five percent of adult Internet users have created content online, according to eMarketer.

So if you could tap into this ever-growing universe of social media, do you think it would benefit you? Absolutely! In fact, many companies today are trying to figure out how to get involved. They are shifting money from traditional marketing budgets to social media marketing. Here are some reasons why:

- It can help to manage company or brand reputation.
- It can be used to build brand awareness.
- It can help you get closer to customers by learning about their needs and responding through discussion, conversation, and debate.
- It provides creative and effective ways to gain insights not previously available.
- Customer support can be provided using new and inexpensive methods.

- It's typically less expensive than traditional forms of advertising.
- It can be measured in various ways to track performance.

As you can see there, are many benefits to adding social media to your marketing mix, and you should learn how to leverage them all. As you do so, you will be able to add a whole new dimension to your business.

Now that you have a basic understanding of social media marketing and its associated benefits, the next step is to learn more about building your own social media strategy.

Social Media Strategy

As I just illustrated, there are many benefits to adding social media to your marketing mix. Many companies are simply unsure of where to start or how to develop a plan. Social media is useful for many types of organizations, whether they are national brands or small businesses. By using social media correctly, you can engage your audience in new ways, be more personable, develop new connections, and maintain the ones you have.

The first point to make here is that you have to think of social media differently than traditional advertising. The traditional approach is to research your target audience and understand their demographic profile. From there, you can discover what TV shows they are likely to watch, magazines they typically read, and so on. You can then customize your messages and advertisements, push them out there, and hope to make an impression.

Being involved in social media is like walking into a large room with many people. You see people in different groups listening or participating in a conversations. As you walk by, you listen to what they are saying and decide if you want to join them or move on to the next group. Once you find a group that is discussing something that interests you, you join in. After you gather enough information about the topic, you add your own contribution to the discussion, which can influence the course it takes. Later on you might be so bold as to start your own conversation around a different topic and draw people into your group.

One of the keys to drawing people to you is to have smart, fun, and relevant content. Content should include keywords. This should be at the core of any social media strategy. Great content should reflect your brand and give people a reason to stay engaged.

I will outline the development of a social media strategy with these six steps, summarized in Figure 8.2:

1. Listen in on the conversation (conversation mining).
2. Identify or refine your goals based on what you learn.
3. Develop your plan and time your content.
4. Develop your content.
5. Engage in the conversation.
6. Measure success.

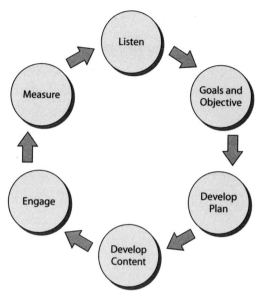

Figure 8.2 Social media strategy

1. Listen

One way to begin developing a plan or strategy is to get out there and listen to what is being said. I call this *conversation mining*. How are people feeling about you and your brand? What are their points of view? Identify the key people who influence others. What topics are they discussing? Is the tone of the conversation heated? Do people favor one point of view over the other, or is it mixed?

The first step to take before you start developing a strategy is to simply listen. Determine your audience and where they are online. Blogs are great places to start looking. Technorati (`http://technorati.com`) is a good tool to help you search for blogs and blog posts that have content related to your niche. Twitter and the Twitter network is another great place to gain insight into conversations that are happening in real time. The advanced Twitter search (`http:search.twitter.com/advanced`) is one of many tools that will let you isolate specific conversations and monitor them. I will go into this in more detail later in the chapter.

Once you have identified where your audience is, listen to what they are saying. What are their issues, opinions, and needs? How does this information fit with your value proposition? Understanding this information will help you determine how to best contribute to the conversation.

Next, find out who is driving the conversation or who has a strong influence? These people are called *influencers* because people respect them and they possess the authority or experience to shape opinions. A good example is Lance Armstrong. Since I am a cyclist, I follow what he has to say. If he endorses a product, you can be sure I will check it out. Find the people who influence your industry or niche. They are not necessarily the most popular people, but maybe they are the ones that are the most vocal online. As you follow these influencers, you can learn much from what they are saying. To find influencers on Twitter, look at WeFollow (www.wefollow.com). WeFollow breaks down influencers by category and lists them by the number of followers they have.

2. Identify Goals and Objectives

You should now be in a better position to establish some goals. You may already have some goals for what you want to accomplish, but you may need to refine them based on your "listening" exercise.

An important point to make here is that you need to consider not only your company goals but the goals of your audience. You will get much farther with social media marketing if you offer something of value. I see many people who are simply promoting themselves, hoping they will attract new customers or site traffic. This really doesn't work well with social media. One of your goals should be to identify what you can offer of value to your followers. It could be links to relevant articles, tips, white papers, coupon codes, and so on.

Once you have given people something of value, you have earned the right to plug yourself a little. I recommend that you spend about 90 percent of your time providing value and 10 percent promoting yourself. This may differ slightly within your own industry, but you will find that you can build more influence by providing value than you can by just promoting yourself.

3. Develop Your Plan and Time Your Content

In this step you map out your approach to delivering your products or services to satisfy the needs of your audience. Will you reach out and leverage influencers? Will you provide free material or samples? How will it be delivered? Maybe you have products that are environmentally friendly. Will you moderate and lead a conversation about environmental issues? There are many creative ways to approach your audience. Be innovative.

The next part in developing your plan is to create a 12-month timeline and identify any events, promotions, or product launches that you are aware of. Now identify the content you want to deliver that can supplement those events. Look for opportunities to reuse assets each period or year as you obtain new followers who may not have been exposed to it previously.

Consider it as kind of a media plan where you are timing your efforts so they are consistent and relevant. You will find that it will be much easier to manage content creation efforts with this method and allow you to plan ahead.

Another aspect of developing your plan is to pick the right social media platform. Is Facebook the right platform for you? Is it a combination of social media sites? If so, you should develop a mini plan for each site and decide how you will consistently use each site to accomplish your goals and objectives. Be careful not to go after too many sites too quickly. Make sure you start with one or two sites at a time so they are firmly planted and grow as you intend them to.

Pace yourself so you have time to produce quality content that will engage your readers.

As I discussed in Chapter 2, reach out to your team and delegate to others. I recommend having a solid social media policy in place before you do this so your team members know how much latitude they have to respond and interact with others. There may be some issues that need to be dealt with at a higher level, and that should be clearly defined.

A good social media policy will outline the dos and don'ts for those who are speaking on the organization's behalf. You may have designated employees to monitor social conversations and react to them quickly. Since they are speaking on behalf of the company, your policy will act as a guideline so they do not overstep their bounds. If there are sensitive or legal issues, for instance, they should be taken to legal counsel or a supervisor before a response is given.

4. Develop Your Content

The next step is to develop the content you have outlined for your timeline. This is where you really need to understand your audience and your brand. You need to be highly creative, and much of what you say within social media channels should reflect what you want your brand to represent. A great example is Skittles, which does this very well. Look at some of the comments in Figure 8.3. I've seen some of the status messages attract more than 1,000 comments, and over 8,000 likes on Facebook.

Skittles
What's the weirdest place you've ever eaten Skittles? Post a pic!
Yesterday at 12:00pm via The Rainbow

👍 1,563 people like this.

💬 View all 871 comments

Skittles
I wish that screech owl would use his inside screech.
Sunday at 12:00pm via The Rainbow

👍 8,682 people like this.

💬 View all 515 comments

Skittles
My computer is out practicing jump shots. I think it's tired of just beating me at chess.
Saturday at 12:00pm via The Rainbow

👍 8,095 people like this.

💬 View all 583 comments

Skittles
Writing an autobiography of the Rainbow. What should the title be?
April 29 at 4:00pm via The Rainbow

👍 6,039 people like this.

💬 View all 3,680 comments

Figure 8.3 Skittle Facebook posts

This content is successful because of the way it is written. The posts are like the candy, which is colorful, playful, and imaginative. The brief, daily observations are very creative and interesting. People enjoy each bite-sized posts just as they enjoy Skittles candy.

Facebook and other social media sites are great places to optimize your content with your targeted keywords. Armed with a solid keyword research report with relative categories, you should be able to derive some great ideas for content that is relevant and will resonate well with your audience. This content can come in various forms. Here are a few ideas:

- Promotions with deals for participants, daily deals
- Tips or how-tos
- Little-known facts or factoids
- White papers
- Relevant and timely statistics
- Community polls
- Guest authors
- Top ten lists
- Case studies
- Guides to help educate
- Interviews
- Live events
- News
- Opinions
- Photos
- Gift ideas

It doesn't take much if you have a good plan. Again, make sure you leverage your targeted keywords as appropriate. This will help you build your brand around messaging that will be associated with it, which is invaluable.

5. Engage

Armed with smart objectives, a solid timeline, great content, and the right social media sites, you are now ready to post your content. Engage in the conversation and ignite a debate or express your point of view. As you become a proactive participant, it is important that you invest the time to keep the conversation going. Social media marketing is not something to get involved in for the short term. You should make sure you have the resources and time available before you begin.

You may be taking a passive approach to social media and have just developed a reputation management plan to listen in and respond to situations. This is a viable strategy, especially for building your brand and your customer service function. I developed this strategy with one of my clients. We were monitoring branded keywords and were alerted whenever a tweet or post came up using that keyword.

We would reach out to these individuals with thanks for positive comments. In some cases, the comments were negative. I remember one instance where a customer had a problem with a late shipment. They vented online as we all like to do. We reached out to them and apologized for the inconvenience and helped to expedite the shipment. They were blown away that we were not only listening but proactively helped them. They became a wonderful advocate for my client's company and began tweeting their praises.

6. Measure

As you know, the ability to measure the effectiveness of marketing activities is imperative to any company's marketing strategy. Measuring social media marketing isn't straightforward, but it can be done with the right tools and mindset.

You might look at content consumption. Who is reading your content and where are they coming from? You can also look at how much or how little is being contributed and the number of visitors who are interacting with your content.

Here are some of the social media metrics you should be looking out for:

- Share of voice and sentiment
- Awareness
- Engagement
- Influence
- Popularity

Share of Voice and Sentiment

In social media, share of voice refers to the number of conversations about your brand versus your competitors or your market. You will want to use a monitoring program that can assist you in keeping track of all mentions of your brand and your competitors' brands over a given time period. Make sure you track positive, negative, and neutral sentiment. Then you can assign a weight to each of these categories and calculate your average sentiment.

It's good to track your share of voice and sentiment over time so you can see how your social engagement and promotions are affecting your overall trends. Also, if your sentiment/share of voice jumps or drops suddenly, you will want to investigate why and act accordingly.

Radian6 (www.radian6.com) and Social Mention (www.socialmention.com) are excellent social media tools that can help you measure share of voice and sentiment. Let's look at an example of how you can measure both of these with Social Mention.

On the Social Mention site, type your company name in quotes ("organization name") and click Search. Make sure you select All from the options above the search box. This will make sure you are getting only exact, relevant matches. For this example, I will analyze the top fast food burger chains.

On the results page, you can see the total number of mentions at the top right, as shown in Figure 8.4. In this case, there are 353 mentions. You can adjust the date range if you like. You should then scan through the mentions to get a feel for what is being said and by whom. This will help you put the mentions in proper context.

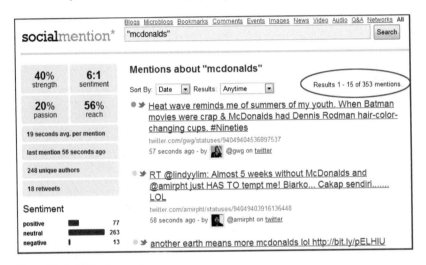

Figure 8.4 Social Mention report

Now look at the sentiment data in the chart on the left. You will see positive, neutral, and negative sentiment. If you add these up, it will equal the total mentions.

Open up a spreadsheet and enter each of these numbers as I have done (Figure 8.5). Then do a search on each of the competitors you are tracking. Record the same numbers in the spreadsheet for each competitor.

Now add up the positive and neutral mentions for each company and divide by the total number of mentions. So for McDonald's, I would add 77 + 263, which is 340. Now divide this by 1,723 to get 19.73 percent. This is the share of voice for McDonald's. So here is the formula:

(positive mentions) + (neutral mentions) / (total mentions for all companies-

To get the average sentiment, I will use a 5-point scale with positive = 5, neutral = 3, and negative = 1. For each type of mention, multiply by the scale number and divide by the total number of mentions. So for McDonald's, the calculation would be $(77 \times 5) + (263 \times 3) + (13 \times 1) / 353 = 3.36$. Do this for each company to get the average sentiment. Here is the formula:

(positive mentions $\times$ 5) + (neutral mentions $\times$ 3) + (negative sentiment $\times$ 1) / total company mentions

Now, in your spreadsheet select the organization column and the share of voice column and insert a pie chart to get a nice graph you can show your boss.

Mentions

Organization	Positive	Neutral	Negative	Total	Share of Voice	Avg. Sentiment	Type	Weight
McDonalds	77	263	13	353	19.73%	3.36	Positive	5
Burger King	52	263	20	335	18.28%	3.19	Neutral	3
Wendy's	37	128	10	175	9.58%	3.31	Negative	1
Hardees	70	219	19	308	16.77%	3.33		
In-N-Out	59	213	6	278	15.79%	3.38		
5 Guys	46	212	16	274	14.97%	3.22		
Total Mentions	**341**	**1298**	**84**	**1723**				

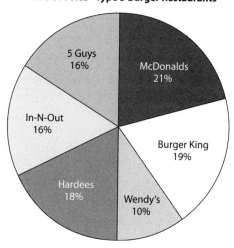

Share of Voice - Type 5 Burger Restaurants

Figure 8.5 Share of Voice report

Awareness

Building brand awareness should be one of your goals for social media. As you begin your campaign you might be starting from scratch, and it takes time to build awareness. Once you do, you'll get some traction and begin moving forward, and it will begin to accelerate. You need to be able to measure this trend and keep track of your progress. While there are no perfect and direct ways to measure increases in brand awareness, there are some signals you can observe that can give you some ideas of your brand awareness:

- Amount of website traffic/site visits/page views
- Number of searches for brand keyword terms
- Video and content views
- Number of followers

Engagement

Engagement is the extent to which people interact with you and your content. Engagement shows that people are interested in what you are offering and are interested enough to participate. Measuring engagement is important so you can see how much and how often users participate with your content. Look for the following signs of engagement:

- Likes (of a Facebook page and of your content)
- Shares
- Mentions (positive, negative, neutral)
- Blog comments
- Ratings
- Retweets

Influence

Influence is the likelihood that what you're doing is inspiring action from followers. Being able to measure influence tells you to what degree you are able to motivate people to action. Here are some signals of influence:

- Number of (and quality of) inbound links to your content
- Twitter links that are retweeted or commented on
- Facebook posts that are commented on and liked
- Content that is shared/liked (and to what extent)

Popularity

Online popularity is basically the number of people that subscribe to your content. Some say the quality of your following is more important than the quantity. That holds true to some extent, but if you're looking for advertisers or sponsors, you will have more luck having 12,000 followers on Twitter than 800. This is some of the information you can use to measure social media popularity:

- Number of RSS/email subscribers
- Number of followers on Twitter
- Number of members of a LinkedIn group
- Number of people who like your Facebook page

Social Media Monitoring Tools

If you are looking for a tool to help you in your measuring efforts, there are several to choose from. Tools you need to buy include Lithium (www.lithium.com), Radian6 (www.radian6.com), and Trackur (www.trackur.com). Free tools include Social Mention (http://socialmention.com) and of course Google Analytics (http://analytics.google.com) for seeing where visitors are coming from. These tools can also help with step 1, researching and listening.

Measuring can be a challenge because the medium is conversational in nature. You can measure the number of followers or those who are participating in the conversation. You can measure web traffic increases due to your social media efforts. You might gauge the tone of the conversation and what percentage of participants was influenced by your involvement. Whatever mechanism you use to measure, be sure you do it often. Pick a time to do this regularly and stick with it.

Social Media Keyword Research Tools

Now that you are grounded in the basics of social media with an understanding of the role keywords play and are versed in the six steps for developing a social media strategy, we are ready to take a closer look at keyword tools directly related to social media at these social media sites:

- YouTube
- Twitter
- Facebook
- Blogs

Before we begin, let's consider the basis on how these tools work. Each social media site has its own network of conversations and interactions. Twitter, for instance, is a vast network of mini messages flying around in real time. The unique thing about Twitter, though, is that there are many applications that can tap into this network. Facebook, on the other hand, has its own network that is self-contained and is generally accessed through its own tools.

I don't have the space to go all of the many sites and tools that are out there. So for a comprehensive, updated list of these tools, please visit this book's site at www.keywordintelligencebook.com.

Keyword Research for YouTube

Using videos is increasingly one of the fastest and most popular ways to connect with your audience online. There are many video sharing sites, but YouTube is really the largest. It is even challenging Google as the second largest search engine in the United States. For marketers, the goal of researching keywords for YouTube and online video marketing is to determine three things:

- How users are searching
- Which search queries are more popular
- The best ways to get your content found

YouTube has two tools that can help you as you conduct keyword research specific to video marketing: YouTube Suggest and the YouTube Keyword tool.

YouTube Suggest is a keyword suggestion tool similar to the Google suggest tool. It has an enhanced search function that uses a predictive model to display popular search queries in the YouTube search box, which is available on all pages within YouTube, as seen in Figure 8.6.

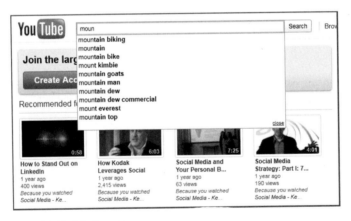

Figure 8.6 YouTube Suggest

YouTube also has a rather robust keyword tool (https://ads.youtube.com/keyword_tool) that can be used to research keyword use on its site. It is closely related to the Google Keyword Tool in appearance and functionality, as seen in Figure 8.7.

You have the option of beginning your search by using descriptive words or phrases, a YouTube video ID or URL, or demographic information. If you use the first choice, you should enter a seed keyword phrase. Remember, when using video and images, people tend to use longer, more-descriptive phrases rather than shorter ones. Instead of "sea kayaking", they may use "sea kayaking with Orcas in the San Juan Islands".

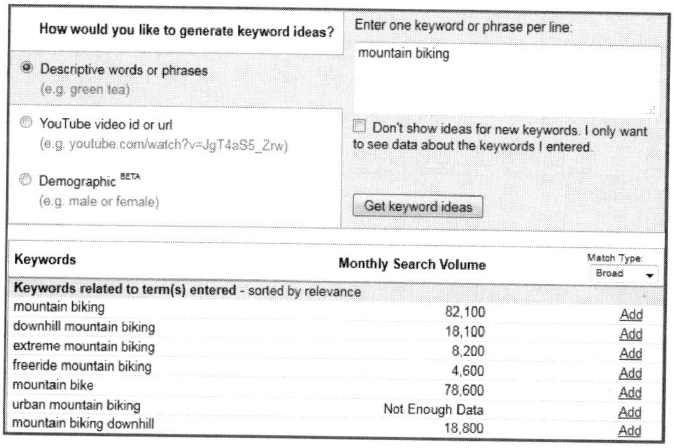

Figure 8.7 YouTube Keyword suggest

Keyword results are sorted by relevance and offer monthly search volume. The demographic choice is actually quite interesting. You check off the demographic modifiers like male, female, age range, region, and even topical interests. Then you get results for that segment. This can be a great tool for grouping keywords around specific categories.

By using these two tools, you will gain insight into keyword popularity and frequency on YouTube. The keyword suggestions can of course be integrated into your video optimization efforts. Remember that to do this properly you should place these keywords into the title of the video, the tags, the video description, and any associated relevant links.

Keyword Research for Twitter

Twitter has emerged as a major force in the social networking space, and marketers who ignore Twitter as a viable channel do so at their own peril. The amount of content generated by Twitter users on a minute-by-minute basis is staggering. It makes Twitter a powerful tool to help marketers not only listen in on this growing conversation in real time, but also to engage. It also provides another platform in which to perform keyword research. And given Google's recent move to integrate tweets into real-time, blended search results, marketers who leverage Twitter for keyword research effectively will gain even more visibility for their landing pages.

What Is Twitter?

Before I get into the specifics of keyword research for Twitter I would like to review what Twitter is, what its benefits are, and how to use it. Twitter (`www.twitter.com`) is a social networking tool that lets users send out short messages, or *tweets*, that are picked up and read by friends or followers. It is also referred to as *microblogging*. I like the idea of limiting your message to 140 characters because it forces you to be succinct and to the point, as in headlines.

There are several benefits to using Twitter. To understand the benefits of Twitter, you need to go beyond just looking at the Twitter site, which is a little limited on features. You need to think more of the network of conversations, or tweets, that are happening in real time. Twitter.com and other sites allow you to tap into this network and leverage it for the following tasks:

- Personal promotion and broadcasting
- Business promotion and broadcasting
- Reputation/brand monitoring
- Competition monitoring
- Event monitoring
- Information gathering/research

If you decide to use Twitter for more than just monitoring and start tweeting, think about your conversation and how you can provide your followers with value. You are basically building relationships, and to do so you need to give before you receive. People like things like tips, statistics, opinions, and links to relevant articles.

Managing your tweets from Twitter.com can be a challenge. As a matter of fact, when I first started using Twitter, I was unimpressed with the tools and capabilities offered on the Twitter.com site. Most of us like to use an application like Microsoft Word that is self-contained and has all of the tools built in. With Twitter it is just the reverse. Twitter's strength lies in utilizing many external tools and applications, each with its unique approach to enhancing your Twitter experience.

The first tool I would like to share with you is TweetDeck (`www.tweetdeck.com`), which was recently purchased by Twitter. This application allows you to view all of your friends' tweets in a columned interface, as shown in Figure 8.8. The neat thing about TweetDeck is that you can group your friends into themed columns. Looking at just one column of "all" of your friends' tweets can be overwhelming. I like to create a column (or group) for what I call search-related tweets, one for specific influencers, and one to track tweets relating to keyword research.

If you are an iPhone user or have a smart phone with access to the Internet, you are in luck. There are several tools that will help you follow your tweets while you are on the road. There are even widgets (Mac OS), sidebars (Windows OS), and other kinds of tools you can use. You'll find a list of all of these tools on the Twitter applications page (http://twitter.com/downloads).

Figure 8.8 TweetDeck interface

Once you are set up, one of the first things to do is to find people to follow. A good place to start is on search.twitter.com. On this page you can find people you might want to follow or search for by topic, or you can find a company. Another useful site is WeFollow (www.wefollow.com), and Twellow (www.twellow.com) that will display influencers by category and number of followers.

Understanding Twitter Lingo

Now that I have armed you with tools to get up and running, let me review some simple terms that you will need to know. When I first started looking at tweets, it seemed as if everyone was speaking in some sort of code. Once I learned the lingo it all made more sense. Let's demystify some of the most common signs:

@ If you want to "talk" directly to someone and let everyone see your tweet, you will use the @ sign. For instance, if you were to send me a tweet, it would look like "@ ron_jones thanks for book on keyword intelligence."

RT The RT is short for *retweet*. If you are reading your tweets and find one that you would like to share with your followers, you would put an "RT @username:" in front of the tweet and then send it on. This lets people know who originally started the tweet and in a manner of speaking gives them the credit. It is a good practice to retweet often. Tools like TweetDeck provide simple options to help you retweet. One thing to remember is that when you retweet, you add more characters to your tweet, so you might need to shorten it to make it fit into the 140-character limit.

A word preceded by the number sign is called a hashtag and is used to label parts of your message. For instance, Search Engine Strategies (SES) designates "sesny" to be the official hashtag for its conference in NY. Everyone who tweets during the conference places #sesny somewhere in their tweet. So if you wanted to keep up with the specifics of the event in real time, you could just do a search on "sesny" and you would display all of the tweets related to that conference. Or, maybe you are tuning in to *American Idol* and would like to monitor real-time tweets about everyone's opinion about Idol contestants or even the judges. Just search for the hashtag #idol.

DM This stands for *direct message*, which is the Twitter equivalent to email. You can only send direct messages to your followers. If you want to automatically set up direct messages to thank people for following you, there is a free tool called Social Oomph (www.socialoomph.com).

Tools for Using Twitter and for Keyword Research

There is an endless assortment of web applications and listening tools that can help marketers conduct keyword research for Twitter by tracking popular hashtags, trending Twitter topics and eavesdropping on conversations. Here are some of my favorite sources for Twitter keyword research:

TweetBeep (www.tweetbeep.com) TweetBeep is a tool that allows you keep track of any keyword mentioned on Twitter. You basically set up the keywords you want to track and TweetBeep will send you any tweets that include your keyword set. This is great for reputation management, keyword research, and competition analysis.

Hashtags.org (http://hashtags.org) Hashtags.org provides graphs on Twitter #hashtags and hashtag use; find the most popular and newest hashtags people are using, especially around events and trending topics.

Twitter Advanced Search (http://search.twitter.com/advanced) Twitter Advanced Search is a great tool for accessing all of the real-time conversations, or tweets, that are within the Twitter network, as you can see in Figure 8.9. You can find tweets based on the following variables:

- Words (in more than a dozen languages)
- People (from, to, or referencing people of interest)
- Places (near a place or within an X mile radius)
- Dates (since or until a date)
- Attitudes (positive, negative, or asking a question)

The first three are specific to keyword research since any of these variables can be keywords or search queries. It will help you isolate any of these keywords used in real-time tweets and track the hottest trends. You can click on the stream to pull up a feed of the public conversation.

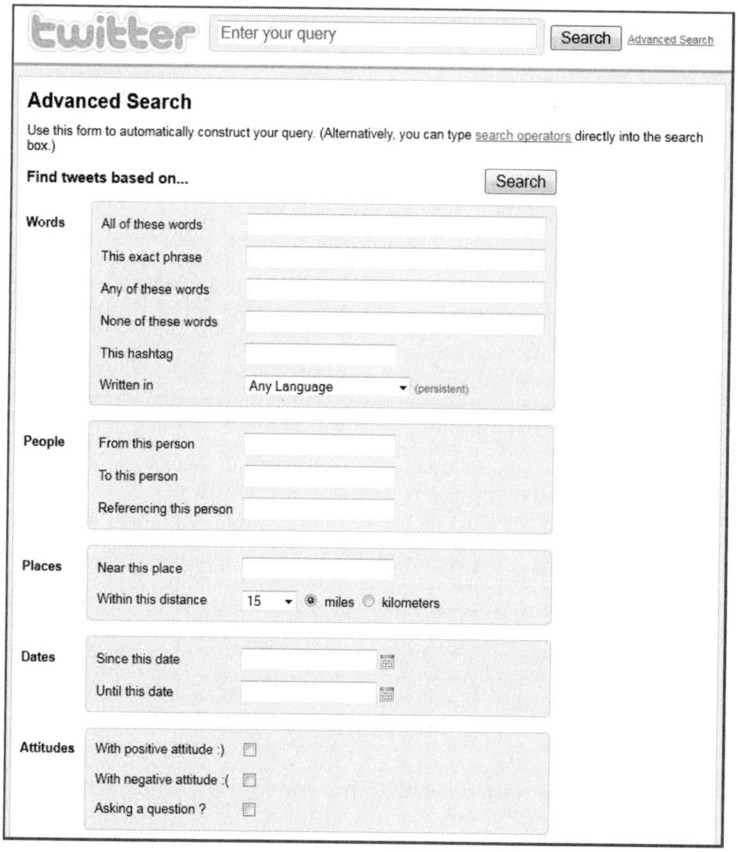

Figure 8.9 Twitter Advanced Search

Trendistic (http://Trendistic.com) **and TwitScoop** (http://www.twitscoop.com) Trendistic and TwitScoop are tools that will show you trending keywords on Twitter in real time.

TweetVolume (http://tweetvolume.com) TweetVolume allows you to enter your keywords and see how often they appear on Twitter.

Twazzup (http://www.twazzup.com) Twazzup is another tool for analyzing twitter buzz around specific search queries. It will display not only relevant tweets but also news, live pictures, top links, highlights, and influencers.

Tweet QA (http://www.tweetqa.com) Tweet QA is similar to the other twitter tools but it focuses on question- and answer-related tweets. Many people are asking questions and others are providing answers. This is a great tool for mining those threads.

Social Mention (http://socialmention.com) Social Mention, as I have already shown, is a great tool for measuring share of voice and sentiment, but it is also a great tool for monitoring Twitter traffic and Facebook. The nice thing about Social Mention is that it tracks top keywords based on your search query, as seen in Figure 8.10.

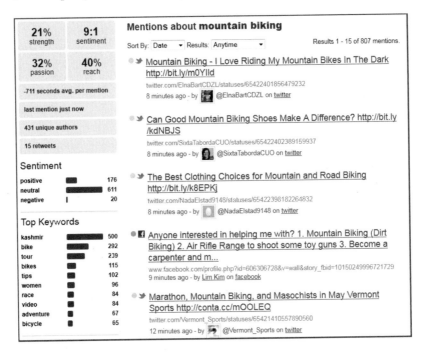

Figure 8.10 Social Mention

These are just a few of the tools available to tap into Twitter and the many real-time tweets happening every second of every day. For a comprehensive and updated list of these tools, please visit www.keywordintelligencebook.com.

As Twitter continues to grow in popularity and relevance, marketers need to pay careful attention to trends and data to find out what people are talking about and what questions they're asking and to figure out where their brand and business fits into the conversation.

Keyword Research for Facebook

Facebook is continuing to increase and has even managed to push out Google as the top visited website according to Hitwise (www.hitwise.com/us/datacenter/main /dashboard-10133.html), as shown in Figure 8.11. So as a marketer you should be finding ways to leverage this channel if you haven't already.

Top 10 Websites

Top 10 visited US websites

The following report shows **websites** for the industry 'All Categories', ranked by **Visits** for the **week** ending 07/02/2011.

Rank	Website	Visits Share
1.	Facebook	11.03%
2.	Google	9.53%
3.	YouTube	4.07%
4.	Yahoo!	2.94%
5.	Yahoo! Mail	2.33%
6.	Bing	2.05%
7.	Windows Live Mail	1.20%
8.	msn	1.19%
9.	Yahoo! Search	1.17%
10.	Gmail	0.88%

Top 10 visited Real Estate sites

The following report shows **websites** for the industry 'Business - Real Estate', ranked by **Visits** for the **week** ending 07/02/2011

Rank	Website	Visits Share
1.	Yahoo! Real Estate	8.52%
2.	Realtor.com	7.42%
3.	Zillow	5.47%
4.	Trulia.com	4.93%
5.	AOL Real Estate	2.72%
6.	Homes.com	2.40%
7.	Rent.com	2.30%
8.	Apartment Guide	1.67%
9.	ZipRealty	1.35%
10.	Apartments.com	1.34%

Top 10 Travel Websites

The following report shows **websites** for the industry 'Travel', ranked by **Visits** for the **week** ending 07/02/2011.

Rank	Website	Visits Share
1.	Google Maps	18.74%
2.	MapQuest	6.35%
3.	Expedia	2.81%
4.	priceline.com	2.12%
5.	TripAdvisor	2.01%
6.	Southwest Airlines	1.84%
7.	Yahoo! Travel	1.61%
8.	Yahoo! Maps	1.52%
9.	Bing maps	1.50%
10.	Orbitz	1.40%

Top 10 Social Networking sites

The following report shows **websites** for the industry 'Social Networking & Forums', ranked by **Visits** for **week** ending 07/02/2011.

Rank	Website	Visits Share
1.	Facebook	61.08%
2.	YouTube	22.51%
3.	Meebo	1.73%
4.	Twitter	1.33%
5.	MySpace	0.98%
6.	Yahoo! Answers	0.92%
7.	Tagged	0.66%
8.	myYearbook	0.43%
9.	CafeMom	0.36%
10.	Linkedin	0.31%

Figure 8.11 Top 10 Websites according to Hitwise

Like Twitter, it represents a vast network of individuals who are sharing their thoughts and opinions online. Unlike Twitter, it allows you to post messages that can be longer than 140 characters. So these posts can be more conversational than headline oriented.

Listening in on conversations on Facebook is not as easy as on Twitter, where you can follow anyone you wish. On Facebook, you can only monitor conversations of those who you are "friends" with. You can, however, engage your audience on fan pages and group pages and with paid advertising. There used to be a keyword tool for keyword research and monitoring called Facebook Lexicon, but it has been removed. According to the Facebook website, they are working on the development of an analytics tool for "page owners, advertisers and Platform developers."

For now, you can use the internal search functionality on Facebook to help you with keyword research. With each search, you can monitor and view messages, links, and notes of Facebook users and see which keywords they are using.

To do this, start your search by typing in your search query. You will notice that the results change for each letter you type, just as with Google's real-time search. "See more results for *your search query*" appears at the bottom of the list. Then on the left side, you will see the various type of results (Figure 8.12). You can choose any item on the list or just select Posts By Everyone for the full list.

Figure 8.12 Facebook search

Keyword Optimization for Facebook

Now let's take a look at some tips for optimizing Facebook around your targeted keywords. Just as SEO increases visibility to your website landing pages, Facebook SEO will do the same for your Facebook pages.

Fan Page Setup: URL, Title, and Picture

If you haven't already, you should use the name of your business or organization as your fan page name. This is not the place to stuff too many keywords that aren't relevant to your organization. Since Facebook is a social networking site, you will likely turn people off by doing this. You want people to have a strong impression about your page. I would also recommend using a good-sized picture for your profile image. This picture should be a nice-looking quality image that will help support your and your brand.

If you have more than 25 fans, you can request a vanity URL. They make it easier for people to find and remember you. A vanity URL would be facebook.com/ *yourname*. When selecting a vanity URL, you should stick to using your organization name, which may have a keyword or two that is very core to your business. The idea here is to link the URL with the name and the profile picture to create a memorable brand for you or your organization. This will benefit you well as you continue your Facebook SEO efforts.

Fan Page Information

There are two places you should make sure you fill out on your fan page that will increase your SEO power. Make sure you fill out the information tab for your fan page. The more information you fill out and complete, the more information Facebook can pull from to have your page show up in related searches.

Additionally, you should fill out the About box, which is currently located on the upper-left side of the page. It will give you a couple hundred characters to help visitors and Facebook know what your page is all about. Remember, when filling out this information, use your targeted, relevant keywords.

The AutoComplete Box

The Auto complete box is the search box that follows you around everywhere you go within the Facebook interface. Currently this search box is right in the middle at the top of every Facebook page (Facebook has a tendency to change their interface every so often). Depending on what you are searching for, you will see results that will "autocomplete" as you type in each letter of your search.

Going back to Figure 8.12, you can see that I didn't complete my search query on the search phrase "mountain biking". All I typed was "moun" and Facebook knew what I was looking for. The result is influenced by popularity and account history. If you are looking for increased visibility within Facebook, this is an important place to rank well.

Top Ranking Factors for AutoComplete Box

Here is a list of things that rank when you do a search in the AutoComplete box.

- Your name (from your profile)
- Events that you are invited to
- Friends (or friend of a friend) that have the keyword in their name
- Apps you have used
- Groups and pages you have joined or liked (including any relating to your interests)
- Questions with the keyword in it

This should give you a good idea of how to utilize your keywords to help with increased visibility when people use the AutoComplete box.

Link Building

Just as link building is very important to regular SEO, it is also very important to Facebook SEO. A high number of inbound links to your fan page will help to boost your visibility. Again, think of links as "votes." The more votes you get, the more popular you are. There are two ways to use links to your advantage. The first is to use links to build up your fan base. More fans will help increase the popularity of your fan page.

The second way is to use external links that point to your fan page. Make sure you have links on your site or blog that promote your fan page. Promote it to your friends and partners and have them link there as well. One of the best ways to do this is to use the Find Us on Facebook badge.

Facebook is indeed growing and becoming an important part of most organizations' marketing efforts. By using some of these tips, you can start developing the right framework for your Facebook fan page generate more traffic and increase brand awareness.

Now that you have your new Facebook page setup, it is time to reach out to your customers and make them aware of it. A promotion is a good way to start. Offer a discount or prize drawing for customers that become fans. Let them know that you would like them to share their feedback on your products or services. It goes without saying that you need to be prepared to receive this feedback first. This should be a given with any type of social media marketing strategy.

As previously discussed, when your customers (or fans) interact with you on Facebook, their friends will see those comments on their news feed. This is one way to leverage the power of Facebook as a viral marketing tool, and in turn, it should attract more fans to your page and thus more prospective customers.

Engagement and Conversation

Many people are fixated on the goal of acquiring new fans. It is a metric you cannot ignore; the more fans you have the more successful your campaign is, right? Not exactly. The real goal is to engage your fans in conversation. If you don't communicate and converse with your fans, then your fan page will become dormant and fans will disperse to other interesting sites. It is important to note here that you need to be committed to spending time doing this. Many businesses create a fan page with the mentality that "if you build it, they will come" and don't invest the time to interact with their fans, a lost opportunity.

Facebook provides some great tools to help you engage with your fans. You have the ability to send videos, photos, messages, and links to each fan. Each time you send out one of these forms of communication, you show up on their personal news feed. This in turn helps to keep you and your products or services top of mind with your fan base. Be careful not to "spam" them, but spread out your communication pushes and make them meaningful and relevant.

A cool feature of Facebook is that it also provides you with the ability to segment your audience by region, age, and gender. This will help you send the right messages to the right demographic group. So learn who your audience is and plan your messaging strategy around those groups. Facebook also provides a helpful reporting tool called Insights. This tool will help you understand the various types of content your fans enjoy interacting with.

As stated earlier, you need to be prepared to invest time to manage your Facebook page. Make sure you set aside the time to read through comments and other posts from your fan base. You might find, since you are encouraging open and honest conversations, that you occasionally get some objectionable posts. Facebook does provide tools to help moderate and even block users. But you should have a plan for how to handle this ahead of time and communicate to your fans up front so they understand the policy. Regardless, you should use these tools sparingly. If fans feel their comments are being edited or you are watering down the Kool-Aid, they will be less likely to engage in conversation in the future.

One advantage to search marketers is that search engines are working with Facebook and Twitter to integrate updates into their search results. Getting found in real-time searches is another strategy for promoting your fan page.

Keyword Research for Blogging

Blogging too has grown in popularity for the past several years. Millions of people worldwide read blogs every day, and 77 percent of active Web users read blogs according to eMarketer. Because of their growth and popularity, many people are questioning if they need to get one started. If you have been wondering about blogs or planning to start one, then you should consider the information in the following sections.

What Is a Blog?

A weblog, or *blog*, is essentially a personal (or professional) journal on the Web. It is a type of website that can be maintained by an individual or an organization. They cover many different topics and express lots of different opinions. Some blogs are influential and have many readers. Then there are some that are merely intended for family and friends.

The main purpose of a blog is to provide commentary or news on a particular subject. It is also a tool to inform and educate and to make a connection with people to help them make a decision about your product, service, or business. And because there is little to no cost to setting up and maintaining a blog (except for your time), many individuals and organizations now have a platform to share their thoughts and opinions.

The Importance of Blogs

Blogs allow millions of people to easily publish their ideas and many more to respond with a comment. They should be thought of as a form of two-way communication between a publisher and interested readers. If you get enough people participating in a blog, you are essentially having a conversation or discussion online. Blogs enable us to become active participants in the conversation instead of just passive readers.

How to Set Up a Blog

First of all, you will need to think up a name for your blog. With so many blogs out there, you will do good to think of something unique and relevant to your blogging content. Once you have a name, you should lock in a domain name for your blog. If you already have a domain name, you can choose a domain name like www.*mydomain* .*com*/blog or maybe blog.*mydomain.com*. If you are starting from scratch, you can go to a domain registrar like Network Solutions (www.networksolutions.com), GoDaddy (www.godaddy.com), or MyDomain (www.mydomain.com) for help. If you can get your main keyword(s) into the URL, it will help with your SEO efforts as well as help readers identify what your blog is about.

Picking a Blogging Platform

The next step is to pick a content management system that provides you with the tools to manage your blog. The best part about this is that most of the tools are free. The top two platforms are Blogger (www.blogger.com) and WordPress (www.wordpress.com). Blogger is 100 percent free but can be fairly limiting. If you choose to go with WordPress, there are two versions: wordpress.com, which is a hosted solution but limited in features, and wordpress.org, where you need to have a server to host your blog.

Once you pick your platform, you will want to design your page. There are several tools out there that will help you with customizing the design of your blog: WordPress Themes (themes.wordpress.com), Template Monster (www.templatemonster .com), and UniqueBlogDesign (UniqueBlogDesign.com), to name just a few. You will probably need to have some knowledge of HTML or CSS, or know someone who does, to get the design the way you want it. Or you can pick one of the built-in designs provided by your blogging tool.

You will need to make sure the ability to leave comments is turned on. This will help to make it feel more like a conversation is happening. It is good to get positive and negative comments. This will make your blog appear to be real and down to earth.

What Is RSS and How Does It Work?

RSS stands for *Really Simple Syndication*. Basically, it is the most common way of promoting your blog online. Most blogging tools will automatically produce an RSS feed for you. This "feed" can be subscribed to just like a news feed or Podcast, and it gives blog subscribers a way to stay up-to-date on your latest blogs. Your blog feed can also be submitted to sites like Feedburner (www.feedburner.com), which is now a part of Google, to allow people to find your blog in much the same way they might find your website via search engines.

Adding Social Media and Links

Add links to all of your social media profile pages including Twitter, Facebook, LinkedIn, and so on. You should also add links to any other personal or corporate pages you have. Additionally, you should link to your blog from all of your social media profile pages. There are many social bookmarking plug-ins you can use to help promote your blog, including these:

- Google +1 (www.google.com/plus)
- Digg (digg.com)
- Sphinn (www.sphinn.com)
- Twitter (www.twitter.com)
- Delicious (www.delicious.com)
- Stumbled Upon (www.stumbleupon.com)
- ShareThis (www.sharethis.com)

Now that you have your blog set up, the next step is filling it with content. For most of us this can be a challenge. The first point is that most people write blogs because they are passionate about a topic and they have knowledge to impart or an opinion to share. This makes for interesting reading because people enjoy reading from authors who are emotionally attached to their subject. This should be a major consideration when deciding on the subject matter of your blog. Let's look at some other tips.

Tips and the Top 10

Speaking of tips, people love to find tips about how to do something better. Thanks to David Letterman, we all love top 10 lists. They have a way of attracting readers' attention. Go out and find good tips on your topic and post them to your blog. You don't always have to use 10. It's perfectly okay to post something like "The top 6 Twitter SEO tips" to your blog.

Solve Problems and Ask Questions

One of the best ways to approach your blog posts is to put yourself in the shoes of your followers and identify a question they might have. Your assignment is to then answer that question with a post. This makes your post more conversational. It will also help you get more followers because you are answering a question that is likely already on your readers' minds.

Look for Growing Trends

By staying on top of current trends, you might be able to identify a topic that will be of interest to your readers within a specific time period. Let's say there is a growing buzz on a new iPhone app. If you use a tool like Twitter or hang around blogs or forums related to iPhone apps, you can write about it on your blog. You might just be the go-to blog on that topic if your timing is right.

Take a Poll

A good way to find unique content is to poll your followers. Ask a question that solicits a response. Get out on Twitter and invite people to your blog to take the poll. You will be surprised at the response. People like to have a platform on which to express their opinions. You can follow up with some rich, relevant content.

Networking and Partnerships

Get out there and interact with people outside your blog. Set up a Facebook or Twitter account and find out what is on people's minds. Read their blogs. Not only will you find new readers, you will find some fresh ideas that you can bring back to your blog as well.

If you come across a difficult topic, don't feel like you have to do days of research to make sure you cover it accurately. Find other experts who have the answer and refer your readers to them for the specifics. You will find that you can build some great relationships and probably get some quality referrals that come your way.

How Often to Blog

Getting a blog started and launched can be really exciting. Once the honeymoon is over, you need to be prepared to stick with it for the long term. Some people blog every hour, some daily, and some weekly. This is all fine, but you need to pace yourself. If you blog every day and then stop for a week or two, you will likely lose your momentum and your followers. Just be consistent.

Blogging and Keyword Research

Now let me discuss how to leverage blogs to gather keyword research intelligence. Just like Facebook, blogs allow for posts. However, these posts are more like articles than quick statements or even tweets. So for keyword research, you will need to look at the various blog posts that are out there on the Internet. Some blogs have multiple posts a day and some have them once a week or less. The best place to start is with some good tools to help you find these conversations.

I recommend starting with these tools to help you mine keyword-specific conversations:

- Technorati (http://www.technorati.com) is and has been the place to go to research blog posts by search query. Notice you can search by posts or by blogs. Note that the results also displays trending arrows, authority, and positive or negative change, as seen in Figure 8.13.

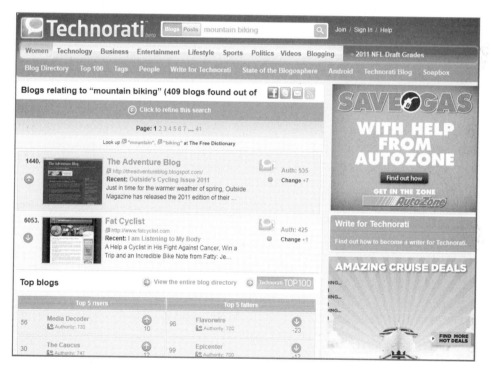

Figure 8.13 Technorati

- Surchur (http://surchur.com) goes a little beyond just showing blogs and blog posts. It also displays related news, pictures, video, and products. It will rank topics by keyword and ranks them for Twitter, Surchur, and Blogosphere on a scale of 1 to 10.

With these and other tools, you should be able to monitor conversational posts that are happening and learn from what people are discussing online. With this insight, you can use this information for keyword research purposes and identify the needs and wants of your audience.

Summary

By performing keyword research for social media and analyzing search term usage, you can really get to know your audience better. This can help you gain an advantage over your competition, assuming they are taking a more limited approach to their keyword research activities. This is especially true when you understand that user behavior varies from search engines to the social Web. Keywords and their usage won't always be the same. By following the steps laid out in this chapter, you will be well on your way to having a solid social media strategy that utilizes the right keywords for each social media channel you use to promote your brand, products, and services.

Using Keywords for Mobile and Local

Have you ever been traveling and found yourself in need of finding a local restaurant or something specific at a store nearby? What do you do? Pick up your mobile phone, and in some cases you use keywords to search for local stores that have what you are looking for. Alternatively, if you are a local store, you want to optimize your site for those who are tying find you locally. Optimizing for local search rankings as well as mobile search devices should definitely be a part of your Internet marketing program. In this chapter, I will discuss both mobile and local search, how to do keyword research, and apply keywords to these two important channels.

9

Chapter Contents

Local Search Visibility
Optimize Your Site Using Local Keywords
Mobile Keyword Research
Developing a Mobile Strategy

Local Search Visibility

A marketing channel that small businesses often overlook is achieving visibility in local search listings. Consumers, whether they are searching from their desktop computers or mobile devices, are often looking for local businesses. Chances are they are only a few miles away from you when they do their search. This chapter will show you how you can tap into this marketing channel and drive more traffic to both your website and your local store. The other day I was out running some errands, one of which was to send a package. I figured I would run into a UPS or FedEx store somewhere along the way. Well, I didn't, and I was running out of time. So I picked up my iPhone, opened a search app, and voiced a search query. I was instantly given several results. I picked one that was less than a mile away. I found the place quickly and delivered my package. I was rather pleased with myself.

So how can you tap into that type of experience and connect with more customers? I will first share with you some local keyword research tools and methods and then show you how you can use those keywords to optimize for local search.

Local Keyword Research

Choosing the right keywords is especially important when it comes to local search. This is because searchers have learned to include a location-specific modifier in their search if they want to get localized search results. All too often we type in general search queries expecting to get local results and end up instead with results from all over the world.

Additionally, the search engines are making an attempt to serve up local results even if we haven't typed in a location-specific keyword. They learn from our search history, IP address, and other methods to deduce our current location so they can show us local search results.

I will now share with you an approach to modifying your current keyword list to create localized keywords that you can use for your site, business directory listings, and mobile channels.

Step 1: Classify Keyword Phrases

First you will need to take the list of keywords that you developed from Chapter 4. If you also read Chapter 5, you will have already segmented those keywords into relevant groups or themes. Here you will do the same, but you need to consider two specific additional keyword classifications: informational and transactional. This mimics the buying cycle scenario discussed in Chapter 2, where *informational* represents searchers who are seeking information on products and services and are not yet ready to make a purchase and *transactional* represents specific long-tail keyword phrases that suggest they are close to making a purchase decision.

So the informational group will include keywords that are broad or less specific in nature, like "bicycle" or "plumber". Transactional keywords would be more specific, like "bike shop in Cleveland" or "Jacuzzi plumber in Seattle". When people search these types of phrases, they are looking for something specific and are likely ready to make a purchase.

Step 2: Localize Your Keywords

Now take each of your keyword segments and start making a list of prefixes or suffixes that will localize them. The most obvious is to think of the cities and towns you have in and around where your business is located, like "Jacuzzi repair in Austin" or "Austin plumber".

Remember that people will try to localize their search on keyword modifiers other than just the city name. Consider county, state, zip code, and neighborhoods. Make a list of neighborhoods, counties, zip codes, and so on that your business serves. Keep in mind that your business might serve multiple regions depending on where you are actually located. You may also serve only a small portion of a larger city. You might be located in New York but more specifically in SoHo, for example. If you can attract visitors from SoHo, you might have the best chance of increasing business. People searching New York might be looking uptown or in another neighborhood.

A couple of great tools to help you with this assignment are Local Marketing Source (www.localmarketingsource.com/local-keyword-research-tool/) and Generate Local Adwords & Keyword Lists (http://5minutesite.com/gen_keywrds.php). Both work very similarly. Figure 9.1 shows the Local Marketing Source tool, and you can see that there is a large box for entering keywords. Then there are several modifiers that will help you adjust for best results, like your current zip code, radius from the zip code, including state names in locations, and so on.

So you simply add both your informational and transactional seed keywords into the box and select any modifiers you like. Once you are done, you click the Generate Keywords button and presto, a new list of keywords that have been localized. You can export them as a CSV file to incorporate into your spreadsheet.

There is another set of tools that will also help you as you research localized keywords. To demonstrate these tools, I will use the health club market as an example search. I will also narrow my focus not just into one city but across the United States so you can see the breadth of how these tools can work. Keyword research should be done nationally first to understand overall user search behavior. People generally search for a health club the same way in California as they do in New York.

To start gathering population data around cities and metropolitan areas, visit the US Census bureau website (www.census.gov/popest/datasets.html), which provides a wealth of knowledge, even though the navigation and interface leave much to be desired. Another site that offers helpful population and demographic data is City-Data.com (www.city-data.com/top2/toplists2.html), which I prefer. You can gather information on zip codes that have the highest gross income or get really focused and zoom in on a plethora of data around a single zip code. These tools are great for gathering this type of data but do not help you identify pockets of keyword opportunities.

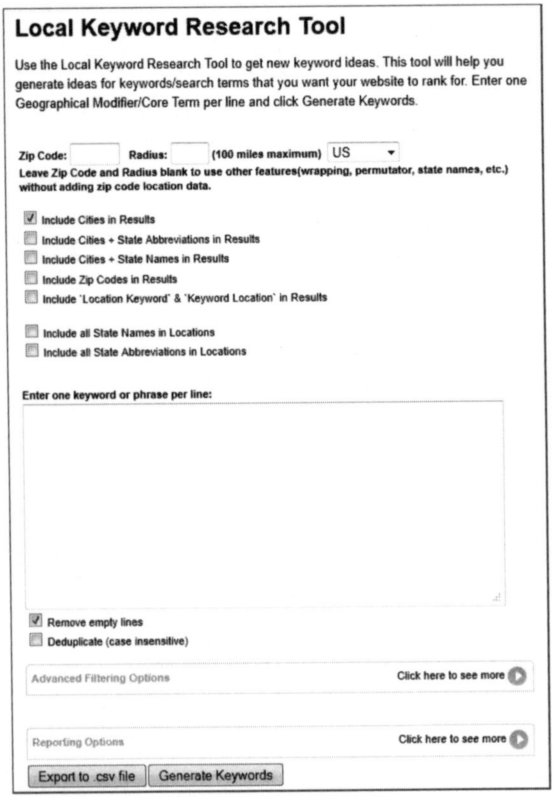

Local Keyword Research Tool

Use the Local Keyword Research Tool to get new keyword ideas. This tool will help you generate ideas for keywords/search terms that you want your website to rank for. Enter one Geographical Modifier/Core Term per line and click Generate Keywords.

Zip Code: [ ]   Radius: [ ]   (100 miles maximum) US ▾
Leave Zip Code and Radius blank to use other features(wrapping, permutator, state names, etc.) without adding zip code location data.

☑ Include Cities in Results
☐ Include Cities + State Abbreviations in Results
☐ Include Cities + State Names in Results
☐ Include Zip Codes in Results
☐ Include 'Location Keyword' & 'Keyword Location' in Results

☐ Include all State Names in Locations
☐ Include all State Abbreviations in Locations

Enter one keyword or phrase per line:

☑ Remove empty lines
☐ Deduplicate (case insensitive)

Advanced Filtering Options   Click here to see more ▶

Reporting Options   Click here to see more ▶

[Export to .csv file] [Generate Keywords]

Figure 9.1 Local Keyword Research Tool from Local Marketing Source

For that you need to venture on to Google Insights (www.google.com/insights/search/#). So I did a US search on "health club" and found the data you see in Figure 9.2.

It seems that the District of Columbia, Massachusetts, New York, and Kansas yield the highest search volumes. If you drill down into the New York metro area, the highest search volume is in the lower part of the state, as you can see in Figure 9.3. Furthermore, if you zoom into the city view, there should be no surprise that New York is the largest, as shown in Figure 9.4.

This gives you a macro-to-micro approach to finding geographical areas where your keywords might have the most impact. In Google Analytics, a similar tool exists that shows you where your traffic is coming from but it doesn't break it down by keyword.

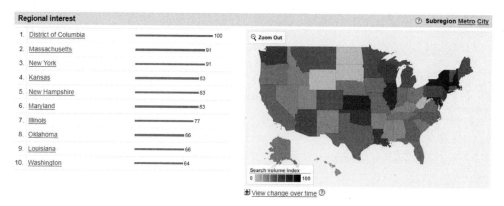

Figure 9.2 US detail in Google Insights

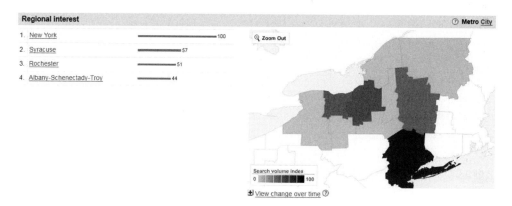

Figure 9.3 Metro detail in Google Insights

Regional interest

1. New York ——————————————100
2. Jersey City ——————————70
3. Brooklyn —————————51
4. Newark ————————44
5. Livingston ———————35

Figure 9.4 City detail in Google Insights

Step 3: Combine Keyword Parts

In step 2 you identified a list of cities, neighborhoods, zip codes, and so on. Now you will combine them with your transactional and informational keyword segments all into a list of new keywords that are localized. You end up with the following possibilities:

- plumbers atlanta

- plumbing services atlanta

- atlanta plumbers

- dunwoody plumbers

- plumbing services 123 elm street, atlanta

- stone mountain, atlanta plumbers

- plumbing services 30324

As you can see, this list contains the different variables we have discussed. Also notice the placement of the location in the keyword. You may want to have the location at the front and at the end. In your testing, you can determine which will perform best for you.

A handy way to manage the merging of each of these parts of the keyword phrase is to put each term into a spreadsheet like the one in Figure 9.5. You can see that I have a column with the keyword "plumber" and another with local neighborhoods or cities. In column C1, for example, I added the formula =A1&B1. This combines the contents in cell A1 with that of B1. I use this often to help me as I am working on and managing local keywords. Depending on which version of Excel you are using, you may need to add space between the words or a column so you don't get "plumbersatlanta". Also, you will need to make sure the cell has been formatted as a text field and not a number or other type of field.

	I18		f_x	=A1&B1
	A	B	C	
1	plumber	Williamson	plumber Williamson	
2	plumber	Whitesburg	plumber Whitesburg	
3	plumber	White	plumber White	
4	plumber	Waleska	plumber Waleska	
5	plumber	Waco	plumber Waco	
6	plumber	Villa Rica	plumber Villa Rica	
7	plumber	Union City	plumber Union City	
8	plumber	Tyrone	plumber Tyrone	
9	plumber	Turin	plumber Turin	
10	plumber	Tucker	plumber Tucker	
11	plumber	Temple	plumber Temple	
12	plumber	Taylorsville	plumber Taylorsville	
13	plumber	Tate	plumber Tate	
14	plumber	Talmo	plumber Talmo	
15	plumber	Suwanee	plumber Suwanee	

Figure 9.5 Spreadsheet to combine words

Step 4: Local Business Competition

If you followed the methods outlined in Chapter 4, you will have already gathered data on how competitive keywords are. Additionally, you should have scored the keywords based on a competitive scale. At this point you should also look at the number of local business listings in search results for a given keyword phrase, as in Figure 9.6.

Places for **health club** near **Kansas City, MO**

(A) 24 Hour Fitness - ✰✰✰✰✰ 24 reviews - Place page
www.24hourfitness.com - 8600 Ward Parkway Center, Kansas City - (816) 276-2466

(B) Gold's Gym - ✰✰✰✰✰ 27 reviews - Place page
www.goldsgym.com - 4050 Pennsylvania, Kansas City - (816) 931-9888

(C) Quality Hill YMCA Express - 6 reviews - Place page
www.kansascityymca.org - 1051 Washington Street, Kansas City - (816) 842-9622

(D) Picture Hills Fitness - 1 review - Place page
www.picturehillsfitness.com - 6501 N. Cosby, Kansas City - (816) 505-1200

(E) 24 Hour Fitness - 12 reviews - Place page
www.24hourfitness.com - 301 N.E. Englewood Road, Kansas City - (816) 453-8824

(F) Solid Fitness Sciences - Place page
www.solidpft.com - 4711 Central, Kansas City - (816) 960-1077

More results near **Kansas City, MO** »   Rate places to improve your recommendations »

Figure 9.6 Local business listings

If you find that there are too many listings for a particular keyword, it will be more difficult to rank for. On the other hand, those that have few listings will be easier to rank for, which represents an opportunity for you. Going after keywords with many listings is not bad; you just need to set your expectations and goals accordingly.

Now that you have further refined this set of keywords, you can begin the process of optimizing your website using them. You will also need to incorporate them into local listings.

Optimize Your Site Using Local Keywords

Optimizing for local search is a process of making sure search engines and potential visitors know where you are located. This is especially so if you have several locations and it gets to be a little more complex. You will want to optimize your website and/or your blogs to help you attain higher visibility with search engines.

Let's start by looking at your current website. You should look at each and every page and map your new localized keywords to each one. If someone were to search on the phrase "Dunwoody dentists", which page of your site would be the most relevant? How about "cosmetic dentists in dunwoody ga"? To help you with this process, you can enter your site map on a spreadsheet and then take your localized keywords and place them next to the most relevant pages. If you find you have pages with no keywords, you may need to identify new keywords or ask yourself if those pages are needed and possibly remove them.

Another place to consider is where you place your contact information, specifically your address and zip code. Is it only on your Contact Us page? Don't miss a good opportunity to have your city, state, and zip code (local keywords) on *each* page of your site.

Additionally you need to make sure you have the location of your store or office on each page. If you have multiple locations, make sure they are listed as well. You can place this information at the bottom of your page or get creative and maybe develop a tagline that includes each location.

As you are optimizing your site for SEO, make sure you include your local keywords in HTML tags, links, filenames, and image/video descriptions as discussed in Chapter 6. For title tags and meta descriptions, you can keep it simple:

```
<title> company name, San Francisco, CA - tag line </title>
<meta name= "Description" content= "company name, San Francisco, CA - tag
line"
```

You should also read your body copy and see if it makes sense to include a local keyword like a city name. This again will help search engines and visitors know where you are located and will increase your chances to be found via local search queries.

Solicit Local Links

Next, you should to submit to local organizations and their directories and get your company listed there. Consider joining your local chamber of commerce, Better Business Bureau, or other type of organization that serves the community. Reach out to other web directories that are local to your area as well, and ask them to link to your website. The more local links you can get, the better. This helps you establish that you are an active participant in your community.

Each time you get an opportunity to get listed with an organization, you will likely have the opportunity to create a profile. The following profile information for local search will be the most notable:

- Company name
- Company address
- Company website address
- Company product/service

Remember to use the local keywords you just created in these fields. Elect to make your profile information public. Where possible, link your keywords to the relevant pages on your website.

These local links are very important to your site's search rankings. These inbound links are like votes to your site. The more you have, the more "popular" you are, and you will see your visibility increase as a result.

Use Keywords for Local Listings

Next you will want to get listed with some specific sites that are designed just for local listings. Again, for the sites on which you submit your business listing, make sure your information is complete and correct and that you are consistent with your use of the local keywords you just created. Before you embark on the process of listing your business with each of the directories, you might want to create a profile in a spreadsheet or a Word document with all of your company information. Make sure you have simple descriptive statements about your company, and be sure you use your local keywords.

When it comes time to fill out each of the business listings, you can simply copy and paste, ensuring you will keep all of your information consistent. This will help you keep your messaging strong and focused.

Now let's look at a few of the places you can go to get your business listed:

- GetListed.org (www.getlisted.org), the place to start because it will help you understand what listings you have and what listings you should pursue
- Supermedia (www.supermedia.com/business-listings/)
- Local.com (https://advertise.local.com/)
- The Yellow Pages (http://adsolutions.att.com/internet-solutions)
- Localeze (www.localeze.com/)
- Universal Business Listing (www.ubl.org/Signup.aspx)
- Merchant Circle (www.merchantcircle.com/)
- Hot Frog (www.hotfrog.com/)
- InfoUSA (www.infousa.com/)
- Yext (www.yext.com/pl/free-listings/index.html)

Not only will listings with these directories help you with local search, they will also feed many other services, like GPS, and other listings, like Yelp.com. So it is wise to get into as many listings as possible to ensure that you are represented everywhere.

Update or Add Your Site on Local Search Engines

Now let's look at the major search engines and their local sites. If you chose to use GetListed.org, you are probably already listed in these local search engines. However, if you would like to double-check, I will review each of them. Let's start with Google Places (www.google.com/places/). You will need to set up a Gmail account prior to filling out the form. You should also know that this is the way to get your listing to appear on Google Maps as well.

As with most of Google's tools, once your listing is up and running, you can gather some general analytics data on its performance, as seen in Figure 9.7. As you can see, the tool gives you a visual representation of the number of impressions. It also shows you the number of actions. This is represented as a click on the map, clicks for driving directions, or clicks to your website. For those that click on the map, you can see the city name and zip code where the requests came from. This will help you get an idea of the area from which the local demand is being generated.

Google Places will also display the top search queries that triggered your listing. This is another great source for keywords, especially those that provide visibility for your business.

There is even a place to share an update, like upcoming events or maybe a promotion. You have 160 characters to post your message, and it expires in 30 days. Use relevant keywords if appropriate.

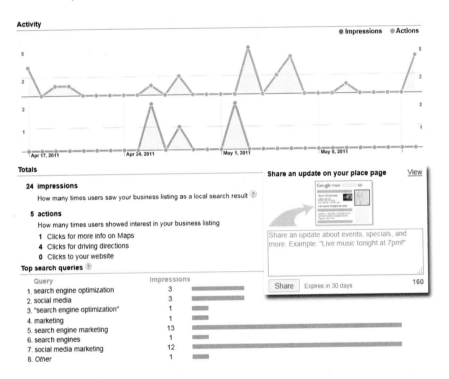

Figure 9.7 Google Places

Next is Yahoo!'s Local Search (http://listings.local.yahoo.com). As with Google, you will need to set up an account before you proceed with the listing. A listing on the Yahoo! Local page will also help you get listed on the maps page.

Finally, there is Bing's Business Portal (www.bing.com/businessportal/), and yes, you guessed it, you will need to set up a Microsoft Live account. As with the others, you will be placed on the Bing map.

Now that you have taken the time to set up your business listings, you are on your way, but there is still work to do. Reach out to your customers—the satisfied ones—and ask them to rate your business and/or write a review. This is important because when people are searching to find you, they are likely to come across your competitors as well, and positive reviews will add more credibility and help you stand out in the crowd.

It may be time consuming, but consider employing a reputation management program to monitor what is being said about you and your business. Make an effort to go out of your way to serve your customers well to earn their positive feedback. As you do this, you may not even need to ask for ratings because your customers will be eager to provide positive feedback on their own.

Mobile Keyword Research

There are many people who feel mobile search has finally come into its own. According to eMarketer, the US mobile advertising spend was estimated at $743.1 million in 2010 and is expected to reach $2.5 billion by 2014. Furthermore, the development of apps for mobile wireless devices continues to grow. This has caused many to sit down and consider their own mobile strategy and how they are going to compete in the market-place. Another report, this one by Performics, predicts that mobile search queries will account for 16 percent of all search clicks by September 2011. That represents a lot of clicks you might be missing out on if you do not have mobile in your marketing mix. The iPad and tablet devices have caused a disruption in the mobile space and need to be factored into the equation. A report by Yahoo! Inc. found that there were approximately 10.3 million tablet users in 2010, and that number is expected to reach 82.1 million by 2015.

As the use of these devices continues to grow, we will learn more about behavioral trends that come from keyword research. However, there is some research that has been done by Google that illustrates different ways people search on mobile devices and those who use a keyboard and the impact it can have on keyword research. The Google Research Blog (`http://googleresearch.blogspot.com/2009/05 /bar-bet-phenomenon-increasing-diversity.html`) explains that new high-end smart-phones like the iPhone are changing the landscape of mobile search. People using these new devices mimic, to some degree, computer web search patterns. It cites that there are about 3 words per query for computer and iPhone queries as opposed to 2.5 words for conventional mobile queries. Additionally, there is a white paper titled *Deciphering Mobile Search Patterns: A Study of Yahoo! Mobile Search Queries* (`http://www2008.org/papers/fp846.html`) that outlines the differences between modes of mobile search like SMS (text messaging), mobile web search, and mobile apps. This makes the task of keyword research for mobile a little more challenging.

Time will tell how tablet devices will affect this behavior because they typically come with built-in keyboards that will allow people to type in search terms as if they were on a desktop or laptop computer.

For our purposes, we will focus on keyword research as it relates to handheld devices like the iPhone and Android devices. Because this mobile platform is so large, it requires additional keyword research. Once you understand user search behavior on mobile devices, you can identify more closely with their wants and needs through your keyword research. The knowledge learned from this research can benefit your optimization of the following items:

- Web content
- Mobile web content
- Mobile links
- Mobile paid advertising
- Mobile applications
- Local listings

Let's now look at some methods for conducing mobile keyword research.

Google Suggest Mobile

Just as with Google Suggest on desktop PCs and MACs, when the first characters of the search query are entered, Google Suggest Mobile attempts to "predict" what you are looking for and serve up recommendations for you, as shown in Figure 9.8. The predictive results are derived from high search volume, search history, and your current location. So as you test keywords using this method, you should keep this in mind.

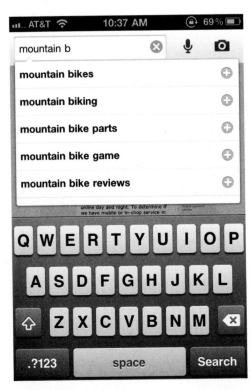

Figure 9.8 Google Mobile Suggest

Google Keyword Tool for Mobile

The Google AdWords Keyword Tool for Mobile was introduced back in 2009 and was difficult to use. It also didn't paint a complete picture, in that it only contained volume for feature phones, which represents a smaller amount than volume from smartphones. However, the tool has been upgraded and enhanced to show volume from smartphones as well. This provides better insight into mobile searchers and what they are actually looking for.

To use the Google Keyword Tool for Mobile, simply go to the Google Keyword Tool site (`https://adwords.google.com/select/KeywordToolExternal`) and click the Advanced Options and Filters button to reveal a new window like the one in Figure 9.9.

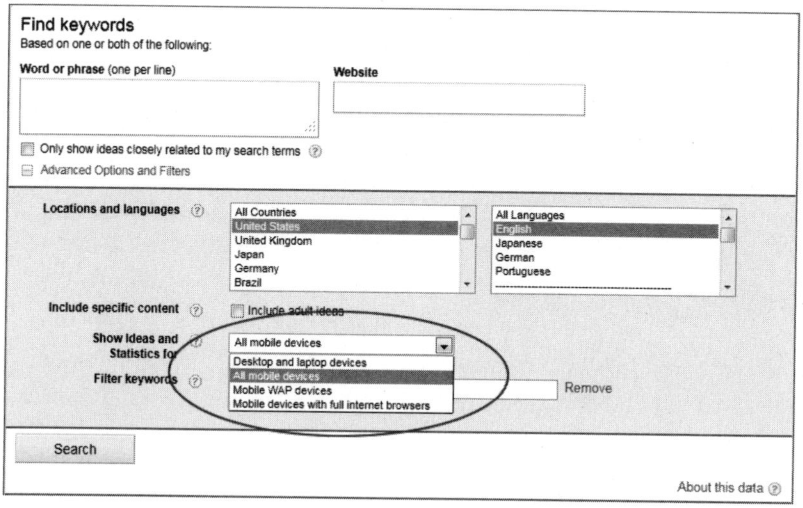

Figure 9.9 Google Keyword Tool for Mobile

You now have a list of modifiers to refine your search. We are interested in Show Ideas and Statistics For. The drop-down menu lets you filter by the following criteria:

- Desktop and laptop devices
- All mobile devices
- Mobile WAP devices
- Mobile devices with full Internet browsers

To use this tool, input your seed keywords into the search box. Or even better, if you have Google Analytics installed, you can grab all of your organic keywords driven by smartphone devices and paste them in. This will give you some great results based on your current site performance with mobile devices. Next, uncheck the default Broad Match type and select either Phrase Match or Exact Match as your match type. Then select Mobile Devices With Full Internet Browsers.

You can continue selecting different modifiers, like Global or Local, depending on your business type. Then do a search and download into a spreadsheet. Once this has been done, go back and do the same with Desktop And Laptop Devices. This will show you variances in demand from mobile to desktop searches.

Go back to your spreadsheet and match the mobile and desktop demand volumes to the actual organic traffic you have. With this data, you should be able to calculate the mobile search CTR and its demand across all of your search terms.

Google Webmaster Tools Query Stats

Google Webmaster Tools (www.google.com/webmasters/) has a statistics report that displays the highest impressions for your site based on various keywords. You can even segment mobile devices and mobile images in this report, allowing you to visualize mobile search queries for which your site is appearing.

Developing a Mobile Strategy

After you have researched your keywords for mobile, you should consider the best way to use them for mobile sites, mobile apps, SMS, and so on. I will share with you a six-step method for outlining your mobile strategy that leverages these new and exciting small devices.

I was impressed by a presentation that Jeremiah Owyang from Altimeter gave in May 2011 on mobile strategy (www.web-strategist.com/blog/2011/05/09/keynote-how-to-develop-a-mobile-strategy-video-and-slides/). He made a very compelling point that we should consider looking beyond just features (which is tactical) and align our mobile strategy to the entire customer experience. He maps out this customer experience in seven phases:

Awareness Customers seek out a solution to problems or issues they are having and become aware of your product or service.

Consideration Customers identify several solutions that help them solve their issue, and they compare to find which solutions suit them best, one of which is yours.

Intent Customers have decided that your product or service meets their needs the best and they are intent on making a purchase.

Purchase This is where the customer makes a purchase.

Support Now that the customer has made a purchase, they are likely to need support and assistance.

Loyalty As the customer continues to use your product or service, they become loyal participants and continue to use your product or service over the competition.

Advocacy A loyal customer becomes an influencer and sings your praises. They share with their friends and help promote your product or service.

Understanding each of these phases in the customer cycle will put your strategy into better perspective. In the next sections, I will outline six steps that you can use to develop your mobile strategy with the customer cycle in mind.

1. Define Target Audience and Personas

Identify and define your target audience and break them down into personas or audience segments. A persona is an archetypal user or searcher that represents the needs of larger groups of users, in terms of their goals and personal characteristics. They act as "stand-ins" for real users and help guide decisions about website functionality and behavioral site design. Personas will help you become more personable with your target audience, and you can map out specific needs with each persona you define.

2. Conduct Your Research

As with any strategy, you need to conduct the proper research to learn more about your audience and their needs. Find out from your customers what devices and platforms they are using. Are they using any tools or apps? If so, which ones? Find out what their pain points are. You can do this by polling them, participating with them on the social web, or doing market research. Make sure you conduct this research for each persona because the needs and goals might differ.

3. Develop Your Mobile Solution

With the research you have conducted, you now have the basis to decide how you are going to meet your customers' needs. You know what their pain points are and can develop a solution that will alleviate that pain. As you develop this solution, continue to ask yourself how your mobile solution will help meet the needs of each persona. This will help you stay focused.

Remember that you want to deliver valuable services and solutions that are optimized for mobile devices. Using a mobile device is different than using a PC to access the Internet. Take advantage of GPS and location-based services and provide information as it is needed and not all at once. You should be sensitive to the small-form factors of mobile devices and design content to show only what is needed as customers interact with your solution.

4. Design Your Pricing Model

As you are building your solution, consider how you can reduce the friction and allow purchasing to happen in very few clicks. Consider how you can enable customers to prepay for your product or service. Owyang even suggests we may see future models where we can postpay to help speed up the process. He also mentions that the point of purchase is no longer limited to the physical location. A great example of this is the app that Starbucks started offering at the beginning of the year. Figure 9.10 shows how

Starbucks is offering the ability for mobile payments for customers. The left screen shot shows the store card and the amount it has left to make a purchase. The screen shot on the right shows the ability to add more money onto the card. To make a purchase, you simply "touch to pay" and the item amount will be deducted.

Figure 9.10 Starbucks app

The goal here is to reduce the friction and allow the purchasing to happen in very few clicks, making as easy as possible for the customer to make the payment.

5. Develop Your Support Model

It is not over after the purchase has been made. You need to continue to nurture the customer experience further by providing the proper support and help them when they need it. This can be done with self-help mechanisms like frequently asked questions (FAQs) or other documented information the customer can access on their own.

You can also create ways for them to get support from their peers through social media tools or support forums. Finally, make sure you have ways for them to contact you directly if need be. There is nothing more frustrating than not being able to find an answer to a question online and then realize there is no way to contact a company directly.

Your support model is also a great device you can use to listen and get feedback for suggestions and proposed improvements. Many good ideas for future product features can come directly from your customers.

6. Develop Retention or Loyalty Program

Loyalty programs can help you develop long-term relationships with your customers. What kind of program can you put in place to build your customers' loyalty? Can you offer any kind of rewards program or incentives? One thing to consider as you develop this model is how to reward not only long-term customers but also those influencers who are willing to share their recommendations with others.

By having a great customer support model and loyalty program in place, you are creating advocates for your brand. If your customers are treated well and consistently nurtured, they will share with their friends and become a new source of leads for you.

Consider each of these steps and how you might make them actionable within your own company. If you remember to keep your customer and their needs in focus, you will be on your way to developing compelling solutions that will help you prosper in the mobile space.

Summary

You should now have a set of keywords that have been localized for use on your website and local listings. Many times there is less competition at the local level. This allows you to employ keyword research to give you a competitive edge. So be sure to take advantage of the knowledge that comes from the tools and tips in this chapter to help you strengthen your position within your local market.

These same keywords can also be used and integrated within your mobile strategy as you consider the development of content for mobile devices. As your business changes and moves, remember to go back and revisit your keyword lists to validate them and maybe find new ones that will work for you. Also remember to revisit your listings and ensure that the information is correct, especially if any of your listing information has changed. Keep them up-to-date.

Keywords and Site Architecture

With your keywords in hand, you now, whether you realize it or not, have a model for how your website should be structured. The keyword research has given you insight into what search queries are most relevant and popular, and you will want to steer people to the most appropriate page on your site. This chapter will guide you thought the steps to create a site architecture that leverages your keyword research efforts. You can develop a highly relevant site that maps directly to the keywords you will be using in your marketing campaigns. This will translate into a higher conversion rate and more user engagement.

Chapter Contents

Understanding Site Architecture

Just as an architect designs a structure in blueprint form before it is built physically, an information architect (or site architect) builds a site in template form before it gets developed and launched. There are two audiences to consider when developing your site: your users and the search engines.

An architect has to consider many variables as they conceptually build a structure, things like the number of people who will be using it, traffic patterns and flow, electronic systems, and so on. These are all taken into consideration before the pencil hits the paper.

Once you have decided to develop a website, you should take the same approach. You should consider your users and their behaviors and intent and anticipate their needs and wants all before you do any development on your site. A site architect's job is to collect important information up front, then begin the conceptual work of developing a structure that represents the website and where the information will be located.

In Figure 10.1, you see a very simple depiction of a simple site diagram and wireframe of your home page. The wireframe is blocked out with rectangular place holders that represent where actual content goes. Wireframes can be used to spec out any page on your site. Once you have created a site structure diagram and wireframe, you can start populating them with content. There are programs available now that help with site diagramming and wireframing, like ProtoShare (www.protoshare.com), Justinmind (www.justinmind.com), and Pidoco (www.pidoco.com). These tools not only allow you to conceptually develop your site, but also to plan ahead for your SEO work.

Regardless, the most important aspect of this type of activity is to account for all of the information, establish its relevance, and make sure there is a logical flow. To make your users happy, you need to ensure that the navigation is fluid and information is easy to find and access.

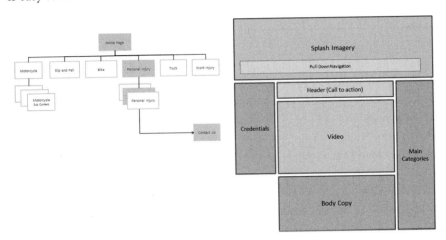

Figure 10.1 Site diagram and wireframe

In other words, site architecture is all about improving how users find their way around your site. The goal is to get the best, most relevant content in front of users and reduce the number of times they have to click to find it. This is also important for search engines.

Now, what does this have to do with keywords? In Chapter 5, "Refine Your Initial List of Keywords in Seven Steps," you learned how to refine your list of keywords and then categorize them into logical groups or themes. If you have already done your keyword research and finished this step, you have already taken a large first step into gathering the information you need to start architecting your site. For each category of keywords you have developed, you are likely to have a corresponding site that has content relevant to that keyword group.

Essentially, if you were to map out all of the categories you developed, you would likely have a pretty solid site map. Or if you already have a website, you can still map out all of the categories you came up with and compare them to the pages on your site. Find all of the variances and note where you are missing content or keywords. It is like performing a gap analysis and finding the holes. Your job is to then fill in those holes with either relevant content or keywords.

I will now outline five steps to incorporate keywords into your information architecture processes and explore some practical tips and methods you can use. The importance of these steps is critical because it has to do with keeping your content and keywords relevant and in the proper context. Remember the keyword success formula: the right keywords + relevant destination content = conversions. If you do this right, you will have driven the right audience to your site and they will be happy to find relevant content that addresses their needs and wants. What are they likely to do? Convert. That is the name of the game.

Step 1: Your Site Structure

My good friend Richard Baxter from SEO Gadget (www.seogadget.co.uk) is a master at site structures and has his own digital agency where he shares the insight about developing a flat structure. Ask yourself this question: How many clicks does it currently take for your visitors to access the deepest content from your website?

Richard points out a simple site architecture (Figure 10.2) that demonstrates the downfalls of a deep, multifaceted site structure, which as you will see is not ideal to your visitors or the search engines.

Imagine that this sitemap describes a very simple site layout. To get all the way to the bottom (the very deepest layer of content), search engines and users are expected to embark on a six-click descent. That's a lot of clicks! That level of depth certainly isn't ideal; you might expect pages that are deeply buried in the architecture to have fewer internal links and be less visible in search engine results, even for very long-tail or specific search queries.

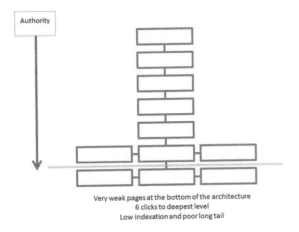

Very weak pages at the bottom of the architecture
6 clicks to deepest level
Low indexation and poor long tail

Figure 10.2 Poor site architecture

Pages buried very deeply in the architecture might not receive enough link authority, or "link juice," that is passed on from the home page. The concept here is that your root or home page has a certain amount of authority. When you click to go to a subpage, there is some equity that is passed on but usually not as much as the value of the home page.

If you click to go to a third level or more, the authority is diminished to the point where there is has no value at all. This link authority needs to have some value to be visible in search engine rankings. Certainly it remains true that by promoting content "up" the architecture, you can improve its overall rank. This process is called *flattening*. This is illustrated in Figure 10.3.

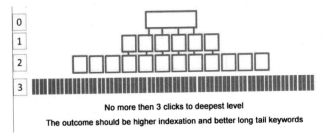

No more then 3 clicks to deepest level
The outcome should be higher indexation and better long tail keywords

Figure 10.3 Flattened site architecture

Here, we've increased the number of links on each page and reduced the number of clicks to the very deepest level of content, effectively flattening the site architecture. Using this kind of architecture is good for both your users and for the search engines. It is important, however, that you are careful about the number of links on each page and that your visitors have clearly defined paths for them to take to get to the information they seek. Take care to place the most relevant content on your site and insure the links are relevant. Too much information can overwhelm people and create confusion.

Step 2: Keyword Modeling

This next step is derived from the exercise you did in Chapter 5. As you segment your keywords into logical categories, you can start to see a kind of site diagram (sitemap). Categories will emerge from the keyword research, identifying different subsets of your products or services or information that your potential customers would find useful. I came up with a list of top performing keywords for a fictitious retirement investment company outlined in Table 10.1. This company provides online retirement information and advice as well as a subscription to premium content.

▶ **Table 10.1** Top-scoring keywords

401 k plan	403b account	independent investment advisor
401 k plan contribution limits	after tax 401k rollover to roth ira	independent registered investment advisor
401k account	best roth ira investment	
401k advisor	early retirement planning	independent retirement account
401k contribution limit	early retirement strategies	individual 401k contribution limits
401k contribution limit 2011	employer 401k plans	individual 401k plan
401k contribution limits irs	estate planning	individual retirement account
401k contribution limits over 50	estate planning asset protection	investment advisory firm
401k early retirement	estate planning living trust	ira accounts
401k employer contribution limits	estate planning strategies	ira contribution limits
401k for self employed	family limited partnership estate planning	ira investment account
401k management		manage 401k
401k plans for small businesses	fee based financial planning	manage my 401k
401k retirement savings plan	fee only financial planning	personal financial management
401k rollover advice	how much do I need to retire	personal retirement account
401k rollover into ira	how much money do I need to retire early	portfolio analyzer
401k rollover options		portfolio asset allocation tool
401k rollover rules	how to manage 401k	retirement account
401k rollover to ira rules	how to manage your 401k	retirement calculator
401k rollover to roth ira	how to retire early	retirement financial advisor
401k savings plan	how to rollover 401k to ira	retiring early
401k to roth ira rollover rules	how to set up a self directed ira	rollover ira
	independent financial advisor	

Continues

rollover ira account	self directed ira	self managed 401k
roth ira	self directed ira 401k	sep 401k
roth ira account	self directed ira account	sep ira contribution limit
roth ira investment	self directed ira investing	simple 401k
roth ira investment choices	self directed ira investment options	top investment advisors
roth ira investment limits	self directed retirement account	ways to retire early
roth vs traditional 401k	self directed roth	wealth management software
sec registered investment advisor	self directed roth ira llc	what happens if I retire early
self directed 401k rollover	self directed solo 401k	what to do when you retire early
self directed individual retirement account	self employed 401k contribution limits	why rollover 401k to ira

With these top performing keywords I will now segment them into these relevant categories:

- Retirement Advisor
- Managing 401k
- Tools and Calculators
- Roth IRA
- Rollovers
- Type of Retirement Accounts
- 401k plans
- Self Directed IRA
- Contribution Limits
- Early Retirement
- Estate Planning

I will now organize each of the keywords from Table 10.1 into one of eleven categories as you can see in Table 10.2.

▶ **Table 10.2** Investment keyword groupings

Retirement Advisor	Managing 401K	Tools and Calculators	Roth AIR
401k advisor	401k management	portfolio analyzer	roth ira
manage my 401k	manage 401k	retirement calculator	roth ira investment
independent financial advisor	manage my 401k	wealth management software	self directed roth
independent investment advisor	personal financial management	portfolio asset allocation tool	best roth ira investment
investment advisory firm	self managed 401k	how much do I need to retire	roth ira investment choices
retirement financial advisor	how to manage 401k		roth ira investment limits
top investment advisors	how to manage your 401k		roth vs traditional 401k
independent registered investment advisor			401k rollover to roth ira
sec registered investment advisor			self directed roth ira llc
best retirement planning newsletter			401k to roth ira rollover rules
			after tax 401k rollover to roth ira

Rollovers	Type of Retirement Accounts	401k Plans	Self Directed IRA
rollover ira	401k account	401k account	self directed ira
401k rollover advice	403b account	sep 401k	self directed ira 401k
401k rollover options	ira accounts	simple 401k	self directed ira account
401k rollover rules	retirement account	401 k plan	self directed ira investing
rollover ira account	401k savings plan	401k savings plan	self directed retirement account
401k rollover into ira	independent retirement account	employer 401k plans	self directed solo 401k
self directed 401k rollover	individual retirement account	individual 401k plan	self directed individual retirement account
401k rollover to ira rules	ira investment account	401k for self employed	self directed ira investment options
why rollover 401k to ira	personal retirement account	401k retirement savings plan	how to set up a self directed ira

Continues

▶ **Table 10.2** Investment keyword groupings *(Continued)*

Rollovers	Type of Retirement Accounts	401k Plans	Self Directed IRA
how to rollover 401k to ira	rollover ira account	self directed solo 401k	
	roth ira account	401k plans for small businesses	
	401k retirement savings plan		
	self directed ira account		
	self directed individual retirement account		

Contribution Limits	Early Retirement	Estate Planning
401 k plan contribution limits	retiring early	estate planning
401k contribution limit	401k early retirement	estate planning strategies
401k contribution limit 2011	early retirement planning	estate planning asset protection
401k contribution limits irs	early retirement strategies	estate planning living trust
401k contribution limits over 50	how to retire early	fee based financial planning
401k employer contribution limits	ways to retire early	fee only financial planning
individual 401k contribution limits	what happens if I retire early	family limited partnership estate planning
ira contribution limits	how much money do I need to retire early	
roth ira investment limits	what to do when you retire early	
self employed 401k contribution limits		
sep ira contribution limit		

If you are conducting a site redesign and are using this exercise to enhance your site, then you might compare these categories with the pages and structure you already have. For instance, you might find that you do not have any content on your website that covers "Early Retirement" or "Estate Planning". With this modeling exercise, you can identify missing content that would be beneficial for you to add based on your keyword research. It is like performing a gap analysis and identifying where the holes are in your content strategy. It is also good to validate the content that you do have.

From a site structure point of view, you might start outlining your site architecture with these categories as part of your main navigation, especially since they line up with your personas and the information they are looking for, which I will cover next.

So a basic architecture already begins to emerge. The top-level categories and subcategories might look like those in Figure 10.4.

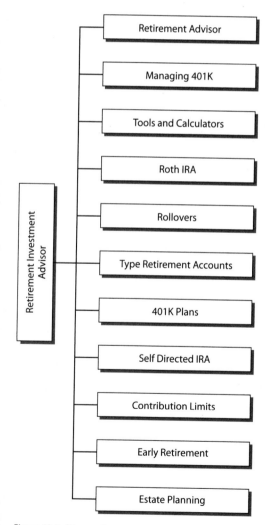

Figure 10.4 Site mapping

The beauty of this architecture is that it essentially mimics the way your prospective customers are thinking. You're using the keywords they will use for your top-level categories. This will help them connect with your site and quickly recognize where to find what they want, and it will therefore increase their engagement. All of this and we haven't even started on the benefits to SEO yet.

The main SEO benefit is that this will allow you to develop pages that have page titles and other page tags using the most relevant and searched-on keywords. This again increases relevancy and engagement because you are essentially speaking your prospects' language.

Mapping keywords to your site structure is an excellent way to build a solid site foundation. To do the job completely, you need to look at the rest of the keywords in your targeted list and outline them in logical places. As you can see in Figure 10.5, I selected one of the top-level pages and added the appropriate subpages based on targeted keywords.

With an existing site, you have to be more selective in your approach. It may be difficult to completely restructure your site. However, this approach will help you identify the biggest problem areas, those where you should focus most of your attention.

Now that you have a site structure in place, you can move on to your pages and work on the content layout and information flow using your keywords.

Step 3: Developing Your Personas

Having established that having a well-thought-out site architecture is important, we'll now look at specific ways to leverage keywords to facilitate a cleaner and more relevant site structure. I'll begin with an example. Let's say you wish to build a site that provides up-to-date information for the retirement investment community.

This site is for individuals who are seeking advice for retirement planning.

The first thing to do is to attempt to learn more about the target audience and establish the personas. Some of this can be done by simply looking at your keywords and the segmentation I just did. Then we can derive the search phrases that your visitors will likely use. A review of the keywords and segments as seen in Table 10.2 leads to four types of personas:

- Seasoned investors
- Entry-level or do-it-yourself (DIY) investors
- Individuals seeking help with retirement
- Individuals seeking financial advice

Now I will attempt to predict the various objectives for each of the four personas, with some overlap:

- Buy advisory service—to manage money
- Buy advisory service—to manage money for others
- Get free retirement information, investment ideas, or DIY information
- Find financial advisor or planner
- Get premium service advice subscription

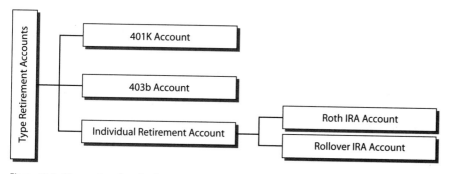

Figure 10.5 Site mapping of top-level pages and subpages

With the keywords and personas listed, I can map the objectives to the personas to get a better picture of keywords that will likely draw a certain profile of individual who has a particular objective, as you can see in Table 10.3.

▶ **Table 10.3** Persona development mapping

Keywords	Personas	Objectives
estate planning strategies, early retirement strategies,	Seasoned and Experienced Investors	Get premium service advice after subscribing; renew premium service subscription
how to manage your 401k, how to retire early, how much do I need to retire	Entry-level or DIY investors	Get free information, investment ideas, DIY information
401k advisor, independent investment advisor, retirement financial advisor, 401k rollover advice	Individuals seeking retirement investing advice	Find financial advisor or planner; buy advisory service

I have classified each persona based on the relevance scores from the keyword research report. I also placed them on a scale to show purchase intent, which seems to be higher when an investor is looking for a subscription-based advisory service, as you can see in Figure 10.6.

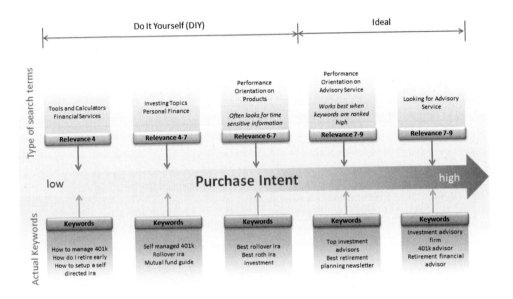

Figure 10.6 Search term types used by personas

If you are in a situation in which you are redesigning your site and you already have conversion numbers for keywords that brought traffic to it, you can compare relevance scores to current conversion data, as seen in Figure 10.7.

Relevance Score	Visits/Yr.	% Total Visits	Conversion Goal 1	Conversion Goal 2	Bounce Rate
9	4,676	7.2%	11.2%	6.4%	36.5%
8	367	0.7%	21.5%	8.6%	49.4%
7	14,223	18.4%	4.2%	2.3%	63.2%
6	29,629	43.8%	1.5%	1.2%	70.5%
5	16,021	22.2%	1.2%	0.6%	77.4%
4	1,569	1.8%	0.9%	0.1%	78.6%
3	4,732	5.3%	0.3%	0.4%	80.2%
2	157	0.4%	0.0%	0.0%	72.6%
1	243	0.2%	0.0%	0.0%	97.2%
Totals	71,617	100.0%	4.5%	2.2%	69.5%

Figure 10.7 Relevance versus conversion

In this case, you can see that conversion is higher with a relevance score of 7 and above. Traffic is heavier at relevance scores between 5 and 7. Also note that 69.3 percent of all traffic came from keywords that scored between 6 and 9. This is one of the advantages of scoring keywords with a relevancy scale. To learn more about this relevancy scale, please read Chapter 5.

Step 4: Content Design

With your site structure complete, you need to strategically place your content in the right areas to enhance the relevance of each page. Here are a few general guidelines for planning your content design.

Focus on one major keyword phrase per page, plus one or two permutations. Your top-level pages, which are your home page and primary navigation pages, should focus on the more general head keyword phrases. As you drill down into your site, use more long-tail keywords. Usually, your content will naturally support this keyword strategy because your content generally gets more specific as you go deeper within the site.

Starting with your home page, branch out into the logical components of your website. The research you did earlier should assist you with additional content ideas. If you're selling products, make sure you plan ecommerce elements like a shopping cart if applicable and product detail pages. Do you need any other interactive elements? Now is a good time to plan for all of these things.

In this example, I could use the home page and top-level pages to focus on the primary keywords that I have already defined. You might use a blog section to capitalize on long-tail keywords and provide some incentive to draw more specific traffic to your site.

Now that you know how to structure your content, it's time to make a keyword mapping document. This document will aid in your ability to place keywords in the right areas within page tags as well as within your body copy.

First take all of the content pages from your site mapping diagram and list them in a text document. For each page of your site, list the primary and secondary keywords. Using these keywords as a guide, create the actual keywords you will use for your title tags, URL strings, H1 tags, and so on. Here are a couple of examples:

Home Page (Retirement Advice)

Keywords: 401k advisor, retirement financial planner, retirement planning

URL: /www.yoursite.com

Title: Top Retirement Planning and Financial Planning Advice—*Name of Company*

H1: Retirement Planning Advice

Managing 401k

> Keywords: 401k management, manage my 401k, how to manage my 401k

> URL: /401k-management/

> Title: 401k Management | *YourCompany*

> H1: Managing your 401k

Estate Planning

> Keywords: estate planning, estate planning strategies, fee based financial planning

> URL: /estate-planning-advice/

> Title: Estate Planning Advice | YourCompany.com

> H1: Estate Planning Advice

Now that you have this document in place, you should share it with your development team. Your programmer can use the keywords to build a site structure that uses them as filenames, which will help to form a keyword-rich URL string. They can also build each page to include the tags from the beginning. Your content development folks can make sure they develop content that includes the exact keywords you have in your document. This will ensure that you have consistency for the entire site development process even though you have many people working on it.

Step 5: Wireframes and Prototyping

Now that you have a site structure with all of the pages mapped to your top keywords, you can start the process of developing a wireframe or prototype for the content. This will need to be done for each page of your site. A wireframe is basically a schematic representation of your website that houses the navigation, functionality, and page content. The process of developing a wireframe in the planning stage enables top-level functionality to be viewed and tested prior to any development that takes place.

The wireframing process is a great way for you and others to view the site's information flow before going to production. There are many tools out there that can help you with this process. The one I use is ProtoShare (www.protoshare.com). Figure 10.8 and Figure 10.9 show four stages of a wireframe: Lo-Fi, Med-Fi, Hi-Fi, and Comp.

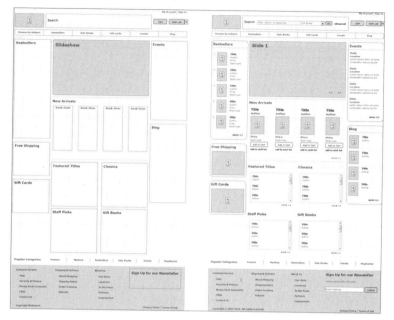

Figure 10.8 Lo-Fi and Med-Fi wireframes

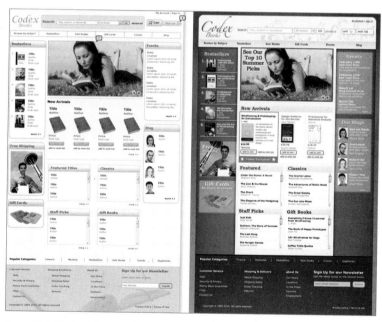

Figure 10.9 Hi-Fi and Comp wireframes

You can start off with a Lo-Fi wireframe with very few details, and as you progress, you can add more detail until it looks just like a finished comp. This tool will allow you to then export your wireframe into HTML to give your developers a jumpstart.

You can develop each page of your site, effectively building your sitemap at the same time. As you add the appropriate links, you can switch to review mode and click around the site as if it were live. This is commonly referred to as a *clickable prototype*. The beautiful thing about this is that it allows you and other users to interact with the site, test the information flow, and get a feel for the content on each page. Then if you need to make any changes, you can do so before the programming starts, which is a much simpler and less-expensive process.

As you then move through the process from Lo-Fi to Comp, your visual designers will be able to add the graphic elements to the page to make it look as intended. Your developers will also be happy because they will be able to see exactly what needs to be built to the exact specs. ProtoShare will even export your wireframe into HTML.

The last element I like about this tool is that you can even enter your keywords for the URL string, meta title, meta description, and meta keywords, as seen in Figure 10.10.

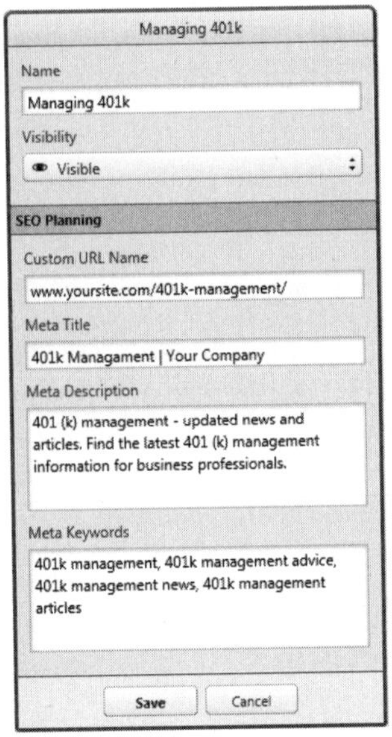

Figure 10.10 Enter keywords for wireframe

If you decide to export your wireframe into HTML, these keywords will be automatically programmed into the site. This eliminates the need for a keyword mapping document because the keywords have been put into place from the beginning.

There are many tools like ProtoShare on the market that can help you with the wireframing and prototyping process, including the ones I mentioned at the beginning of the chapter. The main point here is that you can focus on the user experience and information design up front. Many people take the opposite approach when developing sites. They start with the visual elements and go back and forth trying to get approval on the look and feel of the site. Once it's approved, they start programming the site and stuffing in content. There is little thought to the way information is laid out and the user experience. Making changes to the site after it has been programmed can be time consuming and expensive.

Summary

This whole process of site structure design and mapping your keywords to that structure will help you by providing a more fluid (and less painful) design and development process. Additionally, your keywords will be mapped to your site structure and you will have a landing page for all of your important keywords. This will help you to have a site that is more engaging to your visitors, and you will realize a higher conversion rate.

Creating Great Content with Keywords

You now have a great list of keywords and have mapped them to relevant pages of your site. Next you need to look at the content on those pages and make sure it meets the expectation of your visitors. You can leverage your keywords and the intelligence gained from keyword research to help you with developing great content.

Chapter Contents

The Importance of Quality Content

You have identified keywords, refined them, segmented them, learned from them, and mapped them to your website pages. Now comes a very important part in the whole searcher experience cycle.

SEO and PPC can help drive traffic to your website, but getting people to convert is the responsibility of your website and its content. You might have a wonderful campaign that drives a lot of traffic to your site, but what happens once they get there? We have all been to websites that have underwhelming content. How can you rise above the mediocre and work to produce great content? One great way is to leverage the knowledge from your keyword research.

If you know what keywords people are searching on and you employ social media to add context to your inferences, then you have some very good ideas of what type of content needs to be produced. Furthermore, if you have mapped your keywords to your website pages, you know the subjects that need to be covered.

Another aspect to consider is the impact on search results. As you know, one of the primary factors for gaining high keyword ranking is a large number of links. Google added this factor to its algorithm back in 1998 in an effort to determine which sites had good enough content that people wanted to link to them. The more links, the more popular the site was. This is known as link popularity.

The primary purpose for link popularity was to communicate the idea that sites with good content will generate lots of links. This not only makes the search engines look good by connecting searchers with good content, it works for the site owners as well. When searchers end up on a site that delivers on expected content, they are more engaged and are more willing to buy.

Google and other search engines have always sought ways to match searchers with the most relevant content. In 2011, Google raised the bar even further with its series of Panda updates.

The Panda update is Google's latest change in how its algorithms determine the best pages to present in the SERPs in response to search queries.

Google's goal is to make the search experience and browsing as smooth and as fast as flipping through a magazine. The Panda updates are an effort to achieve the objectives of quality search results and speed. The main focus is on quality content and the usability of the site for the user. Sites and blogs with high-quality content will get rewarded, as will those that provide a fluid user experience with streamlined navigation and easy-to-find content.

Let's look at some of the things that Google considers "quality content." Google has provided a list (http://googlewebmastercentral.blogspot.com/2011/05/more-guidance-on-building-high-quality.html) of questions you can ask yourself as you consider developing content for your site. I will summarize and point out some important points from this list as it relates to our topic on content development:

Written by an expert Content should be written by someone who knows and understands the subject matter well. Make sure you seek out experts to help you develop the very best content for your pages. You can arm them with your keyword list and invite them to write using your targeted keywords. You will find that the content will be more believable and engaging because your passion for the topic is more evident if it is written properly.

Keyword variations Do not duplicate content for multiple pages and then switch out different keywords. You should make sure each page is distinctly written around the main topic or idea. If you have mapped your keywords to each page, you should already have a good idea of what content to write. Also stay away from redundant articles on the same or similar topics. Each page or article should have a purpose and should be unique.

Genuine interest of readers Each page or article should map to the genuine interest of your readers and visitors. To accomplish this, you can first look at your top keywords and analyze them against the buying cycle as discussed in Chapter 1. Specific long-tail keywords suggest that a searcher is at the end of their search and is ready to buy, whereas the broad, less-specific terms suggest that a searcher is in the information-gathering stage.

When you analyze keywords with social media tools, you can put them into the proper context by seeing how they are used in a sentence or a conversation. Using these tools and methods can help you learn what readers really want to know and what their needs and intentions are. With this intelligence, you can produce of content that will be worthy of your readership and will capture their interest.

Good value As you consider the content you plan to produce, you should seek out what has already been written on the subject. How does your article stack up to others that have been written? Is it unique or are you just repurposing someone else's content? Are you providing the right amount of detail or is it just a summary?

You want to have content that is unique from everyone else's. What element will make your content stand out and cause people to want to visit and link to your site? This can be tough, but if you are passionate about your topic, seek to find that one thing that will make your content stand apart from the rest.

As I read over these on Google's blog, they seemed to make sense, and I personally agree that as I search for information on the Internet, I will gravitate to sites that have content that meets these criteria.

Basically, good enough just won't cut it anymore. You really have to dig down deep and find ways to raise the bar and provide significant and valuable content. From what I have read, the search quality algorithms Google deployed in its Panda update are not going away anytime soon because Google seems to like the positive impact it has had on the quality of search results. Google will continue to refine its algorithms, but the underlying principle of favoring great web content will probably always be a primary factor in its ranking schemes.

Rand Fishkin, cofounder at SEOmoz and a well-known and respected pioneer in the search industry, has posted a great chart that helps to illustrate this principle and outlines where you need to be as you consider putting content on your site (Figure 11.1).

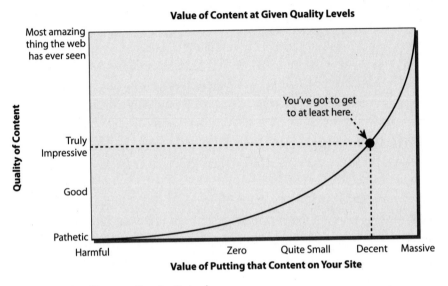

Figure 11.1 Value of Content at Given Quality Levels

He demonstrates that you have to at least provide "decent" valuable content that is more than just "good" quality just to be in the game. So what can be done to build outstanding content that will be competitive and help you stand out from the crowd?

The rest of the chapter will outline several tips and strategies to help you develop great keyword-rich content that leverages the keyword research we've covered in earlier chapters—and that will help you stand out from the crowd.

Writing for the Web

Writing for the Web is a different matter than writing for print. With the incredible amount of information online, it is easy for users to become overwhelmed with all of the content and gravitate to sites that provide tightly organized content in "right-sized" amounts. As they browse the Web, users prefer content that allows them to get what they want quickly and move on without having to scroll through exasperatingly long pages or click on page after page. These days, people also want to be entertained and interact with their content.

We've all seen blogs and websites that are weighed down by content so dense that it goes unread because online readers tend to look for more digestible "content snacks" that are easier to consume and more fun. Consider your audience's needs and give them a page that offers a sample or highlight of what you have to offer, and then move the more detailed information to another page where those who are interested can access it.

Also, with the many interesting ways information is consumed on the Internet, people expect to be exposed to fun choices of media as opposed to just text. Producing a video and adding pictures and audio is pretty easy with the tools currently available. So why not use them?

Writing for Search Engines

As I have pointed out, the game of writing specifically for the search engines is essentially over with the Panda algorithm. Do not make the mistake of writing your content for the search engines. Content that is stuffed with keywords and makes little sense will not help you with higher rankings, and it will cause your readers to flee. If you employ the learning from this chapter, you will be developing content that will help your SEO efforts and attract more engaged readers. It is best practice to always write for your human audience first and foremost, and to integrate keywords into your writing in a logical, sensible way to also ensure that your content is search-engine friendly.

Copywriting

Relevant and expert content that answers a question and fulfills the customer's need is the ultimate goal of copywriting. Integrating targeted keywords into your copy will help you accomplish this goal. Remember to always write to serve your customers' needs first and keyword-rich copy will flow naturally.

Another important aspect of copywriting is to strategically deliver the right words that will get people to take some form of action. Not only are you attempting to provide great content, you're also trying to get your visitors to act in some way. I will not cover the art of copywriting in detail, but I will touch on two areas where you should leverage the integration of this skill with keywords and keyword intelligence:

- Writing great headlines
- Writing web body copy

Writing Great Headlines

The major goal for any headline is to compel the reader to read on. On average, eight out of ten people will read headline copy, but only two out of ten will read the rest. The goal is to increase the number of people who will read the rest by writing a compelling headline that entices them to continue on to the main article or web page content. Each sentence or paragraph should incentivize them to read the next until they reach the call to action.

With this in mind you should consider writing your headline first because it represents a promise to your readers. Then as you develop the content, ensure that you deliver on that promise.

Since this is a book on keywords, let me address the notion of keywords in headlines. There are generally two schools of thought on this topic: those whose sole purpose is having their content found by search engines and purists who insist that headlines are to be written with the sole purpose of enticing readers. In fact, if it is done correctly, both can be satisfied.

Your keyword research has given you insight into what interests your audience, and what words they use to find corresponding content online. Armed with this intelligence, you can write headlines that include important keywords that are interesting to humans who will read them as well as relevant for the search engines who must rank them. It is not writing to satisfy only the search engines, but also the humans who are using the search engines. With this approach, you will see more qualified traffic and engaged readers.

The keywords you select for your headlines should be more specific, long-tail keywords. Since you are going to take the time to provide specific information about a topic, use the niche keywords that will attract people who are looking for that specific type of content. This naturally makes for more effective headlines because it demonstrates to your target audience that you speak their language.

Additionally, headlines that list a number of tips, reasons, types, and so on will work for you because they make very specific promises. Just make sure you deliver on that promise.

These types of headlines will also help you build authority and trust because they demonstrate your knowledge and expertise of a particular topic.

Here are some examples:

- 10 ways to improve your website's search engine ranking
- Five of the best keyword research tools
- 4 types of bloggers—which group are you in?
- Free white paper that tells you the 9 secrets of financial success

You get the idea. These headlines are compelling and cause the reader to want to learn more. You can follow up with a list of bite-sized morsels of information your readers can snack on.

Other headlines that have similar titles are how-to headlines. They provide how-to information that people are interested in:

- Little-known ways to lose weight and keep it off
- How to get rid of [problem] once and for all
- The secret of successful investing

These tips will help you think in terms of capturing the reader's attention with a compelling statement. Next you need to deliver on the expectation you set with the headline by writing compelling copy for the body of your page.

Web Page Body Copy

There is no formula for writing the perfect copy for a web page, nor is there an exact number of words you should have. However, a web page with copy that has fewer than 200 words will probably not contain enough information to provide any value. A good general number of words to target would be around 600 to 800. Much of this depends on what the page is about and how much copy is needed to adequately address the needs of the visitor.

People tend to scan text on the Internet, so keep the paragraphs short and direct. Provide facts and figures concisely and to the point. Use lists and bold and italicized text to direct your visitor's eye to important points, keywords, and concepts.

As with headlines, the goal is to write your copy so you compel your reader to read on to the next sentence, and then the next paragraph, and so on to the end where you will likely have a call to action.

So identify the specific, unique aspects of your topic and write about what sets you apart from the others. If you have a competitive selling point, make sure you point that out from the beginning.

Let's go back to our trusty spreadsheet. Take a broad keyword and break it down into topics and subtopics as I have done in Table 11.1. Next, identify the keywords that fall under each subtopic. You can also add the search volume next to each keyword to get an idea of popularity. Then, for each keyword, jot down the content the searcher is looking for. For example, if a keyword is "road bike reviews", it is obvious that an article or web page comparing different models of road bikes would be a great content idea. It will also help if you add the URL where this content will reside.

Table 11.1 Identify content topics from keywords

Keyword biking	Topics	Subtopics	Keywords	Searches	Content Ideas	URL
	Road bikes	Information	road bike safety, how to buy a road bike, road bike reviews	# of searches for each keyword	How-to content, bike review content	Map to landing page URL
		Road bike types	trek road bikes, specialized road bikes, steel frame, carbon frame		Trek, specialized content, frames content	Map to landing page URL
		Road bike maintenance	bike mainte-nance, how to fix a flat tire		How-to content, fix a flat tire	Map to landing page URL

You can add these columns to the master spreadsheet you created in Chapter 4 and Chapter 5 and track these content ideas as you conduct your research, jotting in ideas that come to your mind. As you conduct keyword research with social media tools, you can find even more ideas of what people are interested in. Add those insights to your spreadsheet as well to provide a better context. Furthermore, you can conduct some competitive research to find out what content you can provide that others are not providing. Add that to your list.

When it comes time to produce quality content, you have a great place to start with some ideas that come directly from the keyword research you have already done. You may then need to find a subject matter expert or creative copywriter to craft it into the type of content your readers will clamor for. You can be assured that it will be the type of content they are interested in and want to consume.

The final stage is to make sure you have an objective for your readers. At the end of the copy, do you want your visitors to download something, call you, or buy something? A good call to action embedded strategically into your content can really help you grow by leading your readers closer to your objectives. A typical call to action is to invite the reader to subscribe to your blog or newsletter. Or maybe your goal is to get them to share their opinion in the comments section. Whatever it may be, make sure you have a call to action and that it is clearly defined. Sometimes getting your readers to act can simply be done by asking them to, especially if you have built up trust by providing high-quality content.

The overall strategy for most companies is (1) how to attract more customers and (2) how to engage them more effectively. The answer to these two questions can be found in the development of great content that utilizes SEO and social media. These will help you attract the right audience, but great content will help you engage them. So your strategy needs to have components of all three: content, SEO, and social media.

Content Management

If you need to constantly develop new content, you may need a way to organize your thoughts and plan ahead. My example in Table 11.1 is a good start, but you can take that idea even further. This next tip I picked from my friend Lee Odden, who is the CEO for TopRank Online Marketing and a pioneer on the topic of content marketing and management. He suggests developing an editorial calendar to manage and plan all of your content.

This example is designed specifically for a blog, but you can also use it for other social media sites, or articles or content you plan to add to your website in the future. This tool will help you plan content using a calendar format, which is essential for producing content that resonates with your target audience. It also represents your target keywords and keeps the authors on track and apprised with great, relevant ideas to write about.

TopRank®
Online Marketing

Example Editorial Schedule for a Marketing Blog
See http://www.toprankblog.com for many more tips on SEO, Social & Content Marketing

Date		Title	Topic/Category	Keywords, Tags	Media	Media	Repost
9/15/09	Mon	Managing Content Marketing for B2B	Content Marketing	B2B, Marketing, Content	Image		Newsletter
9/16/09	Tues	Twitter chats	Social Media, Twitter	Twitter Chat, Twitter Marketing	Image		
9/17/09	Wed	MarketingSherpa SEO Guide Review	SEO	SEO Guide, Report	Image	video	
9/18/09	Thur	BIGLIST SEO Blog Reviews 091810	SEO Blog Review	SEO Blogs	Image		
9/19/09	Fri	5 Tips on social media advertising	Social Media, Advertising	Social Media Avertising	Image		Newsletter
9/22/09	Mon	Facebook Marketing Basics & Tools	Social Media	Facebook Marketing, Tools	Image	PPT	
9/23/09	Tues	Spotlight on Search: (Influential Person) from Famous Br	Search Marketing Interview	Enterprise SEO	Image		
9/24/09	Wed	Book Review: Title by (Influential Person)	Social Media, Book Review	Social Media Marketing	Image	video	
9/25/09	Thur	B2B Thursday: Social Media	B2B, Social Media	B2B Social Media, B2B Marketing	Image		Newsletter
9/26/09	Fri	5 Tips on social ecommerce	Social Commerce	Social Media, Social Commerce	Image		
9/29/09	Mon	3 Things You Need to Know About Facebook Groups	Social Media, Facebook	Facebook Groups, Facebook Marketing	Image	video	
9/30/09	Tues	Is Content Marketing right for you?	Content Marketing	Content Marketing	Image		
10/1/09	Wed	Spotlight on Search: (Influential Person) Yahoo	Search Marketing, Interview	Yahoo SEO, SEO Interview	Image		Newsletter
10/2/09	Thur	B2B Thursday: SEO	B2B, SEO	B2B SEO, B2B Marketing	Image	PPT	
10/3/09	Fri	5 Tips on Geolocation marketing	Geolocation	Geolocation Marketing	Image		Newsletter
10/6/09	Mon	Interview: Social Media Strategy (Influential Person)	Social Media Strategy	Social Media Strategy, Interview, Jay Baer	Image	video	
10/7/09	Tues	BIGLIST Update	SEO Blog Review	SEO Blogs	Image		
10/8/09	Wed	Spotlight on Search: Salesforce.com	Search Marketing Interview	Enterprise SEO, SEO, Interview	Image	video	
10/9/09	Thur	B2B Thursday: Facebook	B2B, Social Media	B2B Social Media, Facebook Marketing	Image		Newsletter
10/10/09	Fri	5 Tips on Social CRM	Social Media, CRM	Social CRM	Image		Newsletter

Figure 11.2 Editorial calendar

The spreadsheet showcases dates for publishing, titles, keywords, categories, media used, cross-posting, promotional channels/tactics, and future repurposing of the content. Organizing an editorial plan like this helps online marketers keep track of all of the relevant content ideas in an organized manner. It helps to keep the content flowing in a methodical, strategic manner. It also makes the task of deciding what to write about easier to manage and plan for rather than coming up with content at the spur of the moment.

Sample spreadsheets are posted at www.keywordintelligencebook.com for your reference. They are basic spreadsheets, and you can modify them any way you like to serve your own purposes.

Content Marketing

Now that I have addressed the importance of developing keyword-rich, relevant content for your website or blog, we'll move on into the area of content marketing and the ability to attract visitors through compelling content. The general idea is to share the great content you have created with others to establish yourself as a thought leader, drive traffic, and improve customer retention.

You may want to develop content that's external to your website to give others a taste of what you have to offer. If you are an expert on a topic, you may want to offer to post a relevant article on a third-party blog that is related to your topic. This allows you to project your expertise on a blog that might already be well known to others. For instance, I write for ClickZ (www.clickz.com), which is a well-known website for digital marketing and online advertising professionals. This site has much more visibility than my company site, Symetri Internet Marketing (www.symetri.com). As I write articles for ClickZ, I establish myself as an authority and help to drive traffic to my own site.

So this concept of reaching out and finding opportunities to share your knowledge can be a great marketing channel. But you need to develop a strategy to help guide you along the way.

How do keywords fit into this? Again, I tapped Lee Odden to help provide some words of wisdom on the use of keywords for content marketing. He states that keywords and keyword research provide much of the insight into what customers are interested in and what their pain points might be. Keyword research also provides insight into what content they are searching for and what they are talking about on social sites.

Content should be designed for your readers first and foremost. At the same time, that content should include keywords that can attract new readers through search and social recommendations. This will help you make your content great as well as findable and shareable.

To illustrate, let's look at an example of a company that sells road bikes:

- Target customers who care about road bikes that cost less and are road safe.
- Target customers who search for "road bikes", "low cost road bike", and "safe road bikes".
- Target customers who socially discuss "save money on road bikes", "road bike safety".
- The content plan outlines an array of content objects supporting search keywords and social topics.
- The content plan tactical execution includes blog hub, video tips, shared customer widget photos, Facebook page for road bike safety tips, email tips and issues newsletter, road bike details Twitter account, guest blog posts using target keywords on road-bike-related blogs, articles contributed to consumer and environmental publications on road bikes, cost-saving tips, and being safe.

The use of keywords helps guide the optimization and findability of your content through search engines. Additionally, it helps to focus in on topics that customers care about and are already discussing through social sites. Keywords can also serve as useful guides for the blogger and for publication outreach.

Keywords drive the "optimize and socialize" efforts of those who employ content marketing to share, promote, and increase the reach of information that is relevant for customers who may buy or refer brand products and services.

As I have already pointed out, don't make the mistake of solely leading with keywords (versus customer needs), thinking that optimizing for the most popular keywords is all that is needed to extend customer reach. Using high-ranking content that isn't relevant with readers and doesn't compel them to share or buy is not an effective approach. Also, customers' needs and the information they seek will vary according to where they are in the research and buying cycles.

Keywords and subjects change over time, so even after a customer is converted, it's important to monitor, measure, and refine as needed.

Digital Asset Optimization

Up to this point I have focused on text as the main content variable. But there are other types of content that cannot be ignored. In the past few years we have seen images and video and audio content appearing in standard search results. As a result, optimizing for each of these media types needs to become part of your strategy.

Many people have a good understanding of SEO and the basic principles of optimization, but with blended or universal search, the natural progression of SEO is one that considers all of a company's searchable assets that can be keyword-optimized and promoted online. This is known as digital asset optimization (DAO). Many of the same principles apply as with SEO, but they can be extended to various media types that are now found on the SERPs, like images, audio, video, PDFs, slide shows, and more. Notice this screenshot of the Google SERP for the keyword "apple ipad": There are news links, video, images, and shopping results.

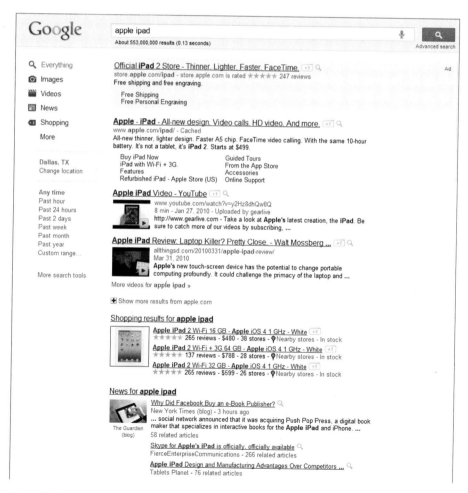

Figure 11.3 Universal search

However, many marketers have failed to take advantage of optimizing for all of their content types. According to a Forrester study

- fewer than 20 percent of marketers insert keywords into filenames of their videos on their sites;
- even fewer marketers write keyword-rich captions or create online video libraries;
- yet video stands about a 50 percent greater chance of ranking on page one of Google.

So what can you do to include digital asset optimization into your campaigns? Here are some tips to help get you started.

Identify Media Types for Targeted Keywords

Grab your targeted keyword list and do some searches to find out what files and media types Google and other search engines are displaying in the SERPs. Different search queries will show a different mix of media types. Get to know which ones are prevalent for your keywords. Remember, these results are dynamic and will change often, so go back frequently to check on any new content.

In the example in Figure 11.3, you can see that the keyword "apple ipad" resulted in four media types: video, shopping, news, and real-time articles. Look for opportunities to optimize your digital assets within each of these areas. You might find that it is easier to optimize for the news section using different assets than for traditional organic results. Certainly it makes a powerful statement to be listed for any of these media types in addition to your web pages.

Use Keywords in Filenames and Tags

This was discussed in Chapter 6, but to recap, make sure you use your keywords in filenames for your digital media assets. Furthermore, use keywords in tags for all images, video, and audio, including alt text for images. This will help identify them for the search engines and for visitors alike. As people do image and video search, they might just find you through any of these media types.

Map Keywords to Digital Assets

Just as with the exercise with web page body copy, you can employ a similar tactic to use keyword research to find out what people are searching for. Then identify the digital asset that will help provide the searcher with the best content. For instance, if you have a keyword phrase "how to fix a flat tire" on your list and it is a popular search, a video is a great way to show exactly how to fix a flat.

Produce the video with a script that uses the keyword phrase, and make sure you tag and use the keyword phrase in the filename, as I just mentioned. Then post the video on YouTube and embed the video on your website. This will allow people searching YouTube and using other search engines, as well as those who visit your site, to find the video.

Summary

Great content is critical to any marketing campaign. There are many reasons you should strive to develop unique and engaging content. The most important is what your target audience wants and is searching for. Great content will also have the effect of attracting more visitors and increasing your visibility.

Keyword research provides the key to helping you know what people are searching for and therefore what you need to develop. Great content can come in the form of text but also as other types of media. Decide which is best for your audience and deploy it on your website.

Using Keywords for Branding and Messaging

One of the purposes of this book is to expand your understanding of keyword research beyond its use as a tool for SEO and PPC. This chapter elaborates on the wealth of information that comes from keyword research and shows how to use that knowledge for branding, messaging, and other traditional forms of advertising.

12

Chapter Contents

Keyword Research for Branding and Messaging
The Keyword Research Brief
Keywords in Press Releases
Keywords in Brand Positioning

Keywords Research for Branding and Messaging

Some of you who come from the traditional advertising side may jump right into this chapter without reading Chapter 1 first. Regardless, I want to revisit the discussion on the searcher engagement cycle (Figure 12.1) because it has a special application for branding and messaging.

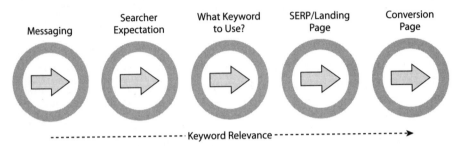

Figure 12.1 Searcher engagement cycle

The cycle begins with some kind of trigger that causes people to become interested in a product or service. There are many triggers out there that are not advertising related. However, the role of advertising is to get in front of your target audience with a message that either leaves a favorable impression or is a trigger to cause them to "act."

Once they decide to act and start the process of gathering information online (assuming it is not a completely offline sequence of events that leads them to the local Starbucks for a cup of coffee), they first form an expectation in their mind, or a visual that represents what they expect to find. Because we are all used to viewing web pages, it is quite possible that this representation in their mind may be web content that includes product information with images or video, comparisons to other products, pricing, availability, and so on.

With that in their mind, they head off to their favorite search engine and attempt to convert the information in their head into *the language of search*, which is keywords. They need to somehow come up with a search query that is a best guess and will hopefully provide listings of sites that deliver on this expectation. At this point, they usually go back and forth visiting different sites, maybe even refining their search queries until they are ultimately confronted with the content they envisioned in their mind.

They view and study the content and get outstanding questions answered before they head to the conversion point, where they decide to buy, download, call, or contact. This conversion happens after they are satisfied that they have all the information they need to take the next step.

If your website is optimized around the search terms they used and it has the content and the structure that helps them realize the expectation they envisioned, then it is more likely they will reach your conversion point and do so quickly. The role of SEO and paid search is to get your site visible within search engines. The role of your website or landing page is to convert. However, getting them to act in the first place depends on awareness building activities, much of which can be traditional advertising and promotion.

So let me introduce a powerful concept. Those who are a part of developing the message for traditional advertising channels like TV, radio, print, and direct marketing must have access to core keywords that have been researched and are proven to drive the right traffic. Once armed with these keywords, they can use them in the messaging for each channel they employ. When a consumer's response to these messages is to seek out a search engine to start the process of finding what they want, they are more likely to use those keywords. In other words, their ability to condense their expectation into keywords has been influenced by the message, and they are using keywords for which the content they are looking for is already optimized.

This is the powerful influence that traditional advertising can exert over online shoppers. An especially powerful application of this strategy is for lesser-known or newly-minted brand names. When you embed your unique keywords into the minds of your target audience with your traditional marketing initiatives, this can influence the search queries they use to find you and essentially push out your competition. You are literally having your audience reach you on your own terms—no pun intended.

Now, there are a number of questions this brings up. How do you get your hands on the keyword research that has already been done? How can you find unique, salient keywords to describe your products and services ? How can you integrate these keywords into copy, messaging, and scripts that will make their way into traditional marketing channels? Let's start with the first of two questions in the keyword research brief.

The Keyword Research Brief

The keyword research brief is a document that is very similar to a creative or technical brief. It outlines only the top-level key insights distilled from your full keyword research and testing. I will share with you an outline of what this might look like. Remember, this is only one example. Once you understand its vital role and purpose in the process, craft one that meets your own needs.

Five Elements of a Keyword Research Brief

To illustrate this more effectively, I will use a fictitious company who is in the business of selling bicycles online and at select storefronts within the United States. (see Figure 12.2)

Keyword Research Brief

Target Audience / Personas

Our target audience is typically individuals between the ages of 18 and 35. For the purposes of the website we have broken down these individuals into 4 types or personas based on intent and their purpose for searching. This will help you put our keywords into better context.

Persona	Description
Newbie	People who have never purchased a bike before
Rookie	Some familiarity with bikes but looking for specific brands or features
Pedaler	Bike owners who are looking for enhancements or maintenance
The Local	People who are looking for a local bike shop

Core Keywords and Data

This is the list of keywords that are the most relevant to our business and which we hope you can use or embed within any content you are developing for our company. We have included some data for each keyword to give you a little insight into their performance potential. We have also mapped the keywords to their personas as well as typical traffic to our website from each keyword.

Keyword	Business Relevance	Monthly Searches	Persona	% Traffic to Our Site	Trends
road bike	9	450,000	All	12%	Peak: April - Oct
road bike brands	8	3,600	Rookie	8%	Peak: April - Oct
road bike maintenance	5	9,900	Pedaler	5%	All Year
mountain bike	6	673,000	Rookie	6%	Peak: July - Aug
trek bikes	9	165,000	Rookie	9%	All Year
bike store denver	10	1,900	Local	20%	All Year
how to buy a bike	7	5400	Newbie	8%	Peak: May - July
best road bike	7	33,100	Rookie	3%	All Year
road bikes online	8	4,400	All	4%	All Year
bike store austin	10	3,600	Local	18%	All Year

Key Landing Pages

To provide you with more context we have attached the main landing pages for each keyword. Feel free to visit each page to learn more about how we are representing each of these keywords on our website. This may provide you with more ideas on how to use these keywords for your work.

Keyword	Web URL
road bike	www.bikecompany.com/road-bike
road bike brands	www.bikecompany.com/road-bike-brands
road bike maintenance	www.bikecompany.com/road-bike-maintenance
mountain bike	www.bikecompany.com/mountain-bike
trek bikes	www.bikecompany.com/trek-bike
bike store denver	www.bikecompany.com/stores/denver
how to buy a bike	www.bikecompany.com/road-bike-how-to-buy
best road bike	www.bikecompany.com/road-bike-reviews
road bikes online	www.bikecompany.com/road-bikes-online
bike store austin	www.bikecompany.com/stores/austin

Keywords with Low Competition

The following keywords that are listed are keywords that have low competition. This means that few people are using this keyword or that they do not know about it. The reason we include these keywords is to give you ideas on keywords you can use in any campaign in which you want to own. If you are looking for a promotional campaign that is new and fresh and need some inspiration on where to start then you may want to consider these keyword phrases.

austin speed shop	bicycle gears	mtb forum	downhill
peddler bike shop	bike supply	cycles direct	dirt mtb
trek speed concept	bike source	road bike rider	city bike
cycle shop	bicycle world	road bike tips	mtb bike review
trek remedy	good road bike brands	bike it	bike components

Figure 12.2 Keyword research brief

Keyword Usage Tips
As you use these keywords be sure to use the word exactly as it is presented in this document. Try not to use variations. We wish to be consistent in the use of these keywords from the website to all other channels we use. The more consistent we are in using these keywords the stronger our position will be.

If you plan to use any of these keywords in a campaign online and you plan to link from those keywords to our website or other campaigns, please be sure to have keyword as the link and not something like "click here". For instance, in the first example the keyword has the link. This is the correct way as opposed to the second, which is optimizing around the word "click here", which doesn't help at all.

For the best in road bike service please visit our website.
For the best in road bike service please click here.

For further questions about usage tips or any other topic on the use of keywords in other online or offline communications please contact:

Ron Jones
Symetri Internet Marketing
rjones@symetri.com
www.symetri.com
336-285-0941

Figure 12.2 Keyword research brief (*continued*)

Element 1: Audience/Persona Expectation

This first stage is to outline the main personas, or target audience, in basic terms. In our example these might be as follows:

- People who have never purchased a bike before
- People who have purchased a bike but are looking for specific brands and features
- People who are looking for enhancements or maintenance on their bike
- People who are looking for a local shop

This helps put the core keywords into proper context based on a range of needs among the target market.

Element 2: Core Keywords to Use

This section is where you will outline the keywords that have been tested and that you want used for online and offline initiatives. For each keyword listed, you should also attach relevant data that will make sense to a colleague who may not be too technical. The number of annual searches per year or relevance rankings (with a brief explanation of each) would be nice to share with them. If you have analytics data for your own site, you might consider showing the relative importance of each keyword expressed as a percentage of your overall site traffic or revenue contribution. Finally, if you have room, you might provide trend data in a simple form that can help your colleagues understand seasonality factors for each keyword. You may come up with other keyword data that you think is relevant and informative to add to the document.

Element 3: Key Landing Pages

You should include a link to the best landing page for each keyword to provide further context. If you have optimized your website around your core keywords, this will not be a problem. Your colleagues can go to your website to see ways you've used the keywords. Additionally, there may be images, video, or other engagement objects that may help to educate and provide innovative ideas.

Element 4: List of Unique, Low-Competition Keywords

As I mentioned earlier, there is value in knowing which keywords have the lowest competition. Whether these keywords are used on your website or not, they can be a source of inspiration for possible brand messages or campaign ideas. Having a list of these keywords can provide a great place to start for those who are looking for new ideas.

Element 5: Keyword Usage Tips

This final section is just for any usage tips you may want to pass along. One of the most important usage tips involves linking. If your public relations folks decide to develop online press releases, they should know that the keyword itself should be the one that is linked, not words like "click here".

This and any other tips you wish to communicate can be placed here for the reader's convenience. Invariably there will be questions or even requests for more detail, so remember to include contact information for someone who can provide answers to questions.

Again, this is a suggested layout of content for a keyword research brief. You should by now have an idea on how this works. Adapt this to your own circumstances and modify it any way you like. If you have any unique uses for what you have done with your keyword research brief, feel free to post your brief or ideas to this book's website, www.keywordintelligencebook.com. I would love to hear from you.

Keywords in Press Releases

Writing a press release can be a great way to incorporate targeted keywords and implement SEO best practices, but it can be a challenge for people who are not familiar with SEO or developing web content. With SEO, you strategically place keywords within pages and in body copy in a consistent way. To optimize a press release, you essentially do the same thing. And just as you do for any SEO efforts, you start press release optimization with your list of targeted keywords in hand and look for opportunities to insert those keywords into your press release without obscuring the overall message.

There are some who place keywords wherever possible on their site just to increase keyword density. This is a mistake for both SEO and for keyword placement for press releases. The idea is to write first for the reader so your content is clear and concise and then attempt to logically place your targeted keywords.

As you embark on writing a press release, you should attempt to use your primary keywords within the first paragraph. It is even better if you can work them into the headline or the first sentence of the first paragraph. In most cases, the first paragraph summarizes the whole press release and its focus. This is one reason it is the most important placement for search engine ranking purposes.

Many writers will include statistics with data and figures at the beginning to create more impact. Regardless of what you use to introduce the article, whether it be a quote, statistic, or even a thought-provoking question, consider how you can embed your keywords phrase from the beginning.

Quotes used in press releases can be especially challenging because they come verbatim from your source, who may not think to include one of your target keywords in their quote. If this is the case, you might try to editorialize their responses. You can use a statement that conveys the essence of their response to any question they were asked and then try to fit in a keyword or two. Or you may keep the quote intact but use keywords in a quick summary that appears afterward.

As you move on in the press release, you should also try to place a keyword within the middle paragraph and then one in the last paragraph. Strive to leave a large enough gap between them. As you continue placing keywords within the article, try not to exceed more than five of the same keywords per release. The use of three keywords is ideal. The best way to test for oversaturation (or keyword stuffing) is to reread the article and ensure that it flows properly and doesn't appear cumbersome. Remember, you want to write for the reader first. It is all about being coherent. Your information must be easily understood and must have continuity.

Here is a quick summary and list of tips for including keywords in your press releases:

- Limit your optimization to one to three occurrences of the same keyword per release.

- Place your most popular keyword in the headline, which carries the most weight with search engines.

- Use a subhead with a keyword phrase if your release is more than a few paragraphs long. The release will be easier to read, and search engines will take note of bolded text.

- Roughly 2 percent of your content should be keywords, give or take.

- Use plurals for your keywords if it makes sense. For SEO purposes, you get credit for both the plural and singular forms of the word. However, avoid excessive repetition.

- Consider using less-obvious (long-tail) keywords. These phrases may get fewer searches but higher results.

- Remember to include anchor text links (the visible hyperlinked text you see on web pages) and write out full `http://www` URLs.

- In your release call to action, insert direct links to separate landing pages set up with further information to aid journalists and any prospective clients.

Keyword Research Techniques for Press Releases

I covered keyword research techniques in Chapter 4, but let's look at some specific techniques for identifying keywords for use in press releases. Or you can identify how others have used keywords in their press releases.

Competition Look at your competition's website and view their press releases. Furthermore, you can choose View Source from your browser window to open up the page source as I demonstrated in Chapter 2. From here you can identify any keywords they may have placed in the title tag, meta keyword, or description tags.

Journalists As you conduct your research, take time to read articles written by journalists writing about similar content. As you do this, look out for their use of keywords and get a feel for whether it flows well or if they simply stuffed in their keywords. You will quickly identify what works and what doesn't.

Internal resources Obviously look at any internal resources you have. Check in with your marketing personnel and grab the list of keywords they have researched or, better yet, get a copy of their keyword research brief if one exists.

PR distribution services There are a couple of great distribution services like PRNewswire (`www.prnewswire.com`) and Marketwire (`www.marketwire.com`) that have SEO features built in. Use them a couple of times to get used to how they work. The nice thing about these kinds of services is that they offer tracking and reporting of impressions, clicks, and prints of your press releases. You can look up results from your past releases to get an idea of which keywords are most popular. Combine this with your own site analytics to get an idea of which keywords from press releases are the best performers.

Since you have already optimized your release around your targeted keywords, it is only natural to add this valuable content to your website. As you do this make sure you adhere to SEO best practices to further optimize your page. Things like title, description, meta keywords, and heading tags are places you will want to make sure you have the proper keywords. Refer to Chapter 6 for more specific information on SEO and keyword usage.

Keywords in Brand Positioning

Every company, product, service, or brand has a position in the marketplace, even if no one is paying attention to it. This is because customers and prospects are continually interacting with various aspects of your business. They are gathering information, forming impressions, and making judgments and even decisions based on actions you take and don't take.

One way of looking at positioning is to consider what people think about your product or service. A position is what the brand stands for in the mind of the consumer or user. It's user focused. It's what sets a brand apart from its competitors in the mind of the target. It's a brief, simple, and single-minded perception of the brand. Positioning is what marketers do to reinforce or modify this perception.

Obviously this is a very important aspect marketing strategy. You want to be in control of this perception. Brand positioning is all about taking charge of the perception and influencing what and how people think about your brand.

Keywords can play a role in this process in several ways. First, you can learn more about your audience by the keywords they use. You can then embed keywords into your messaging to influence their thinking. And as I illustrated at the beginning of this chapter, you can influence the words that come to mind when they get online and start searching.

Let's look at a few ways you can build a strong brand positioning that includes keywords and keyword research.

Six Steps to Stronger Brand Positioning

It is always nice to have access to an experienced marketing team to build your brand positioning, but assuming you don't or you can't afford one, here are six steps you can take that will help you gain more control over your brand positioning and fortify it in the marketplace.

Step 1: Determine Current Positioning

Conduct research among all of your constituents, inside your company and outside. Take time to ask important insightful questions:

- What word or phrase comes to mind when you think about our company?
- What does our company do differently than anyone else?
- What does our company do best? How are we unique?
- What target market characteristics are most important and relevant in affecting their behavior to make a purchase?
- What is the main reason someone would buy from us?

- What is your product's frame of reference? In other words, how would you describe the competitive set or category in which you compete?

- What one user benefit do you want your customers and users to identify with most readily?

For our purposes, the first question obviously jumps out as being very important. You want to know what "keywords" are on the minds of people who interact with your brand currently. Once you know this, you can agree and then fortify this position or modify and plan to place more important keywords into their minds.

The outcome of asking these and other probing questions is to ascertain what assets and strengths you have today. These can be leveraged as potential differentiators for your new or modified positioning. This way you can build on what you already have.

Step 2: Assess Customer Needs

I have covered this several times in this book, and for good reason. By learning more about your customers and their needs, you can craft a positioning statement and branded messages that resonate with them. Often primary needs like high quality, expertise, good service, and low price are rather obvious. The problem, however, is that everyone else is thinking along the same lines. A strong positioning is unique and looks beyond the primary needs by uncovering gems that lie beneath the surface. To help you get to these gems and find any secondary benefits, try answering these and other related questions.

You should rate the importance of the following factors in your decision:

- Increasing operational efficiency
- Reducing risks
- Getting projects completed quickly
- Leveraging existing investments and platforms
- Building organizational capacity for training best practices
- Providing measurable results to management
- Minimizing company involvement with turn-key solutions
- Customizing for unique company needs
- Taking risks to become an innovator and leader
- Possessing domain expertise and competence
- Building human capital for the company

You are likely to find keywords that represent each of these secondary benefits. Make sure you take note of each one. Then you can do further keyword research to learn more about popularity, seasonality, and other statistical insights. This should ultimately have a bearing on your new positioning.

Step 3: Assess Competitive Landscape

Look at your competition and determine the positioning for each competitor. Identify the strong and weak points for each competitor. You may even want to plot these on a graph to visualize where they all fit in the positioning landscape. Are there any holes or gaps? Do these gaps represent opportunities for you to own that space? Maybe there are ways of looking at your competitors' positioning statements so you can appeal to customers in a different way. What keywords are they using to position themselves?

Are there different phrases you might want to use to be unique? What are they? If you have access to a keyword research brief, look at the list of noncompetitive keywords. Do any of these keywords stand out or are they unique? You may not find the exact keyword you are looking for, but this list may spark new ideas.

Step 4: Develop a New Brand Positioning

The best way to think about this step is to understand how you want your target to think about your product or service. A position is what the brand stands for in the mind of the user—what sets it apart from its competition.

The essence of positioning is sacrifice. You must give up something so that what follows is focused. No brand can successfully be all things to all people. To be successful, your position must be long term, unique and protectable (proprietary and ownable), single minded, focused, consistent with product or service delivery, and built on your brand's desired image.

As you gather information from the first three steps, including keywords that have surfaced, start crafting new positioning statements. The key is to attempt to use keywords that are part of your targeted list. Be prepared to create good content on your site around any new keywords that have surfaced. You will also need to add them to your list of targeted keywords.

As you build out new statements, consider generating a list of three to five that can be tested and validated. Here are a couple of examples:

We are the best at _____ because of our ability to _____ .

If you need _____ , choose us because of _____ .

Step 5: Validate the Positioning

After you have identified your sample set of statements, it is time to test all of your alternatives internally and externally to see if they are engaging and believable. Conduct one-on-one interviews with employees and customers alike. Do not focus only on what they say. Observe body language that might speak more than words. You can also ask respondents to rate the statements for favorability, importance, and believability:

- Overall, how do you feel about this statement? (Highly favorable=1 to Highly unfavorable=5)

- How important is this statement to you? (Highly favorable=1 to Highly unfavorable=5)

- How well do you believe 'Your Company Name' can deliver on this statement? (5 point scale: very unlikely to very likely)

- Does this statement take a long-term view of your business? Is it enduring? (Highly favorable=1 to Highly unfavorable=5)

- Is this statement compelling? Does it state a premise worth participating in? (Highly favorable=1 to Highly unfavorable=5)

- Is it simple and credible or does it require further explanation? Is it believable given the proof you have to offer? (Highly favorable=1 to Highly unfavorable=5)

As you do this, you will find what works and what doesn't. In the end you should finalize on a single positioning statement that you plan to go with.

Step 6: Execute and Deploy the Positioning

After you have selected your new positioning statement, it is critical that the whole company gets behind it and is consistent in its use. The website, collateral material, messaging, and all other types of communications should be updated to use this statement. If you have included keywords and keyword research in this process, you will have a positioning statement that includes your best keywords, which is the key to this whole exercise. It is a great opportunity to perpetuate these keywords and any closely associated with them into the mainstream of your company's communications as you "speak with one voice" to the world.

Summary

Messaging and branding are powerful tools for influencing consumer thought and actions. Specifically, they can have an influence on the keywords that might be used for search queries. By understanding this concept and mining the valuable information that comes from keyword research, you can develop messages that will serve you better. The keyword research brief can be a great tool to share with other team members who help develop your brand strategy.

International Keyword Research

For those of you who operate outside of the United States for one reason or another, the process of keyword research internationally can be tricky. There are many challenges and obstacles. This chapter will focus on what you need to know to take what you have already learned in this book and expand your processes to take on keyword research in different languages.

Chapter Contents

The Challenges of International Keyword Research

With roughly 63 percent of the world's online population using languages other than English, international SEO, otherwise known as global SEO or multilingual SEO, is an important component of an effective global Internet marketing strategy.

Most standard search engines and directories have a local version for different countries around the world. You can view a comprehensive list of these international search engines at Search Engine Colossus (www.searchenginecolossus.com).

As you might guess, some search engines are better than others, and they work differently, too. They also have different criteria for inclusion. Some may demand that the site be in the local language, others demand a local URL, and still others expect the search company to be incorporated locally.

Another important point is that Google results may differ from country to country. Achieving a certain rank for targeted keywords for the United States doesn't mean you'll achieve the same results for France, for instance. These are some of the challenges you'll face as you plan your SEO and PPC campaigns for different country sites.

To build out an effective campaign, you will need to do the research. International keyword research is a whole new ball game compared to English keyword research in the United States. For one thing, there are far fewer keyword research tools to choose from. And for those few tools, there may not be enough search volume to showcase any beneficial keyword data, and in some markets only keywords from Google are available.

There are other challenges as well when you get into cultural differences. For example, some languages do not currently have 100 percent agreement on standards for grammar and spelling. This makes it difficult to identify the right keywords to use. To make matters worse, searchers may drop accent marks and space words differently than the proper word style.

If you thought that keyword research in the United States is challenging, welcome to the world of international keyword research. This brings up a good point. Some US English site owners who have a campaign underway but plan to branch out into other languages fall into a treacherous trap. They attempt to convert and translate their current US English keyword list into the desired international language thinking that if a word ranks well in English it will also rank well for other languages.

According to the *Ethnologue* (www.ethnologue.com), there are 6,909 known languages spoken in the world today. This can leave room for misinterpretation if you simply attempt to translate from one language to another, not to mention using native expressions or slang.

For example, the Spanish version of the US phrase *kick the bucket*, which means to die, is *estirar la pata*. If you decided to do a literal translation from English to Spanish, the folks in Spain would think you literally meant to kick a bucket. If you translated the phrase from Spanish to English, the meaning would be to stretch your leg. You can see with this simple example that it is dangerous to use a direct translation of your keywords from one language to another—it can confuse your audience and may not convey the true meaning.

Researching in Other Languages

As you begin researching in a language of which you have little understanding, it may be difficult to practically manage the research process. For instance, if you are researching the Russian, Arabic, and Far Eastern languages, it can be tough to even read the characters, much less translate them. In this case, you will need back translations of keywords to help your team understand the core meaning.

Additionally, you should tap a local team of linguists or translators to help you understand the language, keywords, and their meaning. Linguists are usually versed in their mother tongue. This means they learned the language from their mother's knee as opposed to learning it from books or at school.

A local team is typically made up of individuals you need to hire, but if you have local resources within the target region, you might use them instead. The key is to find someone who truly understands the language and the local culture. They might have little or no understanding of search, so they will need to be trained on the basics of keyword research and search.

In some cases, to get access to these people you may have to hire them from an agency. This can further complicate things because you may have to integrate different approaches and methodologies into the overall process, which can bog things down and strain communication. In other cases, you can use your local resources, if you have them, to be a part of the team. The key is to make sure you have a consistent process that all team members abide by. Training will probably be needed to ensure success.

If you decide you wish to embark in this challenging world of international keyword research, you should set your expectations accordingly. If you live within the international community, you are probably used to these challenges and are doing your best to build a solid multicultural campaign. Many of the principles discussed in this book are still valid, but without solid research tools, you have to lean more on people resources than on automated tools. This basically translates to more work. Because more people are involved, you need to have a solid process that can accommodate these different people resources.

International Keyword Research Process

If you plan to build out a structure around an international SEO and keyword research campaign, you will need a good process to guide your efforts. You will be glad to know that the process discussed in Chapter 4 on finding keywords is still basically the same. The only difference going forward is the person who does the work. The work will need to be done in the local language.

There are four steps to utilize for an international keyword research process:

1. Discovery, refinement, and segmentation
2. Variations in different languages
3. Translation
4. Find the right partner

Step 1: Discovery, Refinement, and Segmentation

It has been determined that the keyword list that is a result of your efforts from Chapter 4 and Chapter 5 is virtually the same. You will have your list of keywords that has been refined and segmented around unique and relevant terms. This assumes that you use your English keyword research as a starting point for your local campaign. Next, you will modify the process to accommodate other languages and cultures. Again, you want to make sure the work is done in the local language. This way, cultural differences as well as linguistic ones are organically integrated into the process. For example, "Dairy Products" might be an odd category on a Chinese food website.

If you are starting your keyword research from within a local language, you can still use the same principles, but you will likely be limited as to the tools you have to work with.

Step 2: Variations in Different Languages

In this step, you begin by looking at your keyword list and asking whether the target language has variations of the same word. You are not translating the keywords but searching for variations. For example, in the United States, the keyword "antivirus" might be a word you would use if you were in the business of selling antivirus software. Another variation might be "virus protection", and there might be one or two more core words. In China, however, there are 21 different ways to form characters to represent the same thing. And if you look at other languages, like French, there might be just one or two.

In languages like Japanese, there are multiple formats for writing. Motoko Hunt of AJPR, who is considered by many to be the leading Japanese search marketing expert, offers the chart shown in Figure 13.1.

"USA"　　　　　　　"High Definition"

*アメリカ　　　　　*ハイデフィニション
*合衆国　　　　　　*ハイビジョン
*米国　　　　　　　*フルハイビジョン
*アメリカ合衆国

Figure 13.1 Variations example

The left column example, "USA", has four popular variations of referencing the United States. These variations include katakana, which uses script fragments to "transcribe" technical and scientific terms where there is no Japanese kanji equivalent. It is essentially a phonetic pronunciation of the Western word. It is also commonly used for country names and foreign cities. In the first variation, the characters represent "a me ri ka". The second and third variations are kanji characters, and the last combines kanji and katakana to represent the formal "United States of America". All four variations are linguistically correct and interchangeable, but each has a different application in formality, written text, and most important, query volume.

In the case of "High Definition", the first variation uses katakana and is a phonetic variation of "high definition", whereas the second is a phonetic variation of "high vision", which is how Japanese refer to "high definition". The last one is yet another phonetic variation, this time of "full high vision".

So the second step, which is a new step as you dive into international keyword research, is to look at each of your target languages and identify all of the variations that might exist for your keyword.

Step 3: Translation

The next step is the translation of the keyword. In the "antivirus" example, 21 variations that exist for the keyword "antivirus" were identified. Now variations need to be translated and added to the list. The important point here is that we started off with step two. Many people just use a keyword suggestion tool and then translate the word into the native language. You may come up with a linguistically correct version, but it may not be the most popular version of the keyword.

To illustrate the downside to this approach, I'll use an example that Motoko Hunt with AJPR has used while doing research for one of her clients. The research was for a Swedish baby carrier called Baby Bjorn. If a Japanese searcher was aware of the brand, they might search using that name. However, without brand awareness, they need to use the product category "baby carrier". The linguist who did the translating decided to go with the phonetic way of writing the keyword. However, there was a Japanese way of referring to the same keyword that was searched on a hundred times more than the phonetic sound of the brand name.

So this is a good example of why you don't want to just translate; you want the keyword localized and then normalized for local demand.

Another example is for the keyword "projectors". The German word for projector is "projektoren". There are fewer than a thousand searches per month for this term. What a German calls a projector colloquially is a *Beamer*. A German would never refer to a BMW as a *"beamer"*—only in the United States do we call it that. The number of searches per month for the term "beamer" is around 40,500, as shown in Table 13.1 So again, "projektoren" is linguistically correct but it is not the correct choice to use on a website and in paid search campaigns.

Table 13.1 Keyword search per month

Keyword Phrase	Search Volume
Projektoren	1,000
Beamer	40,500

Source: Google Suggestion Tool - Germany/Germany - Exact Match

This is why it is often best if you can find a localization firm or a translator that has knowledge in the subject matter. If the translator doesn't have any knowledge of the industry or the products/services you are marketing, this can be a typical outcome. It can often be corrected by having your local marketing teams or marketing partners review the material to ensure that the appropriate words are being used.

Step 4: Find The Right Partner

As you make plans to find the right partners to work with in this process of research and translation, you have three choices:

- Work with an agency (specific keyword research with a local language)
- Work with localization expert (native mother tongue speakers)
- Work with freelance native speaker of the language

All three need to follow the same process and consider any local nuance that you require they add to ensure accuracy.

Working with an Agency

If you feel the work at this point is over your head and you want to hire professionals, an agency might be the thing for you. Companies like WebCertain (www.webcertain. com), Global Strategies International (www.globalstrategies.com), and Localizations. com (www.localizations.com) make up a talented group of multicultural professionals who are mother-tongue linguists and have also been trained in search engine marketing. You may want to engage them if you are new to the area and lack the resources to build out a methodology and team of your own. The key aspect of this kind of relationship is that agencies like this have access to the resources who understand localization and are trained in search. They will likely have access to resources who also have a background in your industry and will pick up on the vital nuances that would escape normal translators. As I illustrated earlier, this can make a world of difference.

Working with Localization Experts and Native Speakers

If you decide to work with localization experts or freelance translators, you will need to do some training and provide some direction before you begin the research and translation process. There are three distinct characteristics that you should look for in a linguist:

- Needs to be a mother tongue
- Simple search experience
- Background with your subject matter

As I stated earlier, a mother-tongue speaker is someone who learned the language at their mother's knee as opposed to someone who studied the language in school.

Having a background in search engine marketing is a major plus. It isn't necessary that your linguist have a vast knowledge of search or links, just that they understand the basics of relevancy. Sharing the worksheets, process, and best practices from the previous chapters would be a great start. This will allow the linguist to understand the workflow and build an accurate and robust keyword list.

Finally, a linguist who also has an understanding of your industry and your subject matter will be a big help because they can provide translations that put your keywords in the proper context.

Ask for Back Translations

Ask your researchers to provide you with back translations of the keywords you are researching. This will allow you and your team to evaluate the keywords in the proper context. *Back translation* is a process of translating a keyword that has already been translated into a foreign language back to the original language.

One of the reasons for this is to define some methods for checks and balances to ensure accuracy. The literal word in one language may not have an exact equivalent in another language. It could also have a completely different meaning in the translated language.

One suggestion is to develop a glossary worksheet on which the local word(s) and the English equivalents are noted. This will allow an easy review by the local teams and can be reused by future localizers. It will also help with the review of paid and organic search reports later in your process.

No translation can be expected to perfectly convey what consumers mean in their own language. This is why there is a need for qualified translators. Back translation can improve the reliability and validity of keyword research in different languages by requiring that the quality of a translation is verified by an independent translator who translates the keyword back into the original language. Then original and back-translated keywords can be compared.

Your Brand and Its Meaning in Other Languages

Because the English language is so prevalent, it is common for English terms to find their way into searches. Take care how your brand and branded key terms are translated from English to another language. They may actually mean something different.

Also, in languages such as Arabic and Russian, you might find that your brands are transliterated into the local character set. If the local character set is used to represent brands phonetically, you will need to be apprised of the resulting keywords. As you work with your linguistic resources, decide how you wish misspellings and grammatical issues to be treated as well.

Keep in mind that a keyword in US English might not have a direct equivalent in some languages.

Your brand name in searches can show different results in search suggestions in local markets. For example, when you type the brand name "Panasonic" in Yahoo! Japan, it shows you options for the brand in katakana and not roman characters, as shown in Figure 13.2. Yahoo! Japan understands the two are the same, but this is not always the case.

Figure 13.2 Yahoo! Japan

Long-Tail Keywords

The principle of the long tail as discussed in Chapter 1 also applies in international keyword research, but it does vary from one language to another. One point to remember is that not every language lends itself to multiple variations of words as English does or multiple characters as Chinese does. Don't assume the number of keywords to be the same in all languages.

Seed Terms

As you work with your keyword research linguist, it is a good practice to provide them with a list of seed terms that have been successful for you in your campaigns. This you should do in your original language. Seed terms help the researcher understand the terms that worked in a given language and will provide them with inspiration as they identify more in another language. The seed terms are not to be translated, however.

When you simply translate keywords from one language to another, it may result in terms that have low search volumes, not to mention they may seem silly in the target language.

For some languages, you may need to use multiple spellings of the same keyword because of the mechanics of the target language, such as, for example, Finnish or Russian. You may also need to vary the content included locally to provide a suitable platform for your selected keywords.

Expanding Your International Keyword Lists

In the localization process, if you have a good localizer, they typically build a glossary. The left column consists of all of the keywords in English. The right column is typically the local market equivalent, as discussed earlier.

The use of memory tools can be effective in this process. Translation memory manager (TMM) tools are essentially databases that store word segments that have previously been translated. They are designed to aid human translators in the translation process. An example of a TMM tool is Trados (www.trados.com).

You'll use this spreadsheet with the two columns as a kind of cheat sheet that provides you with a basic glossary of your keywords in US English and their equivalent in the target languages.

You can run that glossary through a keyword suggestion tool like the Google Keyword Tool and see if the words that you are currently using are the most relevant. This is a great way to find the keywords that are most relevant in the native language you are targeting (as in the "projektoren" versus "beamer" example earlier); then, with a TMM, you simply do a search and replace. For example, if you previously used "projektoren" in the glossary and then change it to "beamer," the TMM should be able to tell you that a certain number of documents or web pages have that word and can see the context of the sentence with the word. In most cases, no action is required. In some cases, changing the word or characters in Asian languages may necessitate the need for changes to the context or sentence structure. It is strongly suggested you review any pages where the search and replace has happened to ensure you have maintained the correct content, message and tone.

Keyword Research Tools

There are many keyword-related tools, but there aren't too many for doing language research. The best tool worldwide is the Google keyword suggestion tool (https://adwords.google.com/select/KeywordToolExternal).

There are specific search engines that you can use to do keyword searches for local markets, like Baidu (www.baidu.com) for Chinese and Yandex (www.yandex.com) for Russian. Some international search agencies may have developed their own tools, but the Google Keyword Tool has pushed away most other tool vendors.

Summary

The challenges of working internationally add a level of complexity to the process of keyword research. The principles you have already learned in this book can still be used, but you need to add new processes to ensure that your campaigns will work within the local culture you are targeting. Your campaign won't necessarily be successful and work well abroad just because it does in the United States. And just translating your keywords into another language should be avoided at all costs. Use the process and practical tips outlined in this chapter to ensure that you will use the right keywords for your targeted region.

Keyword Measurement

The final step in any keyword research process is to test your keywords and validate that they are working for you, as I have mentioned several times throughout the book. This final chapter is dedicated to helping you test your keywords and monitor their performance. Furthermore, you need to learn all you can from keyword usage in each of your campaigns. I will outline various methods to measure keyword performance to help you determine if they are working to your expectations .

14

Chapter Contents

Defining Metrics for Success

I covered the concept of developing a strategy in Chapter 2. I want to reiterate that this is really the place to start because you need to define up front what success means to your marketing campaigns. Without this, you have no way to gauge what success looks like. You need to have a vision of what you expect to accomplish and then set up your analytics to capture as much information as you can to determine if you were or were not successful. Here are some of the most notable goals for a successful outcome:

- Increased overall website visitor traffic
- Increased keyword rankings and top keyword placement
- Increased brand awareness
- Increased generated revenue and ROI
- Specific behavioral insights from your target audience based on keyword usage

Many people think of keyword success as a keyword ranking in the first page of search engine results. This is a goal that most try to strive for, but it is important to note that this isn't the primary goal. Higher keyword ranking translates into more visibility and increased traffic. Achieving visibility and increased traffic is more important than just focusing on keyword ranking.

Another goal that most do not attribute to the use of keywords is market research and human behavioral analysis. This may turn out to be a secondary goal, but it is a goal nonetheless. All current trends suggest that in order to succeed we need to develop extraordinary content. Ordinary content will get buried and will be subordinate to content we "vote" on that is "liked" the best. The study of keywords and what it tells you about their usage can help you learn what kind of content your audiences really want.

Regardless of which goals you have in place, it is important that they are part of your strategy, and mechanisms need to be in place to measure their use.

Measuring Keyword Performance

So you have identified keywords, refined them, segmented them into logical groups, and integrated them into campaigns for SEO, PPC, social media, mobile, local, print, branding, and other marketing channels. Just because you have gone through this process doesn't necessarily mean that your keywords will reach their full potential out of the gate.

Before you start using keywords in channels in which they may take some time to reach their full potential, like SEO, you should test them to give you greater confidence that they can perform as you expect them to. Failure to do this can result in a waste of time and money.

One of the best ways to do quick tests on your keyword performance potential and related messaging is to set up a mini PPC campaign for keywords from your final list.

Using PPC to Test Keywords and Marketing Messages

Let me walk you through an example of setting up a test campaign to measure keyword effectiveness. The testing environment is shown graphically in Figure 14.1. The variables involved in the test are as follows:

- Keywords
- Ad groups
- Ads
- Landing pages

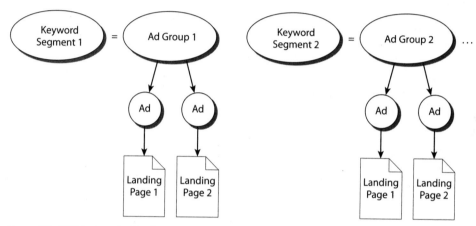

Figure 14.1 PPC Test campaign flowchart

The keywords you want to test should already be segmented into logical groups. These groups become your PPC ad groups. Select exact match for your keywords to give you the best results. Phrase match modifiers can be used, but the tests will not be as accurate. Avoid broad match completely for these tests.

Next, you should build out ads for each ad group. If you are testing these keywords for SEO effectiveness, write your ads with your meta description tags in mind so that your ads simulate your organic search listing in the SERPs. The click-through rate of these ads will help you understand which messages resonate best with your target market so that you can write the most effective meta descriptions for your web pages.

For each ad, you should have a specific landing page that you also want to test. Do this for each keyword segment you want to test. By testing landing pages, you will be adding more complexity and time to the testing procedure, but it will help you better understand how your landing pages will perform relative to your keyword campaign.

On the website, you will obviously make sure you have your analytics set up ahead of time, including your landing pages.

The scenario you want to put together in an SEO test case is to mimic as closely as possible all of the variables you would have if you were running an SEO campaign.

Once your test PPC campaign is in place and your site is tagged and set up, you can launch your campaign. Here are the metrics you will collect and analyze:

- Keyword impressions
- Keyword clicks
- Keyword CTR
- Keyword average position
- Ad impressions
- Ad clicks
- Ad CTR
- Ad average position
- Landing page visits
- Landing page bounce rate
- Conversions
- Conversion rate

Each of these metrics will provide initial insight into the potential effectiveness of your keyword and marketing message choices. The number of keyword impressions and clicks will give you a sense of the popularity and search volume for a specific keyword.

The most important metrics for evaluating your ads during this test are the click-through rate (CTR) and the conversion rate (CVR) of the ads. The CTR will tell you which messages immediately resonated with users searching on your keywords and which did not and will give you actionable data more quickly. The CVR will tell you which ads brought the most motivated visitors, but 5 to 10 times more data will be required to generate a large enough test sample size. Whatever metric you decide to use, you can incorporate the most effective ad messages into your meta description tags and other online and offline marketing initiatives.

The landing page component of your quick test will help you understand how well the keywords you are targeting and the messaging in your ads work together with your web page and if the web page is delivering effectively on users' expectations. Metrics that are important in this part of your tests are bounce rate, conversions (which can be orders or other goals you've set up within your analytics), and conversion rates.

So let's look at an example. I will continue with the bike example and choose to test the following keywords, which make up the keyword segment (carbon frame road bikes). Here are the keywords:

carbon fiber road bikes (2,900 monthly visits)

carbon fiber bikes (14,800 monthly visits)

carbon road bikes (14,800 monthly visits)

I pulled these keyword estimates from the Google Keyword Tool. When pulling your keywords from a keyword suggestion tool, note the number of monthly/annual visits so you can compare to actual visits from your test campaign.

I place these keywords into an ad group and develop a couple of ads to test. Here are two that I came up with for this example:

Carbon Fiber Road Bikes
www.roadrunnerbikes.com
Custom carbon fiber bicycle
frames built & painted in USA
www.roadrunnerbikes.com/testpage1

Carbon Fiber Bikes
www.roadrunnerbikes.com
Best quality carbon fiber
bike frames all hand built
www.roadrunnerbikes.com/testpage2

Notice that in these two examples, I use two distinct marketing messages—one that emphasizes hand-built quality and the other that keys in on "made in the USA." The more separate and distinct the ad copy messages are, the more likely we are to get clear, unambiguous data from our quick PPC test. Notice also how I write the description lines to closely mimic the way it might appear as the snippet in the organic SERP listings. My landing pages will be similar to each other but with slight variations based on the ad message text—one with the USA message and one with the hand-built quality message—so I can test each landing page's bounce rate, conversions, and conversion rate. Now I will go ahead and launch the PPC campaign and test the results, shown in Table 14.1, Table 14.2, Table 14.3, and Table 14.4. I will run the campaign until I get enough data to make statistically valid observations. I like to shoot for tests that run at least two weeks, but I prefer to go longer when I have the time and money so that I have higher confidence in my tests.

▶ Table 14.1 Keyword stats

Keyword	Impressions	Clicks	CTR	Avg. Pos.
carbon fiber road bikes	1,350	40	2.96%	4.6
carbon fiber bikes	11,500	530	4.61%	2.2
carbon road bikes	12,000	220	1.83%	3.5

Ad	Impressions	Clicks	CTR	Avg. Pos.
Ad #1: USA	12,500	540	4.4%	2.9
Ad #2: hand-built quality	12,350	250	2.8%	3.0

► **Table 14.3** Keyword stats

Keyword	Visits	Bounce Rate	Conversions	Conversion Rate
carbon fiber road bikes	40	23%	2	5.0%
carbon fiber bikes	530	33%	16	3.02%
carbon road bikes	220	39%	7	3.18%

► **Table 14.4** Landing page stats

Ad	Visits	Bounce Rate	Conversions	Conversion Rate
Landing Page 1: USA	540	32%	24	4.4%
Landing Page 2: hand-built quality	250	42%	7	2.8%

Based on these figures, I can see that all of the keywords had some decent results; however "carbon fiber bikes" had the highest CTR at 4.61 percent and it had the highest number of clicks. If I move on to the performance on the website, I learn that, as expected, "carbon fiber bikes" had about the same conversion rate as "carbon road bikes". Both of them had a relatively low bounce rates at 33 percent and 39 percent, respectively. There simply wasn't enough volume on the keyword "carbon fiber roadbikes" to draw any conclusions from on the conversions, but the lower bounce rate, even with only 40 observations, appears to indicate that it may be a powerful long-tail keyword. A longer testing period could possibly firm up that conclusion.

So from an overall performance perspective, the keyword "carbon fiber bikes" should be the one that is primarily used within the landing page because it seems to resonate with users better, which can be observed in the higher CTR. The others still had decent performance but not quite as high.

For the ads and the landing pages, I learn that those with the term "USA" seemed to perform better than the ones without. This tells me I need to make sure that the "made in USA" is included within the landing pages as well as the meta descriptions.

With information like this, I can feel more confident in pursuing these keywords, and especially "carbon fiber bikes", and that they are likely to perform as planned. If a test like this had been run for just two weeks, I would consider running it for an additional two weeks to verify the numbers, especially if the data volumes are low. If it ran for a month or more, it would likely yield the answers you need.

The only other thing to consider is to check for seasonality variables. For instance, since I know that most searches for road bikes are made between May and October and I ran my test PPC campaign in January, I would expect my numbers to be different if I ran them in peak season. Alternatively, if I ran them in peak season, I can expect less-impressive results in off-season months.

A tool like Google Insights and Google Trends will help you understand seasonal keyword performance.

Testing Your Google Ads

In the previous example, I touched on landing page testing because landing pages are an important part of the success formula in testing keywords. However, you can also learn a great deal from ad tests that do not take the landing pages into account and primarily use the CTR for measuring performance. One common way is to use Google for ad testing. In Campaign Settings within the AdWords interface, make sure you select the radio button labeled "Rotate: Show all ads equally." If you have checked "Optimize: Show better-performing ads more often," Google will serve the ads with the highest CTR more often. You can be relatively sure that your ads will be served almost equally during the same time periods. However, because one of the ads could be held in editorial review, you should make certain that all your ads are running before you begin testing.

Now you are ready to run split tests on the ads. You'll notice that even small differences can have dramatic effects in CTR and ROI, like changing a singular noun to plural, for example. Even a single keyword in your ad group can have a positive or negative effect on your conversion metrics.

Start by creating four to six ads per ad group, and test messages and styles that are widely divergent. Gross messaging differences—fast versus cheap, for example—will yield faster results and allow you to weed out poorly performing ads and messages.

Once you have reduced your messaging options, you can start testing more specific aspects in your ads, such as singular versus plural, offers, promotions, discounts, capitalization, and display URL variations.

Another good way to perform these types of split tests is to use a feature within AdWords called the AdWords Campaign Experiments (ACE) option. This relatively new feature allows you to create split tests of ads, landing pages, bids, and positions and control the amount of traffic that goes to the ads under test.

The purpose of this type of testing is to see what messages resonate. This will enable you to track each ad and the landing page associated with it. More importantly, it will allow you to test your keywords and how they perform in relation to different marketing messaging.

Keyword Rank Reports

Keyword ranking reports can be an indicator that your SEO efforts are heading in the right direction, or not. However, you need to be careful because they, in and of themselves, do not directly tell you much about your overall performance goals. The true indicators are that you are getting more traffic. So as I discuss this topic in more detail, please keep in mind that keyword rank reports are just a means to an end. You have to put them into a larger context to get a truer picture.

Keyword Monitoring in Google Webmaster Tools

The big advantage of using Google Webmaster Tools (www.google.com/webmasters/ tools) versus other tools is that webmasters can view data on their website as seen by Google. In addition to giving you valuable data about your keyword performance on Google itself, Webmaster Tools helps you identify technical issues such as crawling errors and site performance.

To access the tools that help measure keyword performance, click the "Your site on the web" link, shown in Figure 14.2.

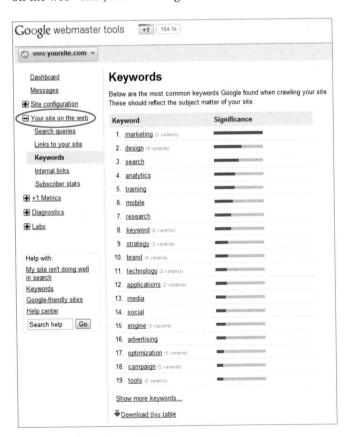

Figure 14.2 Google Webmaster Tools menu

The section you are interested in, of course, is keywords. Click the Keywords link and you will see a list of keywords, as shown in Figure 14.3, that Google thinks are important to your website based on the content of your pages. This page of data basically shows you which keywords are repeated most on your site. You should compare this list of keywords to your target SEO keywords. If you have terms on your keyword list that are not present here, you should consider rewriting your website content to make it more relevant to your target keywords.

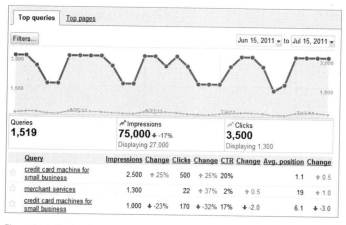

Figure 14.3 Google Webmaster Tools keyword report

By clicking on any of these keywords, you can drill down and see which pages are using the keyword the most. Double-check to see if these pages are relevant landing pages that you intend to target for that keyword. If not, then make the necessary changes.

Search Query Report

The other area within Webmaster Tools that will help you find and target the right keywords is the Top Queries report, shown in Figure 14.4. This report shows you which search queries have resulted in your site being listed in the SERPs.

Top queries	Top pages							

Filters... Jun 15, 2011 ▾ to Jul 15, 2011 ▾

Queries **1,519**	⤢ Impressions **75,000** ↓ -17% Displaying 27,000	↗ Clicks **3,500** Displaying 1,300						
Query	**Impressions**	**Change**	**Clicks**	**Change**	**CTR**	**Change**	**Avg. position**	**Change**
credit card machine for small business	2,500	↑ 25%	500	↑ 25%	20%		1.1	↑ 0.5
merchant services	1,300		22	↑ 37%	2%	↑ 0.5	19	↑ 1.0
credit card machines for small business	1,000	↓ -23%	170	↓ -32%	17%	↓ -2.0	6.1	↓ -3.0

Figure 14.4 Top Queries report

The data shows how each keyword is performing within a given time period. This shows more than the keyword rank or average position; it also shows impressions, clicks, CTR, and the percentage of change. This helps to show more about your keyword performance than just how it ranked, as many rank reports show.

In this example, we'll look at "merchant services" and try to learn more about this search term. In the Google AdWords Keyword Tool, you will see the approximate search volume of this keyword for broad, phrase, and exact matches, as seen in Figure 14.5.

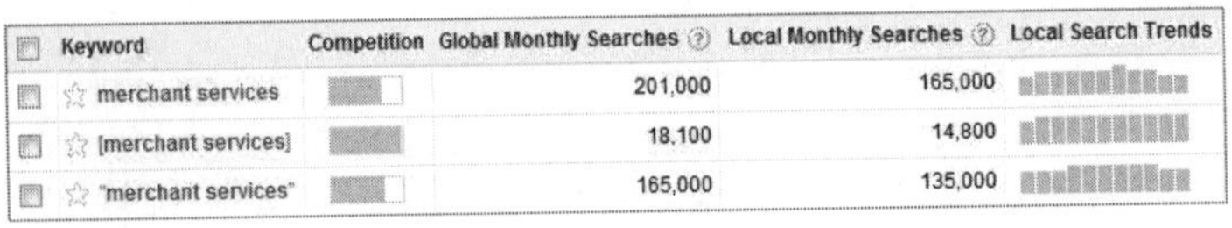

Keyword	Competition	Global Monthly Searches ⑦	Local Monthly Searches ⑦	Local Search Trends
☆ merchant services		201,000	165,000	
☆ [merchant services]		18,100	14,800	
☆ "merchant services"		165,000	135,000	

Figure 14.5 Search volume from Google Keyword Tool

If I take the broad match version of the Keyword Tool's monthly estimate and recalculate for daily estimates, I can compare that data to the data in Webmaster Tools. For example, Keyword Tools suggested I could expect 6,700 impressions per day globally and 5,500 locally, and yet my actual number of impressions as reported by Webmaster Tools was 1,300 impressions per day from the search query, "merchant services". My average position (19) means I am generally showing up at the bottom of the second page of SERPs. This helps put the overall keyword performance in the proper perspective.

The impression data is telling, but the most important data in this report is the number of clicks I get from each keyword. Looking at this example, you can see that there were 22 clicks, which was a positive change from past results. However, the keyword below it shows a negative change. This report is a snapshot in time, so it might not be significant. If, however, you are monitoring this activity over time, you will have a better understanding of keyword performance and the significance of the snapshot data.

This report can be useful for highlighting keywords that you are already ranking without targeting so you can focus your energy on them more directly and make the necessary course corrections to tune them up for optimal performance.

A deeper look at this report can also render insight into user intent behind certain keywords, what searchers are looking for, and how you can better attract clicks once you are ranking well.

While you are looking at Webmaster Tools, take the time to learn all it has to offer. Fixing links and tuning site performance will help you in the long run.

Other Rank Reports

There are other reporting tools, like Web Position (www.webposition.com) and Advanced Web Ranking (www.advancedwebranking.com), that will provide keyword ranking not only for your performing keywords, but also for those that either aren't performing or are just getting started. Many of these tools provide several features, one of which will allow you to measure keyword ranking across many search engines, not just Google.

Most of these tools come packaged with other tools and features that can help you with researching keywords and tracking performance over time. Just remember that if you use these tools, don't get too fixated on just ranking alone. Double-check your results against your analytics tools to help put the keywords in a proper perspective.

Keyword Monitoring in Google Analytics

Let's turn to Google Analytics and find other methods that provide you with a truer picture of how your keywords are performing based on website data. You will of course need to have Google Analytics installed and tracking. Open Google Analytics and choose Traffic Sources > Search > Organic, as seen in Figure 14.6.

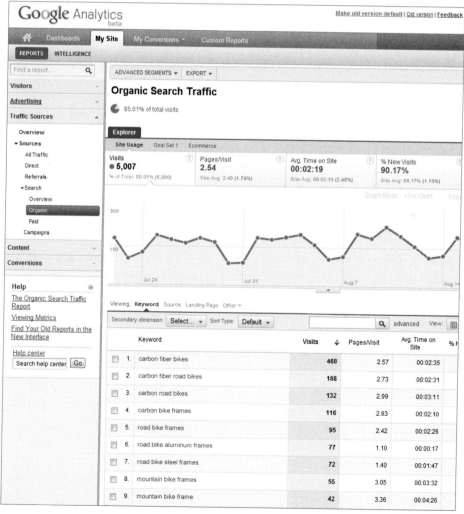

Figure 14.6 Google Analytics menu

I recommend analyzing your brand keywords and other keywords separately because they will have such different performance characteristics. To exclude your branded keywords, click the Edit link next to Advanced Filter and exclude any keyword containing your branded terms, as seen in Figure 14.7.

Figure 14.7 Advanced filtering

This will show you your list of keywords without your branded terms. The first column in Figure 14.8 shows the total number of visits from organic search terms. You should keep an eye on your important keywords over time to see if you are increasing traffic with organic search as you had expected to.

Site Usage	Goal Set 1	Ecommerce		
Visits	**Pages/Visit**	**Avg. Time on Site**	**% New Visits**	**Bounce Rate**
● **4,664**	**2.63**	**00:02:17**	**89.22%**	**57.35%**
% of Total: 75.04% (6,215)	Site Avg: 2.47 (6.36%)	Site Avg: 00:02:01 (13.77%)	Site Avg: 89.16% (0.07%)	Site Avg: 58.02% (-1.15%)

Figure 14.8 Total visits from organic keywords

To get further insightful data, look how each keyword performed, as seen in Figure 14.9. Take extra care to note the bounce rate for each keyword. This will help you understand whether the visitors brought in by that keyword responded positively to the content they first viewed. Additionally, note the number of pages visited. This data gives you insight into behavioral metrics. You are looking for positive trends, such as lowering the bounce rate and increasing the time on site and the average number of pages viewed. However, be careful on these last two metrics. It isn't always the case that longer time on site and more page views indicates a positive outcome. For example, if visitors come to your site looking for pricing information and cannot find it easily, they may bounce around on the site looking for that information and then leave very unsatisfied if they cannot find it.

Finally, if you have taken the time to set up conversion metrics, you can further identify not only which keywords brought in traffic but which ones had the highest conversion rates. With this, you are now connecting the value of your SEO investment as it relates to your core business goals.

	Keyword	Visits ↓	Pages/Visit	Avg. Time on Site	% New Visits	Bounce Rate
☐ 1.	credit card machine for small business	**550**	2.62	00:02:24	85.64%	53.82%
☐ 2.	credit card machines for small business	**289**	3.22	00:02:45	89.62%	49.13%
☐ 3.	wireless credit card machines for small business	**87**	3.84	00:03:44	95.40%	39.08%
☐ 4.	credit card machines	**76**	3.97	00:03:31	92.11%	38.16%
☐ 5.	nurit 8000 manual	**72**	1.32	00:00:51	86.11%	80.56%
☐ 6.	credit card machine	**69**	3.32	00:03:14	75.36%	44.93%
☐ 7.	visa logo download	**56**	1.16	00:00:38	96.43%	85.71%
☐ 8.	how to get a credit card machine for small business	**43**	3.88	00:02:19	76.74%	44.19%
☐ 9.	debit card machines for small business	**40**	2.08	00:02:50	87.50%	57.50%
☐ 10.	card machines for small businesses	**38**	1.76	00:00:53	89.47%	68.42%

Figure 14.9 Keyword performance report

Keyword Analysis Spreadsheet Tracking

As you have seen, there are many tools that can help in different ways, but sometimes if you want to see the data the way you want to see it, you have to compile datasets from different tools and bring it all together into a spreadsheet. This can take more time, but it is well worth the effort. Seeing the data you are most interested in on one spreadsheet page can really improve the quality of your analysis. Here is an example on how you can make this work. First, take the spreadsheet you created in Chapter 5. You should have a set of tabs for each keyword segment or theme, depending on how you set it up.

Next, for each of your segments, add some extra columns for more data. The two I use most often are for keyword ranking and web analytics, as seen in Figure 14.10.

Web Analytics				Keyword Ranking	
Visits	Page/Visit	Bounce Rate	Conversion	Position	Change
Last 30 Days	Last 30 Days	Last 30 Days	Last 30 Days	Last 30 Days	Last 30 Days
500	2.62	53.82%	4.25%	1.1	0.5
22	3.22	38.24%	2.23%	19	1.0
170	2.71	28.47%	1.00%	6.1	-3.0
16	3.84	44.58%	1.38%	11	-0.8
5	3.97	44.25%	2.69%	49	-2.0
12	1.32	15.78%	3.57%	9.6	0.3
90	3.32	51.22%	3.58%	18	-2.0
35	1.16	49.98%	4.80%	2.9	3.0
70	3.88	34.58%	1.20%	9.7	-3.0
23	2.08	41.21%	0.25%	37	0.3

Figure 14.10 Spreadsheet tracking

As you can see, I extracted the keyword rankings from a ranking tool and inserted the data into the keyword ranking columns. I have set my numbers to reflect the past 30 days. You may want to set up future columns to track trending data. Either way is fine; just choose which suits you better.

Specifically, I like to track keyword position and the positive or negative change from the previous 30 days.

Next I do the same thing for web analytics. I set up four columns to track the following variables:

- Visits
- Page/Visit
- Bounce Rate
- Conversions

I gather this data from Google Analytics. It reflects how my keywords are performing in relation to my website. This information grouped with keyword ranking and my other scoring numbers provide a quick glance at the whole spectrum of information related to each keyword, as shown in Figure 14.11.

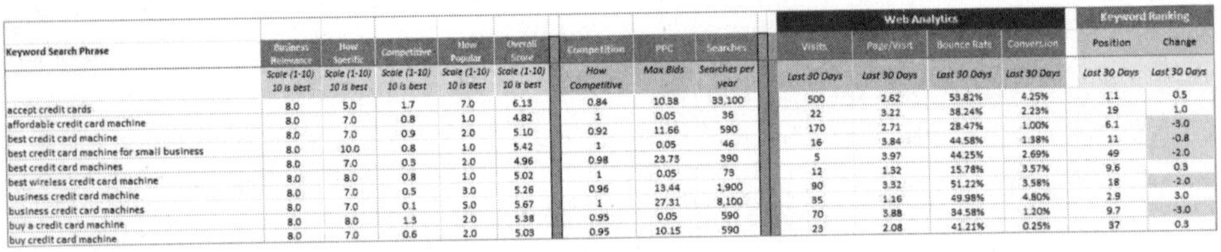

									Web Analytics				Keyword Ranking	
Keyword Search Phrase	Business Relevance	How Specific	Competitive	How Popular	Overall Score	Competition	PPC	Searches	Visits	Page/Visit	Bounce Rate	Conversion	Position	Change
	Score (1-10) 10 is best	Score (1-10) 10 is best	Score (1-10) 10 is best	Score (1-10) 10 is best	Score (1-10) 10 is best	How Competitive	Max Bids	Searches per year	Last 30 Days	Last 30 Days	Last 30 Days	Last 30 Days	Last 30 Days	Last 30 Days
accept credit cards	8.0	5.0	1.7	7.0	6.13	0.84	10.38	33,100	500	3.62	53.82%	4.25%	1.1	0.5
affordable credit card machine	8.0	7.0	0.8	1.0	4.82	1	0.05	36	22	3.22	38.24%	2.23%	19	1.0
best credit card machine	8.0	7.0	0.9	2.0	5.10	0.92	11.86	590	170	2.71	28.47%	1.00%	6.1	-5.0
best credit card machine for small business	8.0	10.0	0.8	1.0	5.42	1	0.05	46	16	3.84	44.58%	1.38%	11	-0.8
best credit card machines	8.0	7.0	0.3	2.0	4.96	0.98	23.73	390	5	3.97	44.25%	2.69%	49	-2.0
best wireless credit card machine	8.0	8.0	0.8	1.0	5.02	1	0.05	73	12	3.32	15.78%	3.57%	9.8	0.3
business credit card machine	8.0	7.0	0.5	3.0	5.28	0.96	13.44	1,900	30	3.32	51.22%	3.58%	18	-2.0
business credit card machines	8.0	7.0	0.1	5.0	5.67	1	27.31	8,100	95	1.16	49.98%	4.80%	2.9	3.0
buy a credit card machine	8.0	8.0	1.3	2.0	5.38	0.95	0.05	590	70	3.88	34.58%	1.20%	9.7	-3.0
buy credit card machine	8.0	7.0	0.6	2.0	5.03	0.95	10.15	590	23	2.08	41.21%	0.25%	37	0.3

Figure 14.11 Full scoring and monitoring spreadsheet example

I can see the following information:

Scoring

    Relevance

    Specificity

    Competition

    Popularity

    Overall Score

Keyword Research Data

    Competition Index

    Avg Minimum Bid

    Search Volume

Web Analytics Data

    Visits

    Page/Visit

    Bounce Rate

    Conversion Rate

Keyword Ranking

    Current Position

    Percent Change

As you monitor your keywords on a regular basis and make updates to this spreadsheet, you will come up with recommendations for small course corrections. It doesn't hurt to have yet another column to note any actions you plan to take to fix keywords that are not performing.

Summary

The topics in this last chapter are among the most important to keep in mind. The work is not over when the initial keyword research is complete. Many people will launch their site and then move on to other things without reviewing any analytics. This is a shame. Setting up goals and tracking performance to see if those goals are met is essential. It is one of the best reasons Internet marketing is so great. You can track everything.

By using the methods and practical tips in this chapter, you will not only know what is working and what isn't, you will learn more about the behavior of your visitors and those searching for your products and services. In turn, you will become a better marketer.

ndex

Trellian Keyword Discovery

Trellian

Keyword Discovery is an advanced keyword research and analysis tool, providing a multitude of search options and features to discover your most relevant keywords. Keyword Discovery compiles keyword search statistics from all the major search engines worldwide in addition to Trellian's exclusive Global Premium database of real users search data, delivering the purest most reliable data.

With over 40 search and analysis options, consider additional features that will impact your traffic immediately:

Also Searched Other searches performed within the same user session. *Great for brainstorming and analyzing user behaviors.*

Successful Searches Keywords resulting in a success click through. *Establish keyword value and ROI.*

Question Phrase Most popular questions searched containing your keywords.

Market Share Identify engine opportunities with less competition.

Seasonal Trending Target your customers when they are seeking your product.

Vertical Industry Terms, Competitive Density Analysis Report, Cross Reference Reports And more advanced features to give your online business the competitive advantage.

Trellian's Keyword Discovery will extend a 35% discount off the annual standard subscription. When ordering please enter the special offer code in the Comment field: **RJ35%AN**. This special offer price is $389.61, saving over $200 on the annual standard subscription (a value of $599.40).

Wordtracker's Keywords tool

For thousands of results-minded marketers around the globe, Wordtracker's Keywords tool is an invaluable resource in the quest for better search engine rankings.

Four reasons why Wordtracker blows other keyword tools away:

Advantage #1: Wordtracker delivers **2,000 keywords per search**, so you can find keyword targets quickly.

Advantage #2: Wordtracker's **competition data** helps you to cherry-pick the most promising keywords.

Advantage #3: Wordtracker gives you **more related keywords** – up to 300 per search, so you can target new markets.

Advantage #4: Wordtracker provides **live support** to help you get the most out of your keyword research. And you get exclusive access to hundreds of helpful articles and how-to videos about keyword research and SEO.

You can try the Keywords tool risk free with Wordtracker's 100% Money-Back Guarantee. If within 30 days you don't feel that the tool has brought you real value, we'll return every penny that you paid – no questions asked.

- Try Wordtracker's Keywords tool risk-free for seven days at www.wordtracker.com/trial or
- Exclusive to buyers of this book, get 13 months subscription for the price of 12 (saving $69) at http://bit.ly/jones-offer.

WordStream Inc.

WordStream Inc. provides software and services that help marketers maximize the performance of their PPC and SEO campaigns driving traffic, leads, and sales for lower costs. The company's easy-to-use PPC management software facilitates more effective paid search campaigns by increasing relevance and Quality Scores in Google AdWords, automating proven best practices, and delivering expert-level results in a fraction of the time.

WordStream also offers a best-in-class Keyword Research Suite for finding and organizing targeted, profitable keywords for use in paid and organic search initiatives. In addition, WordStream provides full-service PPC management and other value-added services to help advertisers who are new to AdWords or strapped for time get stellar results from pay-per-click marketing. Learn more at www.wordstream.com.

Check out our keyword research kit which includes:

- The Keyword Research Cheat Sheet
- The Ultimate Guide to Keyword Competition
- Guide to Keyword Research for Social Media
- Keyword Monitoring Worksheet

Special Offer: Save 15% when you purchase a subscription to WordStream's Keyword Research Suite with code **KRS11**. That's *less than $1 a day* for unlimited access to WordStream's full suite of best-in-class keyword tools. Offer expires October 9, 2012.

SEOmoz

SEOmoz is the world's most popular provider of SEO software. Their easy-to-use tools and tutorials make search engine optimization accessible to everyone. The powerful SEOmoz API delivers Linkscape web crawl data to their campaign-based web app, SEO tools, Open Site Explorer, and dozens of third-party applications. With SEOmoz's deep and fresh data, things like keyword research, competitive analysis, and on-page recommendations have never been so powerful. SEOmoz provides everything you need to succeed in Search Engine Optimization.

Coupon: 10% Off all paid plans, with the coupon KEYWORDS. Does not apply to current subscribers or upgrades.

iSpionage

iSpionage provides PPC and SEO keyword intelligence data for search marketers. Users will be able to find out working keywords, ad copies, and landing pages used by competitors in their niche. Leveraging this data will catapult users' PPC and SEO campaign into a winning and profitable position from the get-go.

Go to www.ispionage.com/KeywordIntelligence to get 15% discount.

SEMrush

SEMrush is the only competitor keyword research tool that regularly scrapes over 80 million SERPs for the most popular keywords. It provides more accurate, "real world," verifiable numbers than any other comparable SEO tool.

SEMrush identifies keywords from both Google Adwords and Google organic search results, exposing both those that are driving the most traffic to competitors and those that are related and potentially exploitable.

SEMrush takes the guesswork out of SEO and gives those who use it the upper hand they need to compete.

Coupon condition: Use code: SDZ0-0C6D-QMJ9-563V. This is a $35 value as we do not offer trials to the general public. You simply create a free account and apply the coupon in your profile page. There are no tricks, gimmicks, and/or any other fine printed conditions. The coupon will be active till the end of 2015.

BrightEdge

BRIGHT EDGE

BrightEdge is the leading enterprise SEO platform and the trusted partner of the largest and most recognizable brands in the world. BrightEdge helps marketers rise above the increasing clutter of the web and drive organic revenue from search engines across the globe in a measurable, predictable way. The BrightEdge SEO technology drives more than $3 billion in organic search for leading brands across industries, including seven of the top ten retailers, and Fortune 1000 leaders in e-commerce, technology, media, Internet, financial services, and consumer goods. BrightEdge is based in San Mateo, CA and is privately held with financing from Battery Ventures, Altos Ventures and Illuminate Ventures.

For a custom discovery evaluation by BrightEdge's SEO specialists worth $200, please visit www.brightedge.com/keyword_discovery_promo and enter the code "**keyword promo**" before November 15, 2012.